Arnold Robert Weiss
Annandale, Virginia
February 18, 1988

The Miller Heresy, Millennialism, and American Culture

THE MILLER HERESY, MILLENNIALISM, AND AMERICAN CULTURE

Ruth Alden Doan

TEMPLE UNIVERSITY PRESS
Philadelphia

Temple University Press, Philadelphia 19122
Copyright © 1987 by Temple University. All rights reserved
Published 1987
Printed in the United States of America

The paper used in this publication meets the minimum requirements of American National Standard for Information Sciences—Permanence of Paper for Printed Library Materials, ANSI Z39.48-1984

LIBRARY OF CONGRESS CATALOGING-IN-PUBLICATION DATA

Doan, Ruth Alden.
The Miller heresy, millennialism, and American culture.

Thesis (Ph. D.)—
Bibliography: p.
Includes index.
1. Adventists—United States—History—19th century.
2. Miller, William, 1782–1849. 3. Millennialism—United States—History of doctrines—19th century.
4. United States—Church history—19th century.
I. Title.
BX6115.D62   1987   286.7'73   86-30163
ISBN 0-87722-481-1 (alk. paper)

FOR MY MOTHER, DONALDA L. DOAN,
AND MY FATHER, HERBERT D. DOAN

Contents

Preface ix

Introduction 3

Chapter I. The Time 31

Chapter II. The Meaning of Supernaturalism 54

Chapter III. Revelation and Authority 83

Chapter IV. Out of Babylon 119

Chapter V. The Individual: Ideals and Control 141

Chapter VI. The Society: Ideals and Control 175

Chapter VII. Epilogue 202

Conclusion 215

Notes 229

Index 279

Preface

Millerites anticipated the breaking open of the heavens, the burning of the earth, and the return of Jesus Christ—before the nineteenth century could reach its halfway mark. A large number of their contemporaries not only thought that Millerites erred in that anticipation but positively looked upon the movement that grew up around the prediction of the imminent end as a threat. To many twentieth-century readers, watching for the second coming seems a peculiar activity indeed. Yet Millerites drew upon a number of elements from the more orthodox religious culture of their day in building their own understanding of the relationships among God, the individual, and worldly society.

Often relegated to the category of curiosity, Millerism is only now receiving full scholarly attention. Historians are beginning to fill in the pieces that will help us to understand who Millerites were, how they fit into the cultural milieu of the antebellum northern United States, with what religious groups they held ideas, activities, or even membership in common, and so on. The angle on this historical curiosity-become-inquiry that I have chosen to take might be summarized thus: What was the meaning that surrounded Millerism in its day? What were the points of conflict, what issues and assumptions were at stake, when contemporaries responded to Millerites with anxiety and anger and with attacks both verbal and physical? This approach can tell us a great deal both about what the Millerite excitement reveals about the America of the 1830s and 1840s and about what effect that confrontation might have had on developments on the American scene through the ensuing decades.

A number of people provided the inspiration and encouragement to begin this study. Professors John Wilson and Emory Elliott at Princeton are, I am sure, modestly unaware of their influence in leading me into the study of American religion. Fellow students and professors at the University of North Carolina at Chapel Hill taught and raised questions, disagreed and cajoled, and generally helped provide an environment in which I could work; among them I would like to mention specifically Julia Hesson and John Nelson.

More specific debts are not meant to imply that broader thanks are not in order. Linda Stephenson made it possible to wade through all the technicalities required on the way to the Ph.D. The staffs at the Department of Manuscripts and University Archives at Cornell University and at the Syracuse University Archives worked the extra measure to assist me in research. The American Antiquarian Society and the Massachusetts Historical Society also proved congenial places to pursue this study. The Department of History and the Graduate School of the University of North Carolina assured me of a semester free for research through a University Teaching Fellowship. Much of the research could not have been completed without the consistent, strong support of the peole in the Interlibrary Loan and Microforms departments at Duke University, the University of North Carolina, and Hollins College. In this regard, the final work on this manuscript owes much to Thomas Mesner. Grant Wacker introduced me to works and debates in American religious studies, pushed me to develop critical skills, and offered suggestions and support both specific and general. Gaines M. Foster and Ronald L. Numbers took time out from their own busy schedules to read the manuscript carefully and to criticize it perceptively. Edwin S. Gaustad helped to clarify some important issues through his criticism of a paper summarizing part of this research. A note of appreciation is also due my colleagues at Hollins College, whose humane treatment of junior faculty made the timely completion of my Ph.D. and the revision of this manuscript possible.

A separate thank you is reserved for my advisor and friend Donald G. Mathews, who has devoted considerable attention and energy to my work, including a number of rereadings well beyond the requirements of his official role. More importantly, though, he has by example encouraged me to believe in the possibility of combining human warmth with intellectual rigor.

Finally, thanks to my husband, Robert K. France, who has seen this study through from beginning to end and assisted on every level, from fixing microfilm readers to reading chapters to providing a rare degree of loving support. And to my stepson, Jaime, who alternately cheered me up and left me alone, and even typed some of the letters.

The Miller Heresy, Millennialism, and American Culture

Introduction

Early Christians wrote and read the apocalyptic books of the Bible under the conviction that God infused history with meaning and that the climax of God's work in history would soon arrive. The Book of Daniel recites, through its peculiar images, a tale that looks to the future of humanity. The Book of Revelation, too, foretells a time of transformation. In the last days, God and history would come together in a great age of peace and in the return of God-become-human in Jesus Christ.

In the first half of the nineteenth century, a New England farmer named William Miller wrestled with the prophecies and concluded, like John of Patmos, that the apocalyptic moment was to come in his own age, "about the year 1843." As he set out to spread his message in the 1830s, a number of people proved ready—even eager—to hope for such a transforming supernatural event. Miller spoke to ever-widening circles during his first decade of evangelism; beginning in the vicinity of his home on the New York–Vermont border, his reach extended finally to seaboard cities and western towns as well as through the hills and valleys of New England. His followers were labeled "Millerites," or sometimes "adventists," "believers in the advent near," and "43 men." Whatever their designation, those who anticipated the return of Christ could generally be found in the established and growing churches. Baptist, Methodist, Presbyterian, and Christian Connection churches, among others, contributed their share of members to the new movement.

In their dual identities—Millerite and Baptist, Millerite and Presbyterian, and so on—adventists were in no way invisible to their neighbors. Indeed, within their existing churches, they often irritated and frightened the other members and disrupted their congregations. But though visible to their neighbors, their dual identities often serve to hide individual Millerites from historians. Many took their places in the historical record only through their membership in established institutions—on church membership lists, for example—and left no trace of their association with the adventist movement. Estimates of the number of Millerites have ranged from ten thousand to one million, and such wide-ranging guesses beg the question of who might properly be labeled a Millerite and who a sympathetic listener. It seems appropriate to label as Millerites only those who would have accepted positive identification with what they called the "advent cause." David L. Rowe has suggested that those who took action as Millerites—writing letters, proselytizing, and so on—should alone be counted. His guidelines are implicitly accepted throughout this study; it is, after all, only the active members of the movement who left sufficient trace to become subject for study. Even so, the line between Millerites and others remains vague. A large number of people attended Millerite lectures, read Millerite periodicals, or discussed the questions of whether, when, and how Christ might return, even with sympathy for those who committed themselves to Miller's conclusions, without actually becoming Millerites themselves.[1]

Even though it is impossible to take an accurate count of Millerites, we can sketch in the general geographical distribution of active members of the movement. Most of the "43 men"—and women—lived in upstate New York, Vermont, and other New England states. The Millerite movement attracted few adherents in the South, but it did move west with migrants from New England and New York. It is fitting, then, to think of Miller's followers as making up a limited, regional movement with appeal almost exclusively in the northeastern United States. However small and localized, though, the movement cast a broad shadow among its contemporaries. Ironically, the greatest legacy of the believers in the advent near arose from opposition to their movement, even though they drew their beliefs, assumptions, and identification from the culture that they shared with their opponents—that of the northern United States in the first half of the nineteenth century—and, further, from deep currents within the Christian tradition.[2]

PROPHECY AND CHRISTIAN MILLENNIALISM

In the Old Testament Book of Daniel, King Nebuchadnezzar dreams "what shall be in the latter days," enshrouded in the symbol of the man with a head of gold and feet of clay (Dan. 2:31–35),[3] and he sends for the Israelite exile Daniel to explicate his dream. From his success with this dream, Daniel moves on to other explications and finally to a vision of his own. All of history is set out before Daniel as a single pattern, culminating in a heavenly consummation, but the symbols revealing the details of that consummation are diverse. There is a second little horn that will take away the daily sacrifice and cast down the sanctuary. Two thousand three hundred days will pass before the sanctuary can be cleansed. He who speaks to Daniel in the vision tells of kingdoms and powers and refers to the last days, but he also says that the vision is to be shut up for many days. (Dan. 8:9–26).

Daniel later learns more of the times to come and the time

of the end. Gabriel comes to him and says that Daniel's people will have seventy weeks "to finish the transgression, and to make an end of sins" and that there will be "seven weeks, and threescore and two weeks," from "the going forth of the commandment to restore and to build Jerusalem" to the time of the Messiah and the time when the Messiah will be cut off (Dan. 9:22–27). And at the end of the Book of Daniel are presented Daniel's last glimpses of the end—a time of trouble; the awakening of many who sleep in the earth, some to awake to everlasting life and some to everlasting contempt; "many shall run to and fro, and knowledge shall be increased"—all of this to be witnessed in the last days. Until these times, Daniel is to shut up the words and seal the book. He is told, before the sealing of the vision, that it will be "a time, times, and a half" to the end of the wonders, that 1,290 days will pass from the time of the taking away of the daily sacrifices to the setting up of the "abomination that maketh desolate." And he is given a final promise, that "blessed *is* he that waiteth, and cometh to the thousand three hundred and five and thirty days" (Dan. 12).

The visions and wonders revealed to the Old Testament's Daniel were matched and echoed by the revelation to the New Testament's John of Patmos. In his Book of Revelation, John sketches the outlines of the times that are to pass before the end. History will proceed through stages represented by the seven churches of Asia, the final stage corresponding to the rise of the "lukewarm" Laodicean church (Rev. 3:14–18). The timing of events to come is presented not only in general stages but also more specifically. Two witnesses will prophesy for 1,260 days before they are overcome by a beast from the bottomless pit. The witnesses will then lie dead for three and a half days before the last scenes appear (Rev. 11:3–12). Similarly, the woman who flees into the wilderness is to stay 1,260 days, there to be nourished for "a time, times, and half a time" (Rev. 12).

When these times have passed, according to the visions of John, the breaking of the sixth seal of the Book of the Lamb—the last seal but one—will lead to terror and desolation: "a great earthquake; and the sun became black as sackcloth of hair, and the moon became as blood," "the stars of heaven fell unto the earth," and "the heaven departed as a scroll when it is rolled together." That day, proclaims John, is the day of the wrath of the Lamb (Rev. 6). Similar excitements will follow the sounding of the trumpets: "Hail and fire mingled with blood," "a great mountain burning with fire . . . cast into the sea," the deaths of many creatures, the fall of a great star called Wormwood from heaven, the darkening of the skies, the opening up of the bottomless pit, which spews out locusts, the loosing of four angels to slay numbers of men (Rev. 8–9). Then, according to John, comes the final earthquake and the final battle. The heavens will open, and a rider on a white horse will come down with a sword that proceeds out of his mouth (Rev. 19). And after the consummation of such thunderous events, John foresees "a new heaven and a new earth" and the "new Jerusalem, coming down from God out of heaven" (Rev. 21).

The beauty of this ultimate scene is perhaps not for all men to share, however. John also sees the final division of mankind in those latter days. Certainly, judgments are to descend upon the "great whore" whose name is "BABYLON THE GREAT, THE MOTHER OF HARLOTS AND ABOMINATIONS OF THE EARTH" (Rev. 17:5). When the warning goes out to others beyond the great city that sits on seven mountains, some will cling to the spirit of the Laodicean church, poor in piety but rich in goods, but others will buy only gold "tried by fire" and wear only "white raiment" (Rev. 3:14–18). In the end, 144,000 "arrayed in white robes" will stand with the Lamb; the others will wear the mark of the beast (Rev. 7 and 13–15). Some will find their names written in the book of life; the others will not (Rev. 20).

The judgments will be swift and sure. The promises will, however, be at least as great. Thus can John repeat the words of Jesus, "Behold, I come quickly," and respond with confidence, "Even so, come, Lord Jesus" (Rev. 22).

Living under persecutions from Rome, John of Patmos saw revealed the impending judgment of his persecutors and the ultimate victory of Christ. The early church held to the hope expressed in Jesus' words, "Behold, I come quickly." They had not forgotten the warnings expressed dramatically by another prophet, Jeremiah. They knew all too well the trials to which the people of God were subjected before their triumph. But they focused on the promise spoken by Daniel and repeated by John. They expected the rapid return of their savior and the consummation of all things. The expectations of the early Christians went unfulfilled. The line of orthodoxy turned against the apocalyptic tradition. The legacy of anticipation left its mark, however, and the hope of the founders re-emerged time and again in the western world.

Through the tradition of the Sibylline Oracles, a set of apocalyptic writings that came out of Hellenistic Judaism and was expanded upon by Christians, the "warrior-saviour" of the Bible took on a double in the form of the "Emperor of the Last Days." During the Middle Ages, influenced by the Sibylline gloss on Daniel and the Book of Revelation, dissenting Christians found roles and meanings for themselves through expectation of the messianic emperor to come. Such Christians often looked to an existing emperor, hoping there to find the promised last emperor. But they could reverse the familiar prophetic tradition, too, and discover evidence that they lived under the Antichrist foreseen by Daniel and John.

In either case, the potential existed for the people to rouse themselves in support of the ruling, emerging, or as yet unseen Emperor of the Last Days. The prophetic tradition of Joachim of Fiore, similarly, looked to scripture to locate the present in the millennial scheme. Joachim fused scripture and history and promoted belief that a leader, existing or to come, would lead true Christians into the final age of the world. The prophetic and apocalyptic traditions were sometimes associated with resurgent mysticism, as in the cult of the Free Spirit, and sometimes, too, with radical egalitarianism, as in Thomas Munzer's revolutionary movement. What all of these variations held in common, as Norman Cohn has pointed out in his substantial study, was an image of salvation as collective, terrestrial, imminent, total, and miraculous. They read into the prophecies special promises for themselves and their age, and they believed and acted out of an assumption that supernatural intervention was to be expected immediately that would transform the earth and grant the special blessings of the elect to their own group.[4]

The Reformation gave new urgency to millennial dreams. With the emergence of Protestantism, the Bible—prophecies and all—came into the hands of the people, and all were urged to read and understand. As they read, Protestants often found the greatest promised by the fact of the Reformation itself. John of Patmos had, after all, identified Rome, the city that sat upon seven hills, as the whore of Babylon. Now the Protestants had escaped from the power of the whore. It was a short step to ask if the final transformation could be far behind.

THE MILLENNIUM IN AMERICA

The founders of the American colonies were, for the most

part, self-conscious inheritors of the Reformation. Their understanding of their mission or "errand," to borrow from Samuel Danforth and Perry Miller, was to build a model society in conformity with the demands of God and so to lead the world forward in the fulfilling of providence. Their sense of a peculiar destiny within the grand scheme led them to expect harsh judgments if they strayed from the ways of God, but they always balanced the threat of judgment with the promise of special hope.[5]

Puritans were accustomed to read their own roles and actions through analogies to biblical figures. The typology through which they connected the Old Testament to the New had its parallel in connections between the Bible and present history. Through this fundamental set of assumptions and correlations, the present was infused with transcendent meaning. The patterns of divine providence and biblical narrative were fused with the patterns of ongoing experience. The millennial hope reflected back to give pattern and meaning to the present.[6]

Through the Puritan fathers, what had been a tradition of millennial dissent in Europe became a foundation of cultural orthodoxy in America. The tying of divine providence and its consummation in millennial glory to the experience of the New World reinforced the power of millennial dreams always inherent in Christianity. Through trials of social, cultural, and political change, the assumptions of the peculiar place of America within the divine plan, and of the special importance of the impending millennium to the American experience, were not cast off, but rather deepened. In the Great Awakening of the mid-eighteenth century, Jonathan Edwards restated the connection—progress through the afflictions sent by God would issue in a millennial dawning, beginning perhaps right there in Northampton, Massachusetts.[7] The revolutionary potential of evangelical dissent did not, finally, break across and against national hopes, but instead reinforced them. When a nation of sons and daughters of the Reformation did break out in revolution, they directed their millennial rhetoric and fervor into a political cause, once again tying the visions of divine direction and godly promise firmly to the destiny of the nation.[8]

The Revolution gave new force to both the sense of opportunity and the increasing commitment to egalitarian ideals that had opened up in the context of the new land. In the Second Great Awakening, both of these thrusts were tied to a culture expressed and defined in evangelical Protestantism. The evangelical system centered on the new birth, the authority of the Bible, a sense of mission, and an anticipation of the coming millennium. That system became the cultural form through which a growing number of Americans tied together identity, community, and nation. Indeed, the new birth itself laid out the pattern for relationships in a community and for an understanding of history. The single, identifiable religious experience at the heart of evangelicalism followed a prescribed course: the individual felt alienated from God and came under conviction of sin, but reemerged, reconciled to God through Christ, after experiencing the depths of isolation. Ideally, that transformation led to a renewed life of increased commitment to God and his demands for moral living. The convert did not necessarily follow this path alone; his transformation could be encouraged by and lead him into a life among a community committed to the repetition and reinforcement of that experience. The convert learned of his alienation from God and the possibility of redemption from spokespersons for the saved. During his experience of trial—of conviction of sin—he was likely to hear of the possibilities for salvation from, and to see the alternative of life in a new community through, the evangelicals around him. Perhaps he pulled through to reconciliation in the midst of a gathering of the reborn, the hopeful, and the similarly convicted. When he reached his moment of turning, he had the opportunity to join into the special relationship of the community of believers. The primary responsibilities of such a community were to validate the experience of the convert, to encourage him in a godly "walk"—in a virtuous and moral life—and, finally, to seek the replication of the conversion experience in those among and around them.

The implications of evangelical experience—both individual and communal—resounded in the nation at large. The purification of conversion promised a sound, individual-centered basis for national virtue and national unity. The evangelical congregation offered a basis for regulating, ordering, and spreading the experience through the nation. Thus could evangelicalism and republican ideology become mutually reinforcing, with evangelicalism providing a basis for the survival of the republic while also symbolizing the underlying moral meaning of being American in the context of the new republic. The millennial hope lent urgency and promise to the American as well as the evangelical mission and gave a biblical basis to the growing sense that a consummation could be achieved within a nation knit together by an "evangelical empire."9

Evangelical experience contained contrary implications, however. The pattern of conversion emphasized alienation from God and a sudden and powerful transformation. Set up as a model for historical experience, that individual transformation implied that the world was left destitute and distant from its maker and ruler until he chose, suddenly, to break through and change the world. On the other hand, the communal experience of evangelicalism increasingly implied that a different model for history was more appropriate. The community had a duty to press change upon the individual. Individuals were told to come together at times when they might especially expect to achieve reconciliation with God. As the timing of those gatherings—revivals—came to be scheduled and planned, so, too, did the means and measures used during them to ensure success. The creativity, the success, and the implications of the "new measures" revivalism associated with Charles Grandison Finney are well known.[10] Gathering together at a set time and place, undergoing well-planned procedures intended to bring about conversion, being told that it was one's duty to accept Christ—all of these implied that individual and community could do something to bring about religious transformation. And as that transforming experience did, in fact, occur, time after time, it began to appear that the millennial dawning did not have to await a sudden, supernatural intervention, but could rather grow gradually and progressively through the accumulating numbers of the saved.

The familiar distinction laid out here has become a favorite among scholars: it is that between premillennialism and postmillennialism. Premillennialism, strictly speaking, is the belief that Christ will return before the thousand years at the end of time. The now-classic understanding of premillennialism is that it is naturally associated with assumptions that the world grows progressively worse, that human beings can do nothing to save themselves, to help the world, or to hurry the course of providential history, and that supernatural intervention alone can halt the downward course of history by breaking across it. The psychological type associated with premillennialism is, therefore, pessimistic and passive. Postmillennialism, on the other hand, is the belief that Christ will not return until after the millennium. Postmillennialism supposedly fits naturally with assumptions that history is a course of improvement growing ever closer to millennial glory, that people can effectively work for that improvement, and that the millennium will appear as one more progressive step in a historical development driven by human effort. The postmillennialist, therefore, is assumed to be optimistic and active.[11]

Postmillennialism became the dominant eschatological position of American Protestants by the mid-nineteenth century. Premillennialism has, since that time, been the rallying point of only dissenting minorities. A problem remains, however, in the sense of inevitability—the rigidity of the stereotype—of the sets of assumptions and psychological characteristics associated with the two positions. The recent research of James Moorhead, especially, suggests that religious Americans were less one-sided than these stereotypes imply. His depiction of the millennialism of the mid-nineteenth century draws elements from both sides: the optimistic hope for progress usually associated with postmillennialism joined with the sense of impending crisis usually attributed to premillennialism. Moorhead asserts that this double anticipation, of both "progress and apocalypse," was most often combined with a postmillennial eschatology during much of the nineteenth century.[12] One caveat should be added here: Although millennialism, including a focus on the prophetic scriptures and an interpretation of them that made them meaningful in terms of the lives of the interpreters, was pervasive in America by the 1830s, it is a mistake to assume that every religiously oriented American had established a clear loyalty to either premillennialism or postmillennialism. It was the orientation and anticipation of millennialism in general that was most important to the generations of the 1820s and 1830s and careful distinction about the chronology of the end took second place to that general cultural tone.

During the first four decades of the nineteenth century, many Americans sought to put into practice the ideals of both the American Revolution and evangelical Protestantism. As the Second Great Awakening spread, its promises and demands issued in a number of experiments through which groups of American Christians sought to give life and structure to their ideals. Many sought to give social and institutional reality to their hopes through organization in congregations and denominations. Yet the churches themselves could not contain the energy unleashed in the new nation. In the early decades, many sought to extend and perfect their hopes through voluntary societies aimed at both the reformation of morals and the spreading of the Christian message. Bible and missionary societies were major legacies of that time. As the years passed, the same impulses fed into broader reform movements and experiments in building ideal social institutions or ideal communities. From antislavery to the Oneida community, a multitude of plans and efforts arose.

The sense of opportunity that existed in the new republic coexisted, of course, with contradictory experiences and possibilities. The assumption of general equality and openness ran up against social stratification. The hope for unity based on liberty faced the problems inherent in unprecedented diversity of population. By the 1830s, some of the conflicting hopes and realities began to open deep fissures in the republic's good earth. Some of those who took part in the booming experimentation of the early nineteenth century seemed to go too far. It was fine to assume that unity and liberty could go forth hand in hand in the American context, but liberty allowed too many to break too forcefully beyond the bounds of the powerful but informal orthodoxy. The logic of evangelical Protestantism itself, through the heat of the revival, cast new forms of religious culture bound up with new hopes for the ability and perfectibility of man. Similarly, from out of the core of orthodoxy itself grew a set of absolute demands for morality and totalistic experiments in social and religious order. What Whitney Cross has called "ultraism" took many forms, from radical abolitionism, to communitarianism, even to the anticipation of the immediate return of Christ.[13] At each point of emphasis, ultraists hit hard upon some existing contradiction within the American cultural and social system. The existence of slavery in the land of freedom, to take an obvious example, found its most uncompromising critics among the sons and daughters of evangelical Protestantism.

The ultraists' alternative proposals for the future of individuals and of the nation appeared alongside a variety of visions and experiments for the future. At some point, however, the majority was bound to take notice of the lengths to which the ultraists had taken certain implications of evangelical Protestantism. Opposition gained force at different times and different places. Anti-Masonic, anti-abolitionist, and anti-Catholic rhetoric and action rose in fervor and frequency by the mid-1830s. By the 1830s and 1840s, that social and cultural efflorescence slowed and gave way to a period of more caution, even suspicion, of difference and experimentation. John Higham has called the shift one from "boundlessness to consolidation."[14] The alternatives—too many alternatives, it seemed—had appeared. It was time to select from among them the few that could be drawn together in a unified balance of freedom and order. If it was becoming clear that the limits of dissent had to be tighter and the structures supporting orthodoxy firmer, it was not yet clear what the limits would be nor what social structures would uphold them.

MILLERISM, DISSENT, AND CULTURAL CHANGE

William Miller grew up in the early years of the new republic. His personal background reflected the fusion of millennial dream and national hope that characterized the broader culture: his mother was the daughter of a Baptist preacher, his father a veteran of the Revolutionary War. Like many a young Vermonter, Miller played the role of the skeptical deist for some years. He read history and scoffed at Christianity. As a soldier in the War of 1812, however, he confronted the paradox faced by so many of his contemporaries. The cause of the nation he believed just, but the virtue of his fellow soldiers hardly paralleled that of their cause. In spite of the failings of individuals, however, victory was bestowed upon the new nation. Miller could only reach back to the interpretations of his parents' generation to explain this surprising result. His deism to the contrary, he was ready to accept the idea that God must have taken a direct interest—even an intervening role—in the success of the United States.[15]

Back at home after the war, Miller returned to the evangelical Protestantism under which he had been nurtured. Following the standard model of conversion, he looked at his deism, his reliance on man and history for final answers, and his bad habits picked up before and during the war as evidence of a profound alienation from God. Cast into a state of conviction of sin, he could emerge only through reconciliation with God through Christ. "God by His Holy Spirit opened my eyes," Miller would later recall; "I saw Jesus as a friend, and my only help, and the Word of God as a *perfect rule of duty.*"[16] Committed to evangelical Protestantism, Miller saw it as his duty to study the Bible. Study he did—for fourteen years. Within a few years after his conversion, he had already come to the dramatic conclusion that Christ would return in the clouds in or before 1843.

Miller joined with hosts of others in developing varied and sometimes idiosyncratic versions of the Christian millennialism that was bound so tightly to American culture. In retrospect, setting a date for the second coming may seem peculiar, even crazy. Perhaps Miller's neighbors thought his particular interpretation of the Bible a bit odd, but they apparently did not find it so strange as to be worth making a fuss about. The broad orthodoxy in place in the 1820s included a general Christian millennialism, but it did not spell out a single acceptable version of millennial hope. No one, as far as the record shows, stood up and shouted "Premillennialist" as soon as Miller began to share his conclusions with others. Miller did say that he believed in the premillennial advent of Christ, but he gave no special emphasis to that adjective. He wrote, rather, of the "personal," "visible" return of Christ as "continually-expected" to come "soon." The issues of deepest concern to Miller were not necessarily those of the stereotypical premillennialist. Nor, more importantly, was Miller rejected because he adhered to a prepackaged premillennialism. It seems, in fact, that at first he was accepted by contemporaries relatively unconcerned with the distinction between premillennialism and postmillennialism.

Miller did see his millennialism as part of a system of assumptions and beliefs that he found consistent and compelling. Some of his ideas fit the stereotype of the premillennialist. He expected Christ to come before the millennium, or the new heavens and new earth. He believed that a person could not effect his own salvation and that human action could not bring on the millennium. He thought that, in terms of what counted most, history was on a downward course. On the other hand, Miller was not entirely what scholars would have him be. He was not passive, but rather a hard worker both in the cause of Christ and at worldly employments. He was not pessimistic, but rather optimistic in his assumptions about the capacities of people for understanding and taking individual action, although not for producing general progress. And he was the ultimate optimist in his certainty of the victory to come.

In 1831, Miller was, in his own terms, called by God to go forth and share his message of the imminent, personal return of Christ. In the still-boundless days of the 1830s, there was room for the likes of Miller to join a throng of lecturers and preachers who promoted their visions and experiments throughout the northern states. Where Miller went, many came to hear. Not all of his listeners agreed with every point of his religious system. He insisted on focusing on the imminent, personal return, and he chose not to tie it irrevocably to his other personal beliefs. He was accepted and encouraged because he carried a message founded upon orthodox expectations and fitted, generally, to the loose orthodoxy of the age.

Miller gained a number of converts during the 1830s. In 1839, the organizational drive of his movement accelerated under the new direction of reformer Joshua V. Himes. The movement accelerated, that is, just as the pendulum was swinging back in the direction of consolidation. Suspicions and fears of ultraism, restrictions and competition because of the economic pinch, and the stepping up of the Millerite movement all came together. The result was pressure toward polarization: one had to become ultra or not, committed financially and otherwise to a particular movement or not, and, specifically, Millerite or not. The debate that ensued fed into the process of defining the new and newly limited orthodoxy that would emerge from the 1840s.

Opposition to Millerism did not appear as a single, coherent argument developed by a few spokespersons dedicated to their role of attacking and putting an end to the adventist movement. Critics spoke from a variety of perspectives—evangelical and Unitarian, conservative and radical, clerical and lay, to name but a few. Although a few became virtual defenders of the faith against the new heresy, most expressed their complaints against Millerism as one part of much broader concerns. Nonetheless, it is useful to refer to opponents of Millerism as a group—practically, because it is unwieldy to remind readers constantly of the fact that this was not the primary role of the spokespersons referred to, and conceptually, because the opponents did, without conspiring or organizing to do so, build up a general argument against Millerism with major points on which most critics could agree.

If critics were arguing postmillennialism against premillennialism, they did not often pose their points in those terms. They spoke to a variety of concerns that reflected not two but rather a range of assumptions about the course and meaning of history, the nature and role of man, and the nature and role, too, of God. Some put the only historical coming of Christ in the past and believed that nature and humankind already possessed the potential to fulfill the kingdom of God on earth. Some believed that people's toil for Christ would lead to the introduction of the millennium, but this group was divided over whether humanity or Christ would provide the final push into the new age. Some thought that the seed of divinity had been implanted in the hearts of people but that that seed could grow and flourish only under the direct encouragement of divine force. Others still assumed that human beings were, by nature, utterly depraved, but that divine intervention would either lead to gradual improvement ending in the millennium or stop the human-based steady decline by putting an end to history. Millerites drew together one set of factors through which faith, identity, action, history, providence, and consummation could be tied together. Their alternative was but one of many. The study of Millerism and "anti-Millerism" is one approach through which we can begin to understand the numerous alternatives available within the American religious culture of the 1830s.

The development of a general critique of Millerism took place through a process of statement, attack, defense, reconsideration, and regrouping. Both those things that Millerites actually said and did and those things that opponents thought Millerites said or did, or meant to say or do, or would have said or done, entered into the emerging public perception of Millerism. The interpretation of Millerism tells perhaps as much, then, about the interpreters—the opponents—as it does about the Millerites themselves. Moreover, as they squared off against Millerites and Millerism, critics refined their own positions and even shifted their ground to distinguish their stance from that of Millerites. The study of Millerism, then, can also be a study of a process of change within American religious culture—indeed, within American culture as a whole.

Americans have never lived with a single, easily defined orthodoxy. Since the Revolutionary era, there has been no orthodoxy in a traditional sense of a single, state-supported religion. Yet to deny that there have been insiders and outsiders in the complex of American religions would be to contradict both evidence and common sense.[17] The status of nineteenth-century Mormons differed from that of Congregationalists. The Unification Church of the present, popularly known as the "Moonies," receives a different reception in any American community than, say, the Episcopal Church. Similarly, Millerites were not welcomed as most Presbyterians were in the 1830s and 1840s.

The challenge is not to assert that there have been boundaries between acceptable and unacceptable religious positions in the American context, but rather to understand what those boundaries were and how they changed. Even if one considers only the northern states, since they became the home of adventism, the story is quite complex. The eighteenth century ended with a sense of deep suspicion among many Protestants about the potential threat posed by religious dissenters. In particular, the fashion of deism among the young and a number of intellectual leaders threw defenders of New England's surviving Congregational establishment into a panic. But deists no more represented the sole manifestation of dissent than Congregationalists monopolized the ranks of the respectable. The challenges of the first three decades of the nineteenth century introduced dissent on a new scale, and the same years necessarily saw a realignment of the forces of multiple orthodoxy.

One vector of dissent originated in the rationalism of the eighteenth century and scandalized new England with its success at Harvard in 1805: Unitarianism. Unitarians would, of course, come to be numbered among the orthodox in Boston, while remaining on the fringe of orthodoxy on the larger scene. Still, the transition from the scandal of 1805 to the establishment of the American Unitarian Association in 1825 proved a large step in gaining the standing from which Unitarians could insist on being heard. They represented, in a sense, one boundary of American multiple orthodoxy; along one edge of acceptability, they provided the limit against which many could define their more broadly respected positions, but they also held the force of social power, which prevented their utter rejection. The vector of dissent that had thus begun to slow into Unitarian structure at one angle was also in part deflected at the angle that took the title Transcendentalism.[18]

Transcendentalists voiced loudly certain sounds of religious change that were as yet only murmurs in other corners of American religious life. They stood for the radically immanent divine, the truth of intuitive perception, the rejection of any outside authority in favor of reliance on the individual who could sense the forces emerging from his own soul. They were proud to remain unorthodox, and they stood beyond the boundaries of acceptable faith and belief. This is not to say that Transcendentalists were not influential, to be sure. Picture the Emerson of the antebellum decades, on lecture platforms, speaking to audiences willing to borrow from such conceptions of self-reliance and individual ability to seek the truth while resisting other pieces and especially the implications of Emerson's system of thought and feeling.[19]

By the time of Emerson's success on the lyceum circuit, other influences in American religious life had predisposed a number of his listeners to attend to some of his ideas and ideals. The evangelicals who gained force from the revivals of the early nineteenth century shared with Emerson, as Martin Marty has pointed out, the conviction that religion "must have feeling, must be feeling."[20] The revivals had originated in pre-Revolutionary days, inspired by the likes of Jonathan Edwards and George Whitefield but also carried out by a number of American religious leaders, among them Gilbert Tennent and James Davenport. Revival fires were rekindled at the turn of the century by sparks set off at Cane Ridge, Kentucky, and at Yale University. For several decades, revival leaders and revival converts remained beyond the pale, relegated to the fringes of religious life and labeled deviant and dangerous. Revivals played on the emotions, threatened established ecclesiastical structures, undermined assumptions of original sin, and generally worked against orthodoxies on a number of points. While the majority of Americans remained skeptical about, and often even hostile to, revivals in the first decades of the nineteenth century, revivals played no small part in the astounding rise of the Methodist Church to the position of the largest Protestant denomination in the new nation by the 1830s. Their competition came not from the old establishment, but from the Baptists, also rising on the revival wave, from the Presbyterians, dividing over just such enthusiasms, and from such new denominations as the Disciples of Christ and the Christian Connection. With the sheer force of numbers on their side, these evangelicals would not be kept beyond the boundaries of shifting American orthodoxies for long. Even in the early years of the century, such "old Calvinists" and former opponents of revivalism as Timothy Dwight, Lyman Beecher, and Nathaniel W. Taylor began to soften their resistance. It is not surprising, then, that the rise of the infamous Charles Grandison Finney and his "new measures" revivalism in the 1820s met with at least two general responses among the orthodox: either they retreated to a defensive position and crowed that they had known all along that this was what those revivals were coming to, or they took Finney as the new measure himself of behavior that went beyond the bounds of the acceptable, and in the process embraced older, quieter conceptions and practices of revivalism.[21]

Thus, by the time William Miller began to preach his message of the imminent, personal return of Christ, several boundaries of America's multiple orthodoxy had come into focus. On one side, Unitarians barely entered into the fold;

on another, Transcendentalists remained outside. Charles Grandison Finney had recently redefined the edge that judged the revival temper and its attendant threat to Calvinism. Inside this vaguely defined polyhedron rested the orthodox of long standing, Congregationalists and Episcopalians. They formed the core of the acceptable less by force of numbers than by the strength of their social, economic, and political power. They were joined by churches that fit safely into the Reformed tradition, especially the Presbyterians, but also by other relatively staid old Protestants churches like the Lutherans. More recently, all of these had begun to make room, albeit reluctantly, for the winners in the new race for religious dominance, the Methodists and Baptists. What defined acceptance into this multiple orthodoxy was only minimally what might strictly be called religious belief. These diverse groups shared little more than the basics of Protestantism: the divinity of Jesus, reliance on grace, a focus on the Bible, points almost unarguable in the religion of the new republic. In the 1830s, Protestant Americans tended to maintain some sense of sin and judgment, to look to God as both designer of the universe and answerer of individual prayer, and to assume that a providential plan was played out in history. Beyond theology, however, they could all agree on the importance of drawing moral force out of religious belief and maintaining the stability of the community, and even the entire American republic, on that basis. In fact, characteristics of the republic that had themselves begun to define tenets of an acceptable American Protestantism included celebrations of republicanism, civil liberty, and the value and rights of the individual.[22]

Kai Erikson, in his classic study *Wayward Puritans*, has introduced a vocabulary and begun to refine concepts that can aid in reaching an understanding of the relationships between forces of orthodoxy and emerging dissenters. Erikson draws on Emile Durkheim for his initial point of emphasis: deviance, say the sociologists, performs a "needed service to society by drawing people together in a common posture of anger and indignation."[23] Moreover, a community of any size must maintain boundaries, and, Erikson notes, the most effective point for "locating and publicizing the group's outer edges" is the point at which those labeled deviant and the community—especially official agents of the community—interact. Of course, such boundaries are not perpetual; they are continually shifting.[24] Erikson labels the dramatic moment at which conflict between deviant and community occurs, a moment likely to signal a shift in those outer edges, a "boundary crisis." He emphasizes that the boundary in question may not be entirely new, but rather that "a different sector of the community's traditional boundary network has moved into focus and needs to be more carefully defined."[25]

The very amorphousness of the American multiple orthodoxy has meant that its definition must take place through action on its boundaries at least as much as through communal reinforcement from within. If there has been little for the religiously orthodox to attach themselves to under the American system, at least there has been plenty—or at least they have created plenty—to define themselves against. Among those negative referents may be counted the Millerites. In the early 1840s, they took part in just such a "boundary crisis." The center of orthodoxy had been shifting and even expanding in the early nineteenth century. Certain alternatives had, however, become less and less popular, or perhaps less compelling to large numbers of northern Americans in the 1820s and 1830s. Yet it was not clear that the Millerite alternative was not acceptable until the crisis arose; until then, the response to their positions and their activities had been largely that to the slightly eccentric but comfortably familiar. Those who would be disdained as Millerites often began as insiders. As certain revivalistic evangelicals came to take a secure position among the orthodox, however, Millerites were cut out and defined as outsiders. Although akin to their contemporaries in many—probably most—ways, Millerites did emphasize one expectation to a degree that came, in the eyes of their critics, to seem out of proportion in relation to other aspects of a Protestant belief system. It was that emphasis that made Millerites seem potentially threatening innovators, even though much of their developing pattern of belief and action was traditional and was shared by their neighbors.[26]

The crisis arose through a confluence of forces from both sides. Millerites became more active, more precise, and more demanding. Perhaps most important of all, they became more popular. But the context in which they worked also changed. The multiplication of dissenting groups in the 1830s finally led to growing fears that they had grown out of control and might threaten the stability of the society around them. It is probably very significant, too, that competition not only for the minds and hearts but also for the resources of Americans became more problematic with the panic and depression of the late 1830s. The transition from "boundlessness to consolidation" that historian John Higham would date from later in the 1840s may have begun in these confrontations, in which Millerites played only one part.[27]

This is not, then, strictly a study of Millerites or Millerism. Nor is it only a study of opposition to Millerism. It is, rather, an examination of the points of intersection of the two, of the points of overlapping concern between Millerites and their critics. The argument about that intersection is twofold. First, the conflict between Millerites and their opponents provides a dramatic display of widely held beliefs and assumptions during the 1830s and 1840s. In attacking Millerism, critics reiterated and reinforced articles of faith already accepted. Second, that conflict became one impetus to change, in that arguments directed against Millerism were reified into landmarks of orthodoxy that differed from previous definitions of acceptable ways of thinking and acting. Although the influence of Millerism in this sense was fairly widespread, its impact struck most strongly defenders of evangelical religion and of a millennialism that balanced "progress and apocalypse."[28] Opposition to Millerism pushed those critics into an unpremediated alliance with another group that took a keen interest in the new heresy and that found its position reinforced in the denunciation of the new deviants. That group was made up of those committed to a conception of God's as immanent and man as full of potential for action and salvation. These included Transcendentalists, some reformers, and "liberals" of several stripes.

Several changes were brought to view and encouraged through the medium of the Millerite excitement. In strictly religious terms, ideas of God and the locus of authority shifted. One of the striking things about attacks on Millerism is the frequency and degree to which the attackers seem to have been already committed to an immanent God, no longer distant and inaccessible, but working in humankind and the world. In this way, a number of evangelicals were moving more rapidly than might be expected into the neighborhood of Transcendentalists and others, and in the direction of the liberalism that flourished later in the century. Similarly, critics of Millerism found authority not in a distant, transcendent Other, but in the souls and consciences of people and in evidence within their world. Perhaps consistent with this, the Millerite excitement began to shake the balance in the conception of the millennium that held sway during those decades. Most antebellum Americans conceived of movement toward the millennium—or its secularized form of progress—as a process that would indeed move forward, but not necessarily with smooth regularity. But the expectation of sudden disruptions did not fare well in the face of the peculiar Millerite expectation, and so that moment gave millennialists a push toward delineating new conceptions of the millennium. In the 1840s and 1850s, those new conceptions included a more steady, gradual, and unimpeded evolution and, as another alternative, a relatively smooth historical course only to be shaken at the long-delayed premillennial return of Jesus.

With reference to American society at large and to the dominant assumptions undergirding that society, the Millerite excitement tended to reveal and reinforce, more than turn in new directions, changes taking place. Such changes can be subsumed under the general headings of secularization and of the rise of Victorianism. For example, disputes between Millerites and their opponents demonstrated how restricted the power of the churches had become by the 1840s. Americans were still religious, and often looked to the churches for a guide to behavior, but the church no longer had the coercive power to enforce its norms upon congregants offered a variety of other options. This becomes strikingly apparent in looking at cases of church discipline brought against Millerites. In other ways, too, the outburst of Millerism and of opposition of it illustrates what might be called the social concerns and the secular efforts to control raised by opponents to the new movement. In the face of the perceived Millerite threat, critics reiterated their new—one could now call them Victorian—expectations for the individual, especially the expectations of the development of character and of disciplined work. If the individual lost his footing on this new path, the society and culture of the 1840s could offer what seemed to be a new solution, incarceration in an insane asylum. In confrontation with adventist deviance, too, opponents rehearsed their fears and hopes for what they conceived to be bases for a secure and better future. For most Americans of the time, the first of those foundations was the family. For some, an equally important root of improvement was social reform.[29]

In the end, the concerns that can be labeled religious and those that can be called secular came together, again, in the notion of progress, especially as it was tied to national destiny. Millerites could protest that they did love God and follow their Bible, that they did stand for disciplined character and hard work, that they did seek the best for both the church—as they defined it—and the family. But the Millerites could not protest that they could go along with their peers in emphasising the fulfillment of providence in the nation's future. Millerites gloried in a vision of no future, or at least no future in the world as it existed. The fact that there was a future was the final blow to their cause.

CHAPTER I

The Time

When Miller began his study of the Bible, he determined to check scripture with scripture, to take literally whatever was consistent with "good sense" and "the simple laws of nature," and to take figures figuratively. Prophecy was fulfilled when its every word could be accounted for either literally or figuratively; otherwise, another or future event must have been intended. The reader required faith, above all, for the correct interpretation of scripture.[1] With this simple program of literalism based on faith and tempered by "good sense" and "nature," Miller approached his long search of the Bible.

TIME AS DATE AND SYMBOL

Miller quickly concluded that such an approach to the Bible precluded the conclusion that either the Jews' return to Israel or the millennium might be expected before the end of the existing world. Nor did his approach allow for a reading that made Jesus' reign spiritual. Miller anticipated, instead, the descent of Jesus Christ "in the clouds of heaven, in all the glory of his Father." He foresaw not a thousand years of peace, but rather the eternal, personal reign of Christ on an earth purified by fire. By moving a set of prophecies beyond the time of the second coming, Miller suddenly saw that coming as immediate, or "continually-expected" as immediate until it actually came.

Miller's principles for interpreting the Bible and his sense of the immediacy of the second advent came together in his reading of the chronology of the scriptures. Man must take scripture as given by God; no portion could be neglected. The rule of taking the Bible literally, when possible, and figuratively, when necessary, opened the way for substantive interpretation of the numbers given in the prophetic books. If the second advent could be expected soon, it would be no surprise if those numbers pointed to a time not far away. Miller began his exercise in prophetic arithmetic with the 2,300 days of Daniel 8:14. Many Protestant commentators agreed that "days" often stood for "years" in the Bible; besides, thought Miller, the 2,300 days were mentioned in the context of "symbolic prophecy," and so were to be understood symbolically as well. The 2,300 days would extend to the advent, and if the days' commencement could be found, the time of Christ's return would surely be known. "God would not bestow on us a useless revelation," Miller reasoned; God must have intended that that end time be known.

The 2,300 years began at "the going forth of the decree to build the walls of Jerusalem"—457 B.C. (Dan. 9:25). Two thousand and three hundred years from 457 B.C. brought Miller to his famous date—1843. Nor did he stop there. Miller's principles of interpretation demanded that he reconcile various parts of the Bible with one another, and the 2,300 days were not the only figure pointing to the dating of the last days. As he read on, Miller found a remarkable consistency among the prophetic numbers. The 1,335 days (Dan. 12:12) began with the establishment of papal supremacy—about 508 A.D. Add 1,335 to 508 and the end is slated for 1843. Miller later claimed that papal Rome rose in 538. Undeterred, he then added 538 to the 1,260 days of the woman in the wilderness (Rev. 12:14) to reach 1798, the fall of the papacy before the power of Napoleon. The last days, then, comprised the 45 years from 1798 to 1843. Or Miller would subtract the 70 weeks of Daniel 9:24—representing 490 years—from the 2,300 days, add the life of Christ (33 years), and come to the same conclusion—1843. Six of seven trumpets had sounded, six of seven "churches of Asia" had passed, six of seven seals had been opened, six of seven vials had been poured.[2] Biblical numbers all led Miller to the same conclusion, that Christ would come for the second time "on or before 1843."[3]

For Miller, setting a date for the second coming of Christ was a kind of shorthand assertion of a complex of assumptions. Miller spoke of "the divinity of Christ, his second coming, office of the holy spirit, eternal punishment, doctrine of grace, election, conviction for sin, regeneration, repentance, . . . faith" as prominent Bible doctrines bound together in a system of truth.[4] Deny any one of these doctrines and, he feared, the entire system would crumble. Beyond this, however, Miller emphasized the hard reality, the absolute literal nature, of these truths. It was this total and concrete reality that Miller found best expressed through the image of the imminent, dramatic, personal return and reign of Christ. In his final rule, "Christ will be present with all his people, and of course personally."[5] No mere "spiritual" reign, no mere "temporal millennium," could present a fitting climax to God's work through mankind. No man-made, temporary improvement could be the final expression of an omnipotent, eternal power. The hope of the Christian, the meaning of Creation, the essence of the Bible message, Miller found revealed in his image of the final scene to come: "The clouds have burst asunder. The heavens appear. The great white throne is in sight—Amazement fills the universe with awe—he comes—he comes behold the savior comes, lift up your heads ye saints he comes!—he comes!!—he comes!!!"[6]

In order to reaffirm the dramatic, literal truths that he found summarized in the fact of the imminent, personal return of Christ, Miller sometimes became adamant about his calculation of the date. Noting that some believed that 1847, not 1843, would witness Christ's return, Miller objected, "if we varry 4 years all is afloat. No, No. I wish I could know my adoption as strong as I believe my calculation is right."[7] Miller was not always so specific about the time, however. His early statements of his anticipation looked to an end "in the year 1843 or before."[8] It would prove more typical of Millerites through most of the movement's history to concern themselves less with whether the 1843 date would prove accurate than with the assertion of the truths associated with date-setting: the power of God, the coming personal reign of Christ, the literal truth of the Bible.

Miller began to make converts to the "second advent doctrine" in the early 1830s. Miller's decision to go forth and preach his message coincided, perhaps not coincidentally, with the revival wave that passed through the northeastern United States between 1829 and 1833. By 1833, anticipation of revival excitement left many audiences ready to listen to a message about the culmination of all revivals—and the judgment of all who remained unconverted. In Vermont, western Massachusetts, and northern New York, and later throughout the northeastern states, individuals and congregations took new or renewed interest in the possible imminent second coming and in the year 1843.

Some who heard Miller's message embraced his system at once and totally. Isaac Fuller, Baptist pastor of Poultney, Vermont, became the first member of the clergy to accept Miller's interpretation of the scriptures. In 1833, Miller counted eight ministers who preached his doctrines.[9] Seth Ransom prayed that Miller's views would quickly replace more popular, "new fangled" beliefs and practices. Abolitionists Lewis C. and Elizabeth Gunn became Millerites in 1841, and Lewis Gunn later wrote forcefully for the position that the time of the end was to be known in the last days—that it would be, in fact, between March of 1843 and March of 1844.[10]

Some came to acceptance of Miller's conclusions more slowly, but proved enthusiastic and certain once convinced. Charles Cole had doubts about Miller's chronology, but believed his dates "settled by Astronomy" by 1838. A resident of Fort Ann, New York, remembered that he opposed Miller when he heard his lectures in 1834, but began to suspect they might hold truth in 1841 and 1842; in 1843 he wrote to the *Signs of the Times* as a convinced believer. Even if the work of spreading the "soul-awakening doctrine" was slow to penetrate the woods of Maine, John Pearson could report, by 1841, that a "goodly number" in Portland had become "strong in the faith" of 1843.[11] Even Joshua Himes was briefly reluctant to throw his influence behind Miller's calculations: "I shall speak again soon—but mean to know what I say and know whereof I affirm. I am coming on—and when I come—look out—all my soul will be in it."[12] Himes spoke for many Millerites when he averred that the doctrine of the imminent second coming of Christ was a truth to which one could commit no less than all of one's soul. For many Millerites, the most compelling expression of that faith was the announcement that Christ would return in 1843. Yet the fact remains that most Millerites did not make the date the central tenet of their system, at least before 1842 or 1843. Hesitation on the question of the year did not prevent commitment to the movement.

William Miller received scattered reports time and again of the new conviction that followed the spread of his ideas. Millerism seemed blessed in its power to "get up" a revival or to feed its fervor. Millerite lectures became the means of bringing many to repentance, of putting off "Indifferency" and ushering in "Penitence" and "Conviction."[13] Millerism could act as a spur to religious excitement, however, without gaining converts to "2nd adventism" or to "43ism." Many who reached their moment of turning under the influence of Millerite lecturers never became committed to the movement. Fewer who heard Millerite views accepted the details of Miller's chronology including the date. Many, it seems, found most compelling "not so much the belief that Christ might come in 1843" as "the certainty of that event."[14] The fact that Christ would come again, personally, and soon, seized the attention of converts new and old. After a series of lectures by Miller in Dover, New Hampshire, one resident found "uniformity in one thing," in that "no one offers argument or evidence against the doctrine of the near advent of our Lord the second time." The "precise time" remained a matter of dispute and uncertainty. Although "we profess not to know how long or short the time to our Lord's coming," the converts at Dover gleaned the central message: "Be ye ready."[15] The news that gripped men's souls was the fact of Christ's imminent return.

Acceptance of the "second advent doctrine" without adherence to the 1843 date penetrated to the very center of the Millerite movement. This was not a case in which a core of believers upheld a strict set of beliefs while more peripheral followers took up a watered-down version. Millerism without Miller's date came early into the leadership circles of the movement and carried far to new audiences through the person of Henry Jones.

Jones ricocheted through a series of enthusiasms, his energetic optimism carrying him into first one crusade, then another. A Congregational pastor in Cabot, Vermont, Jones had angered many of his fellows with a fervent anti-masonry. He compounded his sin by confronting his neighbors and peers with the rhetoric of the nascent abolitionist movement. Soon cut off from access to pulpits, he found new audiences by taking to the road for yet another reform—temperance.[16] The peripatetic reformer was doing verbal battle against "spirituous liquors" and maintaining his personal stance of anti-masonry, abolitionism, and non-resistance when he heard that some were saying that Christ would soon return in power. In 1833, he began corresponding with Miller. From the beginning, he professed himself more interested in what kind of millennium would follow than in when that final drama would take place. Yet his commitment to the cause would be no less powerful because of his disavowal of the specific date. He foresaw, on the very eve of taking up the second advent cause, "the unprecedented self denial, and humiliation of the labors, which my principles and conscience would certainly immediately urge on me" when he came to "obtain a clear conviction" of the imminent, personal return of Christ. When he was settled in that conviction, Jones continued to reject the date.[17] Jones devoted himself to lecturing on the second advent through the late 1830s and early 1840s. There would be, he warned, "no flattering delay of his coming," but a "sudden, swift, and powerful spread of the gospel" would be cut short by the midnight cry, and Christ would come "personally and visibly." Jones felt no need to keep silent on the question of date. While agreeing to cooperate with date-setters in teaching that the second coming was near, Jones asserted that the 1843 date was "founded on human presumption, and profane history" and that the "prophetic *times* and *seasons* were *indefinitely foretold.*"[18]

Jones represented a large part of the Millerite following in his refusal to set a date for the end. It was expedient, therefore, for spokesmen and organizers in the movement to compromise on this question. At the First General Conference of Believers in the Advent Near in October 1840, approval on the record sealed what was already common practice. The year 1843 did not become a test of true faith. Adventists chose, rather, the imminent, personal second coming of Christ as their defining and cohering principle. It was especially crucial that Joshua Himes rallied his organizational powers to this principle. Although Himes himself favored the 1843 date, and although he thought the date "most efficient" in converting people to Christianity and adventism, Himes understood that the greater power of the movement depended on the numbers and unity possible under the banner of "the *Advent near*—Even at the doors."[19]

The decision not to focus on the time was not primarily a matter of expediency, however. As noted above, even Miller used the date as a symbol for a complex set of beliefs and assumptions. The advent near was the true center of the Millerite movement from the early 1830s until 1843. In fact, delegates to the 1840 General Conference had another alternative upon which they might have focused. The second major point in dispute at that meeting was the question of the return of the Jews.[20] Many readers found in the prophecies a clear statement that the Jews must return to Israel before Christ will return. A growing group of Christians in England and America looked for a personal, premillennial second coming, but firmly believed that the advent could only take place after the Jews returned to the holy land. If Himes and others wished only to hold together a good-sized following adhering to belief in the literal return of Christ before the millennium, they could well have turned to this group to form an alliance. Instead, they called them "judaizers" and threw them into a category with the "spiritualizers" who did not believe in—perhaps did not even hope for!—the imminent return of Christ. The Millerites did not reject the Jews' return gratuitously. If the Jews had to return to Israel before Christ would come to earth, then the second coming was not imminent. Waiting for so many to travel to the Middle East would surely carry over beyond 1843, beyond the 1840s, perhaps even beyond the lifetimes of those gathered in Boston in 1840. The immediacy of the threat of judgment and the promise of redemption gave power to the prophecies for the Millerites. They were the believers in the advent near, not in the advent a short way down the road. By 1843 it mattered little whether William Miller and originally thought of the precise time as being crucial to his system. The movement that had grown up around him took as its symbolic center the assertion that Christ was coming, that he was coming to rule in person, and that he was coming very soon—that, as Miller had said, "he comes!—he comes!!—he comes!!!"

OPPOSITION

If for Millerites the setting of a date for the end of time symbolized a web of interconnected assumptions and beliefs, so it was for their critics. Yet the two sets of assumptions about what system revolved around "1843" proved very different. Millerites heard predictions of the advent in that year and interpreted them to mean that Bible truths were as real as a physical presence. Observers and opponents, on the other hand, heard in the cry of "1843!" a series of threats and dangers. Those who spoke out against the Millerites accomplished two ends. First, they tied the image of Millerism to the date so closely that that simplistic picture has persisted for a century and a half. Second, they convinced their audience that such date-setting had inevitable consequences contrary to the interests of religion, social harmony, and national progress.

Ironically, a fairly common method of denying legitimacy to "43ism" was the promotion of a different time scheme. Some alternative dates rose from isolated prophets and marginal groups. Andreas Bernardus Smolnikar arrived from Germany with his interpretation prepared: he was the messenger of Jesus, events ushering in the millennium began on January 5, 1837, at five o'clock in the afternoon, and the final unity of Christians in peace would take place in 1846. "Giles the Prophet of God and Branch of Christ" became a new Elijah on April 7, 1840, and would cast out devils and work miracles until Christ's return to his temple in the year 2000. John T. Matthews claimed that he had a white stone that promised him power against the enemies of Jesus beginning in 1848. One thousand years later, the final end would come. An "Ethiopian" prophet predicted that the white people would be destroyed by April 10, 1844, and the colored race would retrieve its lost power.[21] Although these prophets and interpreters saw themselves as offering alternatives or correctives to Millerism, general perceptions of their position were rather different. They became, in the public press, additional proof of the foolishness, or even danger, of the speculation and calculation associated with the Millerites.

Prophetic arithmetic was not unknown to the respectable, however. Methodists had always to contend with the fact that John Wesley himself had set a date for the end, in 1836. Needless to say, Millerites did not hesitate to recall this fact for any followers of Wesley who forgot their heritage or who became too indignantly opposed to prediction of the time.[22] Nor were the Baptists free of such a tradition; recent predictions from among their adherents focused on 1830 and 1847.[23] Widely varied persuasions had, in fact, representatives who foresaw an end in Miller's year, 1843.[24]

Juggling prophetic numbers did not always lead to the

setting of a time for the end. A number of writers made specific criticisms of Miller's arithmetic while maintaining that the sum of the exercise remained mysterious. The Reverend William R. Weeks outlined 160 points in his "Mistakes of Millerism," a popular series reprinted or recommended in a number of papers. He objected that Miller differed from "common chronology." He denied that pagan Rome fell in 508 A.D.—the year to which Miller added 1,335 to calculate the time of the end. He implied that the relationship between 70 weeks and the 2,300 days was murky at best. As he listed argument after argument, Weeks did not rely solely on numbers and historical chronology to dispute Miller. Nonetheless, prophetic arithmetic formed the core of his contentions. As a sympathetic editor noted, Weeks gave the "facts" with which to combat Millerism, and those proofs were "as simple as two and two are four." One hundred and sixty diverse points left the settled conviction that straightforward addition made the case.[25] Similarly, Samuel Farmer Jarvis refused to accept Miller's particular mix of the visions of Daniel and insisted on separating the 70 weeks from the 2,300 days. He also turned to Bishop Ussher as an authority on Bible numbers. If the world began in 4004 B.C., as Ussher said, then 1843 was not the six thousandth year of creation, but only year number 5,846 (4,003 + 1,843). When Miller argued that there were 4,157 years between the creation and the birth of Christ, he failed to convince Jarvis not only because he contradicted Ussher but also because Miller had reportedly spent only three days calculating this particular sum.[26] Prophetic arithmetic might be legitimate, but only, it seems, if it were difficult and time-consuming.

 The result of criticism such as that of Weeks and Jarvis was, once again, to draw attention to dates, past and future. Such opponents of Millerism usually denied vehemently that the time of the end could be known. Yet they persisted in making all calculations up to the final one. All that was missing, it seemed, was the one fact to locate the totality of prophetic chronology in time, that one beginning or ending date that would make the series fall into place and so name the climactic hour. Neither Weeks nor Jarvis followed the temptation to try to glimpse that final point. That they led to the brink is clear, however, from Jarvis' comments on Ussher. Ussher said that the world began in 4004 B.C. Common orthodoxy had it that the world would last 6,000 years. Jarvis may not have printed the obvious conclusion to this line of thinking, but little sophistication would have been required to read the time of the end from his words: 4004 B.C. plus 6,000 years equals 1996 A.D. Other arithmetic anti-Millerites could not resist edging precariously close to date-setting. John Dowling objected, with others, to Miller's fusing of the 70 weeks and the 2,300 days. He ridiculed Miller for having passed over the point that Christ was probably born in 4 B.C.: would that not put the end in 1839? (Dowling wrote in 1843.) In any case, Miller, according to Dowling, was wrong about the commencement of the 2,300 days, and his arithmetic should properly have led to 1969 or 2132 as the final year. As Dowling dug further into Miller's chronological errors, he got more specific. He declared that 755 A.D., not 538, was the date of the Pope's rise to temporal power. Given that, should the end not come in 2015? But Dowling then had to back off: he opposed the naming of a particular date. Later in the same work, he guessed that the time for the final consummation could very well be about 2000 A.D.—but no, once again, he would have nothing to do with date-setting.[27] The setting of a time for the return of Christ was suspect, but the marking of a date too close to the present was, it seems, heretical. A number of critics walked this careful balance, accepting some fiddling with prophetic numbers as long as the sum did not impinge on the near future, and rejecting date-setting completely if it was associated with a time soon to come.[28]

Some critics set alternative dates and chronologies against those of Miller. Others sought to ridicule the Millerites precisely by pointing to the variety of times that had been established for the end. Predictions of the consummation of history and recurred time and again, and critics of the Millerites often referred to that dubious tradition as an argument against the new group. In some cases, references to past disappointments did not even mention the Millerites by name. The *Christian Reflector* referred to the "Doctrine of the World's Destruction" in the tenth century without drawing explicit analogies to the present. When the *Reflector* depicted the results of that belief—"universal panic" and the abandonment of all responsibilities—the warning could hardly have been lost on its antebellum readers.[29] Other writers and editors presented stories of earlier predictions under titles that made the contemporary reference clear. "Millerism in the XVIIth Century" told the audience of the *New York Evangelist* of London's Reverend Thomas Beverly, who asserted, in 1688, that the end of Popery and the commencement of the millennium would come after nine years. "Credulity of 'Millerites' in 1712" repeated the story, not of Millerites, but of William Whiston's prediction that *"a total dissolution of the world by fire"* would follow the appearance of a comet in October of the given year. Readers required no discussion of the similarity between Beverly or Whiston and Miller and to get the point.[30]

Ridicule by association was not always left to implication. Journals as often drew out the analogy between Millerism and earlier avowals of specific times for the world's end. A writer noting the passing of the last day set by a group of Frenchmen in 1840 commented disingenuously that whether Miller were an equally false prophet "remains to be seen." An Englishman's incredulous and supercilious estimate of the situation was reprinted in the United States: "That the renewal of a rumor, which had periodical currency amid the particular interests had general superstition of the dark ages, should be possible in our day, . . . speaks but little for the state of education in the country where it has obtained."[31] The anti-Millerite James A. Hazen urged his contemporaries to take a lesson from the example of John Howe, whose predictions in the seventeenth century brought about an increase in atheism. Millerite date-setting, Hazen asserted, would do the same.[32] The prominent critic of Millerism Luther Dimmick declared indignantly that the multitude of failures in reckoning "times and seasons" should stop Miller and anyone else from pursuing such calculations. Dimmick put forth the example of Thomas Munzer as a prime example of the dangers inherent in the speculations on the precise time of the end.[33] Another writer, apparently enamored of calculations himself, added up fifty-four theories that had been expounded determining the final date. Thirty-two, he noted, had already been disproven by the passage of time. His coy admission that he could not prove that 1843 would not bring the end only served to drive his point home.[34]

FINAL DAYS

It was not only commentary from outside that led to the association of Millerism with the date, of course. Miller's announcement of the time of the end certainly dramatized his message and facilitated the spread of the movement. Even though many Millerites did not go so far as to accept the 1843 date as absolute, there was a dynamic within the movement, driven by both external commentary and internal logic, toward date-setting. In one sense, that shift can be viewed as a classic example of the formation of a sect out of a movement. The particulars in this case can draw us into further insights as well.

William Miller had originally centered his prediction vaguely on the year 1843. Christ would come, he said, "on or before" or "about" that time. In developing the chronology that led up to the 1843 finale, too, he faced the temptation to formulate a precise timetable. By the mid-1830s he privately forewarned that "the door of mercy will be shut in the year 1839." Those who were saved at that time would be the last of the saved; "he that is filthy will remain so." In the three and one-half years before the end, there would be no "rain of grace," but only "trouble anguish wrath, malice, hattred & distress" for those who had not chosen the way of Christ.[35] When he elaborated his theories in a full-blown set of lectures, Miller made a more public prophecy. The Turkish government, he said, would fall in 1839.[36] Both of these predictions were dangerously subject to disconfirmation. As 1839 passed, a rumor circulated that Miller had admitted to an error of one hundred years and put off the end until 1943.[37] In both cases, in fact, the passing of the year 1839 led to less drastically revised calculations. The closing off of grace Miller now thought likely to take place on August 11, 1840. The fall of the Turkish empire, too, would occur in 1840. Critics jumped on the passing of 1839 and the recasting of the time. Now, certainly, Miller had been shown up as a false prophet. They foresaw the end of Millerite preaching or less confidently urged the public not to trust a man who had proved wrong at the first opportunity.[38] Most Millerites, however, were undeterred, replying that Miller had always presented these forecasts as "a matter of *opinion*."[39] Neither the passing of 1839 nor the passing of 1840 struck a serious blow to the movement. Critics might have taken this as a foreshadowing of things to come; they did not.

At the First General Conference of Believers in the Advent Near in October of 1840, there was some agitation on the question of time. The unity of the movement proved to be the paramount consideration, however, and Millerites stayed together on the basis of belief in the imminent, personal advent of Christ.[40] A year later, the question had not died out; Henry Jones found it necessary to warn that some were alienated from the movement because of talk of the specific year of the end.[41] By 1842, the problem of date-setting neared a crisis. At the Conference in May of that year, disagreements did not prevent the inclusion of a statement confirming the 1843 date in the minutes.[42]

Organizational development paralleled and interacted with movement toward focus on a precise date for the anticipated end. Millerites insisted that they did not intend to organize a new church; their understanding was universal in its application and believers were expected to appear within a number of different religious organizations. Besides, the end was near; precious time was not to be wasted on mere sect-building. Nonetheless, organization proceeded and interacted with changing ideas about the end. From scattered preaching and meeting in the 1830s, Millerites had stepped up activity around 1840. The gathering of the General Conference was carefully distinguished from organization-building, but the Conferences took on some of the functions of denominational bodies. Millerites did not ordain ministers, but the Conference "recommended" certain lecturers. The Conference was not to define a full statement of faith, but it rejected the beliefs of those labeled "judaizers" and progressively narrowed the range of acceptable belief. A central leadership group decided where evangelistic forays should focus and where the Great Tent should be set up. In a parallel development, local bands of Millerites established meetings, separate from their churches, where they might discuss the imminent end. This process, which in retrospect is identifiable as a stage in sect-building, made up the organizational dynamic, which had its influence, too, on narrowing the focus and energies of the movement.[43]

The interplay of internal and external pressures toward focus on the date pressed toward its conclusion. The decision on the date would never be final. Some who opposed the setting of a date remained in the movement through 1843 and into 1844. This was the way chosen by Henry Dana Ward, for example. Others, like Henry Jones, slipped gradually out of the central ranks, their discomfort with date-setting leading to a repudiation of Millerism.[44]

By the climactic year of 1843, then, the question of the precise time when the second coming was to be expected took center stage in a way that it had only in the minds of opponents in earlier years. As they concentrated increasingly on the specific date, Millerites began to refine their conceptions of the time. The major revision took hold after it received the legitimizing stamp of Miller himself. The year 1843, he said, actually ran from March 21, 1843, until March 21, 1844. The prophecies had been formulated under the Jewish calendar; by translating the Jewish dates into the common system, Miller and his cohorts arrived at the revised timing of the final year.[45] Critics once again called "foul": was this not a postponement of the end?[46] And once again, the adherents followed Miller. No decimation of Millerite ranks ensued.

While most Millerites accepted the yearlong range as a generally accurate representation of their belief, outsiders passed on tale after tale of exact days having been set for the final drama. The Millerites of Providence, Rhode Island, were said to have chosen the fifteenth of February 1843 as a likely time for the end.[47] The Methodist writer Samuel Luckey accused the Millerites of having appointed April 3 as the last day, although his evidence consisted only of the assertion that Millerites gave the "impression" that they anticipated the advent in the spring.[48] A favorite misreading focused on the determining dates for the last year. March 21, 22, or 23 became, not a possible day for the end, but the absolute last day.[49]

The most highly publicized date for the end was the twenty-third of April 1843. April 23 on the Jewish calendar was, many pointed out, the same as March 22 under common reckoning. The March dates, therefore, required only a quick translation to lend credence to the April day. This argument probably swayed a number of Millerites as well as feeding the fires of their opponents. Charles Fitch, for example, may have preached April 23. Other Millerite spokesmen remained cautious, however. Fixing on a precise day was dangerously easy to ridicule and disprove, and such exact predictions were also contrary to the dominant spirit of the movement at that point in its development. Although he had to admit that some Millerites had set dates, Silas Hawley carefully distinguished between such individuals and the movement as a whole and insisted that opponents, not Millerites, had made up the April 23 date.[50]

The rhetoric continued. Millerites, one story proclaimed, had changed the date from April 23 to July 4. When a Millerite hypothesized that Daniel's 2,300 days "seem to terminate by the 23d of May," his words gave occasion for gleeful satire under the title "The Day Fixed!" Miller, now supposed to have anticipated the end in the spring of 1843, was accused of delaying the time when he suggested that believers might have to wait beyond the autumn equinox to see their Lord.[51]

The Fall of 1843 passed, as did the winter of 1844. The end of the prophetic year—March 21, or at the outside April 23—slipped quietly by. The continuation of time left the Millerites, understandably, in a state of confusion. Most turned away from date-setting altogether in the spring and early summer of 1844. To set any "definite point" in time for the return of Jesus Christ, a Millerite named Coles declared, was the "consummation of folly."[52] The editors of the *Advent Herald*—forgetting, for the moment, to what degree they had joined in the focus on the date in 1843—returned to the message and tone of earlier years that placed the time in a secondary position in the Millerite scheme. They hoped that the steadfastness of believers in the advent near in continuing to look for Christ's coming would inspire others to examine the question of the advent as a whole, not just as a matter of a specific time.[53]

Some Millerites found the waiting and watching approach unsatisfactory, however. Small dissenting groups within the movement sought a functional replacement for the date—a belief or practice that could set them apart as the truly wise or the chosen of God. Some, like George Storrs, turned to a belief in the annihilation of the wicked, rather than their eternal punishment. Others focused on the potential for a second blessing that would bring entire sanctification and engaged in such ecstatic behavior as is often associated with an experience of the Holy Spirit.[54] These vocal dissidents demonstrated an extreme version of the sectarian impulse that had penetrated deeply into the movement after 1842. Adventism had become a subculture whose definition depended on marking itself off from the world.

Back in the winter of 1844, at least one Millerite had glimpsed the new truth that would reunite the Millerite movement. In February, Samuel S. Snow had begun to speak of the end coming in the fall.[55] Snow believed that Christ would come on the tenth day of the seventh month of the Jewish calendar—a date that he believed fell on October 22 of 1844 of the calendar in common use. A number of Millerites heard Snow preach the new date, but few took up the standard in the confused spring of 1844. By the summer, however, the seed of the idea had been planted in a number of points through the northeast. Millerites ached for a word that could sustain their faith and hope and revive the sense of community that had come with fervent anticipation of the second coming. The yearning and the message came together in July of 1844 and set off revivals that turned Millerite expectations toward October 22, 1844.[56]

The "seventh month movement" grew from the grass roots. It took fire almost before the central leadership of the Millerite movement had noticed it, and those leaders hardly knew whether to fan or douse the flame. Into September they remained doubtful and cautious. Josiah Litch flatly denied that the new date was valid. Editorials in the *Advent Herald* exhibited more sympathy—"If we should look to any one day, in preference to others," said the *Herald,* "we should be disposed to look to that day [October 22]"—but uncertainty ran through the columns of September: The editors hoped more broadly that the end would come sometime before the new year.[57]

Conviction about the October date continued to grow among rank and file Millerites. The old leaders were threatened with being left behind by their own movement. The enthusiasm of adherents to the new date and the rapid spread of the idea seemed, in any case, to indicate the hand of God in the work. Finally, the October date did unify a movement that had faced possible disintegration, and unified it on grounds that were easy to accept—easy, at least, for those accustomed to looking for the imminent return of the Lord. Joshua Himes had to admit that the "fruits" of the seventh month movement were "glorious." The October date, Himes said, "has done away with all Fanaticism, and brought those who are given to extravagance into a sober discrete state of mind."[58] One might be tempted to object that, rather than doing away with fanaticism, the seventh month movement made fanaticism—or, at least, extreme sectarianism—the unifying basis for a renewal within Millerism. Nonetheless, Himes' comment is worth taking seriously. As he perceived it, focus on the October date unified the movement and silenced the dissenting minorities that worried him most. From Himes' perspective within the Millerite subculture, the setting of a specific day for the return of Christ could easily appear to be a logical extension of basic adventist beliefs. Himes could deny that the extravagances of the fall of 1844 were fanatical because it was the rest of the world, of course, and not the Millerites, who were beyond the pale.

By October, virtually the whole Millerite movement had swung behind the new date. George Storrs was for it. Nathaniel Southard, and through him the *Midnight Cry,* favored it. Joshua Himes and Sylvester Bliss put the authority of the *Advent Herald* behind it. Josiah Litch pulled an aboutface and accepted it. Even William Miller, no longer at the forefront of his own creation, but still important as a symbolic center for adventism, came to see "a glory in the seventh month which I never saw before."[59]

Despite Himes' disclaimers, extravagances there were as the seventh month movement gained momentum. Millerites began to fulfill the prophecies made by their opponents: they left crops unharvested, closed businesses, gave away money and goods, and generally acted more as others expected millenarians to do.[60] In those last days, they gave legitimacy to the anti-Millerite arguments that had been amassed over five years and more. It required only the final crushing of Millerite credibility when the day dawned as any other on October 23 to lend the anti-Millerites an aura of righteous authority and their arguments a strong—if negative—proof.

October 22, 1844, found Millerites awaiting the Lord in a variety of poses. A number of watchers for the advent left Philadelphia to camp in the country, under the scourge of inclement weather, to look for Jesus' return. Most Millerites probably gathered in churches or homes. Legend has William Miller standing on a large, flat rock on a hill near his home where he could have taken a last view of the unburned mountains and valleys of New England while preparing for the clouds to burst asunder to reveal the returning Christ. It may not be too much even to credit Millerite stories that a number of scoffers could have been found on their knees. All were disappointed in their hopes and relieved of their fears. The day of the coming of the Lord became the day of the Great Disappointment.[61]

Forces from within and from outside the Millerite movement converged to promote the identification of Millerism with the setting of a specific date for the end. To a great extent, the work of the critics was done for them by the passage of time. Yet it was crucial that before the final disappointment the Millerites had become so closely associated with the date. That association was accomplished by propaganda no less effective because not systematically organized. When the insistent flow of the days confirmed for all but a very few that "43ism" and "the tenth day of the seventh month" were false prophecies, a complex of beliefs and assumptions that had been associated with the date fell into disrepute as well. The passing of the Millerites' dates not only justified opposition to date-setting but also gave implicit justification to the arguments of the critics on a score of other issues. It is to those questions that lay behind and arose with the debate over the time that we will next turn.

CHAPTER II

The Meaning of Supernaturalism

"Y ou regret that I should be so confident of 1843," wrote a Millerite convert. "The reason I am so, is, *I believe God.*"[1] That simple assertion summarized the conviction at the heart of the Millerite movement. Adventists viewed the 1843 date not as a peculiar tenet that stood alone, but as a powerful expression of a set of beliefs and assumptions. At the center of that system stood the fundamental point that there existed a powerful, transcendent, supernatural order under the rule of the Christian God. For the convinced Millerite, expressing faith in the imminent return of Christ was equivalent to expressing faith in God.

The central position of the Millerites, and, in the end, their fundamental heresy, can be summed up in the phrase "radical supernaturalism."[2] The phrase itself was used neither by the Millerites themselves nor by their opponents at the time. Radical supernaturalism does, however, mark the central point of identity for the Millerites and the central point of conflict between that minority and their detractors. Adventists insisted on the absolute reality of a transcendent order. The power of that other order depended on its distance from the human realm. If God were worthy of divinity, he had to be an objective force, separate from the people he ruled, and complete unto himself. Yet that separate, objective divinity could cross over the distance between himself and humanity at his pleasure. The alienation of humanity from God had its corollary in the power of God to break across the gulf and pour out both judgment and mercy. Just as the evangelical, in the classic experience of conversion, sensed himself utterly alienated from God and then reunited through grace from above, Millerites perceived each person and the entire human order standing far from the transcendent divinity, but added that reunion was possible, indeed imminent, through the action of God.

Millerites knew that God would break into history because he had done so before. In the first advent, the divine had entered into human history in personal, physical form. The strength of divine power and the unity of divine truth demanded that God's order existed always, outside of time, as a single force. Change over time belonged only to human history; God was unchanging. His actions, therefore, would always be consistent; they originated in an omnipresent order outside of time. If Jesus came the first time in personal, physical form, he had to come the second time in the same manner. To believe otherwise was to envision a fickle God who subjected himself to the vicissitudes of time—or, as far as Millerites were concerned, no real God at all.

Millerite supernaturalism, as symbolized in the imminent, personal advent of Christ, drew power from the continuing popular belief in miracles in the nineteenth century.[3] The advents—first and second—were, in a sense, but the greatest of miracles. Anticipation of Christ's return was thus related to belief in other interpositions of supernatural forces in everyday life, including the devil's work in bad luck or tragedy and the healing or reviving powers of God and his angels. At Millerism's energetic peak, the fringes of the movement encompassed groups that looked to just such miracles as alternative or supplementary manifestations of the same promise represented by the advent near.[4] In its broader appeal, among the mass of Millerites before as well as during the crises of 1843 and 1844, the movement centered on hope for a miracle that was radical not in its supernaturalism *per se*, but in its elevation of supernatural intervention to the center of faith and life. In rejecting the innovation of that emphasis, opponents often rejected the traditional assumptions associated with it.

Contemporaries of the Millerites confronted a perplexing dilemma. Most knew that they, too, believed God. Yet many of them found the Millerite expressions of belief peculiar. Experience told them that time and action within human history were not meaningless. In fact, they found the American Revolution, the spread of moral reform, and the development of civil and religious liberty invested with ultimate meaning. Millerites seemed to say that such assumptions were mere illusions—that they had to be so, if one believed in a transcendent God. Unwilling to cast off the assumptions that their experience made compelling, many who responded to the Millerite challenge worked out a system of belief that left believing in God consistent with valuing experience and action in time and history. They did not lack existing models from which to draw. Transcendentalists and Unitarians contributed conceptions of immanent divinity. Unitarians and Universalists placed the salvation of the whole human race at the center of the divine plan. Methodists already gave men and women a role in their own salvation. In reaction against the peculiar, embarrassing, even frightening visions of Millerism, many American Protestants sought comfortable compromises with those positions. They cut off from the broad center of orthodoxy anything that smacked of radical supernaturalism, and they drew a new boundary enclosing the insiders or orthodox and separating them from outsiders or heretics. The center of acceptable belief now posited a God who worked within and through people and their institutions. It envisioned an evolutionary providence that unfolded progressively within and through history. It rejected the vision of an eternal, transcendent, supernatural order that stood far from humanity and outside of time. The evangelical sons and daughters of Calvinism found themselves caught in a choice. They could hold fast to the powerful supernatural God of their fathers and find themselves aligned, in truth or in reputation, with Miller's adventists. Or they could embrace the immanent God of historical process and follow the new orthodoxy. Some uncomfortable compromise was certainly possible, but in terms of the major thrust of their assumptions, while many took the first road, more took the second. Indeed, the multiplicity of individual decisions in favor of the second path helped to make it orthodox, for in America the force of popular opinion more than adherence to the God of the fathers contributed to the delimiting of orthodoxy.

THE PERSONAL RETURN

As Millerites sought to emphasize the reality of the supernatural order, they turned to physical images to illustrate their belief. For them, the invisible became tangible. This was the truth embodied in the first advent of Christ. This was also the message of Henry Jones when he insisted that Christ would come again "personally and visibly" and when he reveled in a picture of "the visible, glorious presence of Christ."[5] The physical nature of Christ's return took prominence for Millerites, but it was connected to other physical images that reinforced the hard reality of adventist expectations. Jones added "the personal or visible presence of all the holy angels" to the personal presence of Christ in the coming days, and a later adventist tied together "the premillennial personal Advent, the physical regeneration of the earth after being melted with literal fire, the personal reign of Christ on earth, and the inheritance of the saints in the new earth."[6]

William Miller himself was well practiced at giving tangible reality to supernatural intervention. He may have caught the attention of his audiences with his startling proclamation of the date when he expected Christ to appear, but he won the conviction of his followers, to a great degree, with his forceful presentation of a transcendent reality they could almost see and touch. On the one hand, Miller could predict in a most level-headed and almost offhand manner that "Christ will be present with his people, and of course personally."[7] On the other hand, he could conjure up compelling and dramatic scenes of the end:

These will be the means the dragon will use in his last great struggle to gain ascendancy over the minds, consciences and bodies of men. . . . Not least, he will encourage an intolerable thirst for blood. In which battle Christ will come, chain the dragon, give his body to the burning flame, confine the spirits of all who worship the dragon, beast, or false prophet, in the pit of woe. Raise the saints, purify, cleanse and glorify them with his own glory.[8]

The lines are not such as to win Miller literary immortality, but the simple strength of the vision was enough to leave listeners and readers almost tasting the glory of future life in the presence of Christ. Through such passages Miller spread the message he had summed up for his close correspondent: "he comes behold the savior comes, lift up your heads ye saints he comes!—he comes!!—he comes!!!"[9]

Many of Miller's contemporaries found such images repugnant rather than transfixing. Infidels scoffed at Millerite hopes. "What can be more foolish," asked the *Investigator,* "than the doctrine of Christ's bodily appearance in the clouds with a retinue of angels, &c., all of them sailing through the air and blowing trumpets as they pass?"[10] Believers were perhaps more serious but no less vehement in their objections. One who labeled himself an "Orthodox" Christian called the Millerite vision a "gross material transformation," while another writer found it sadly typical of his times that so many should look for a "literal mundane overthrow" of the existing world.[11] Ironically, while the success of Millerite proselytizing depended on the use of imagery that would make their hope tangible, others read the concreteness of those images as evidence of a basely materialistic religious sensibility.

Instead of the personal, physical return of Christ and the material transformation of the world, opponents of Millerism looked forward to a spiritual reign of Christ and a spiritual change. To romantics of Lydia Maria Child's stripe, the contrast between Millerite physicality and their own conception of the "really real" was perhaps most obvious. Child pronounced her "belief in spirit" to be "so strong" that even if "the destruction of the visible world" did come, it would have "little power to affect" her.[12] She blamed the Millerite error on traditional Christian teachings, which, she said, promoted the belief "that the world would be destroyed by material fire, and that the Messiah would come visibly in the heavens, to reign as a king on earth." She felt sorry that so many could conceive of the "coming of a new heaven and a new earth" only in "external form"; she saw the change approaching, too, but understood that the impetus behind it would be invisible, the transformation, at its foundation, spiritual.[13]

Other believers, many of them more orthodox than Child, echoed similar themes. A Methodist stated quite simply that Millerism conflicted with "the plain doctrines of the Bible," including "the spiritual reign of Christ." A writer in the *Chris-*

tian Reflector was even willing to concede the time of the coming of Christ to Miller, but he objected that that return was to be *"spiritual,* upon the hearts of men, and not *personal."* Another believer who looked for a spiritual kingdom, not for a personal reign,[14] reminded the Millerites that Jesus had said, "My kingdom is not of this world."

Millerites would have none of this. They insisted again and again that there would be no "spiritual"—sometimes they called it "mystical"—reign of Christ.[15] Silas Hawley objected that a spiritual return "evidently supposes a spiritual absence, which is contrary to fact." Henry Jones regretted that the Millerites' opponents took from the last days their "real excellency and glory." A loyal adventist follower asked plaintively whether "these spiritualizers . . . deny the Lord that bought them? Do they not teach that there is no Jesus, possessing a material body . . . ?" If the first advent of Christ was personal, the resurrection of Christ literal, then the second advent and surrounding events had to be equally objectively, physically real. And Hawley raised another crucial point: "we err, if at all," he said, "with comparative safety, because of too great love for the Saviour's appearing!" The "spiritualizers," he implied, did not love the idea of being with the Lord—indeed, did not truly love the Lord at all.[16]

From 1843 opponents seized upon the Millerite "ascension robes" as a most effective form of propaganda against the adventists' physical imagery. The popular press of the time, and the long-lasting folklore that grew up around the Millerite movement, gleefully repeated stories of adventists dressing in long white gowns and traipsing to a high spot to await the coming of the Lord. A favorite version of the tale, elaborated to a greater or lesser degree in a variety of papers, had a Mr. Shortridge climbing a tree wearing the expected white robe. On the rainy twenty-third of April 1843, in Providence,

Rhode Island, a different story ran, "several Millerites . . . walked the streets and fields all day arrayed in their ascension robes, dripping from top to bottom, looking for the Saviour to come in the pouring clouds to receive them and set the world on fire." Local legend in Macedon, New York, had it that one man "dressed himself in white, and spent the whole day, either on the woodpile, or on top of the hog-pen."[17] Through such ridicule, opponents of Millerism once again, and quite effectively, made their point. Millerites reduced the promises of God to the most puny externals. Anyone who would be so foolish as to believe that Jesus Christ was about to descend through the clouds in physical form could also transform the symbolic white robes of the Bible into physical garments and then climb trees and woodpiles in order to be closer to their fleshly savior.

Arguments on both sides of the debate on the nature of Christ's return came primarily from the faithful. Although infidels took part in the fray, objections to Millerism were not generally intended as arguments against religion. The Millerite excitement raised a debate not between belief and unbelief, but between two versions of the proper nature of belief. In 1839, an adventist told Miller of a minister who said that it was not important whether Christ would reign personally or not. By the time Millerism reached its peak, it was much more difficult for American Christians to be so calm about the issue.[18] Millerism had the effect of polarizing religious people. Thousands entered Miller's camp. More joined the opposition in rejecting a conception of the supernatural taking concrete form. The Millerite disappointments reinforced this effect. As Angelina Grimké Weld wrote in a lengthy letter to her sister, Sarah, it was easier to see, in 1845, that Christ would come again without a body. "Once I was a believer in the Second personal advent of Christ," wrote the reformer and former Millerite, "but now I see that his second coming is to be in the hearts of the people."[19]

THE BURNING OF THE EARTH

Like other students of prophecy, Millerites elaborated on their vision of the last days. Miller gave a condensed version of the scenes he expected to witness at the end of time in a letter to his sister's family:

> The dead saints or bodies will arise, those children of God who are alive then, will be changed, and caught up to meet the Lord in the air, where they will be married to him. The World and all the wicked will be burnt up. (not anihilated) and then Christ will descend and reign personally with his Saints; and at the end of the 1000 Years the wicked will be raised, judged and sent to everlasting punishment.[20]

Religious writers had a good deal to say about the chronology and substance of Miller's interpretation of prophecy. Of all these images, however, the one that most caught the attention of Miller's contemporaries—next to the personal return of Christ—was that of the burning of the world.

Miller drew his image of the final conflagration from 2 Peter. The third chapter of that book foretells a time when the Lord will come and "the elements shall melt with fervent heat, the earth also and the works that are therein shall be burned up." Only after the blazing heat and the dissolution of the world are the righteous to "look for new heavens and a new earth, wherein dwelleth righteousness." Miller often returned to the theme of "lightnings" that would "send their vivid stream of sulphros flame abroad" to burn the earth.[21] Adventists followed his lead in contemplating the final scenes as portrayed in 2 Peter.[22] This fearsome expectation fit consistently into a system of belief that took the existence of a powerfully real supernatural order as its guiding center. Again, the physical imagery gave expression to belief in the absolute, even concrete reality of that other order under God. The vision of the burning of the earth raised horrifying specters before the eyes of many of the Millerites' contemporaries. They rushed to the defense of their own conception of the purpose of the earth and the place of the human race upon it. They also cried out in protest against the problems they saw raised by the burning and by the idea of a God who would cast down melting fires.

Some critics of Millerism thought it enough simply to deny the vision of a burning world, to call it an "unsupported assertion," or to ridicule the notion.[23] A Universalist protested that "none but such as possess a spirit of demons *could* desire to witness such a scene as the advocates of Millerism have *predicted*."[24] More often, critics cried out more specifically against the God of force that they saw behind the Millerite fires. "By no whirlwind power, by no exhibition of mere almightiness, is the conquest of the world for Christ to be achieved," protested one writer. Another asked if Jesus would now "abandon the field, and confess that he can rule on earth only by physical force?" A third told "our conflagration friends" that "if Christ touches match to this glorious earth of ours, . . . and burns it up . . . he is not the 'Son of man' revealed in the New Testament." Such perversions of the truth grew from human fault. "It is only when we are wrong and wicked, ourselves," he went on, "that we clothe our God with such an incendiary and revengeful disposition."[25] The God of the Millerites seemed to these commentators to be a God of wrath who acted only through ignoble means.

Critics also objected to the raising of the specter of a forceful God on the grounds of the results such an image would have on people. They perceive in those susceptible to Millerite persuasions emotions that seemed out of place among responses to the gospel—"alarm," "terror," "injurious anxiety and dread." A Congregationalist pastor dramatized the point: "When yonder little girl said, 'Mother, I want to die this summer—I don't want to live next year and be burnt up,' she gave a better view" of the effects of Millerism.[26] The critics believed that such emotions were unhealthy influences in the effort to spread Christian faith. The critics did not deny that Millerism had proved remarkably effective in producing revival excitements. They could deny that the conversions produced in the heat of those moments were authentic or genuinely transforming. In the view of these believers, terrifying people into churches did not serve God. The success of Christianity could not depend on the raising of such fantastic and horrifying images. In fact, the inspiration of the Millerites' alarming visions would only lead to mischief, as far as these critics could see.[27] "Men may be terrified into hopes," commented one orthodox writer, "but they are not wont to be terrified into holiness."[28]

In place of the objective, physical, even violent power of the God of the Millerites, critics substituted the subjective influence of loving spirit. The contrast was apparent to many without reference to the Millerite excitement. Theodore Parker, for example, reminded his audience that force had directed the "'old dispensation,' heathen or Hebrew," while the Christian dispensation introduced the law of love. The Protestant educator George Junkin had Catholics, not Millerites, in mind when he described the "great conflict . . . between government by *physical force,* and government by *moral law.*"[29] In response to the rise of adventism, more American Christians paused to consider such contrasts and gave them greater prominence and more complete elaboration. The writer who objected to the "mere almightiness" of the Millerite God preferred to look to "the noiseless, persuasive influence of the Holy Spirit, operating upon the heart and sanctifying the intellect," to turn the world to Christ. Another critic who denied that Christ would rule by "physical force" foresaw the spread of the gospel under the agency of the Holy Spirit and the "*moral* reign" of Christ.[30]

The internal operation of the spirit that led to a moral reign of grace became the basis of the new conception of "holiness" so important to mid-nineteenth-century Christians. That conception was defined as a purifying force within the hearts of Christians.[31] Opponents could not believe that Millerites promoted that essential internal, moral change. Adventists could protest that they accepted the doctrine of holiness—defined as "*purity of heart and life*" in the words of Joshua Himes—but their detractors would not believe it. One Millerite pointed out that holiness—"clean hands and pure hearts"—could alone prepare a person to meet Christ. For that writer, holiness and the advent went hand in hand.[32] But critics saw only a choice between mutually exclusive means to change. The "elements are melting with fervent heat," said one Christian writer, not through "Miller's heat, from physical fire," but rather through "the heat of holiness," which was "refining the gold" of the earth.[33]

The two conceptions seemed irreconcilable not only because one began with objective, physical force and the other with subjective, spiritual influence but also because the one kind of power worked at once and suddenly, while the other spread gradually and progressively. The Millerites looked forward to a transformation that would take place at a single given time. As their opponents confronted that vision, they drew back from the notion that unfolding processes should be cut short.

Millerites warned that the "troubles" of the last days would "come suddenly." Miller, from the time of his original study of the Bible, looked upon the advent as "a continually expected event." Turning to biblical phrases, he foresaw Christ returning "as a thief in the night" (2 Pet. 3:10) or as the "bridegroom" at midnight (Mat. 25:6). The second coming would arrive as suddenly as a flash of lightning in a dark sky.[34] The sense of immediacy reinforced the urgency of the adventist message, and the anticipation of such a sudden return recalled the total power of the Millerites' God. To those believers, it was a sign of lack of faith in an almighty God to say "my Lord delayeth his coming" or to "cry a little more sleep."[35] As Henry Jones warned, there would be no "flattering delay of his coming"; the judgment was so real as to be immediately present. Yet the promise was as strong as the return was imminent, and Jones also reminded his readers of the sorrow involved in putting off the hope of Christ's coming beyond their own lifetimes.[36]

Opponents saw little to commend such judgments and promises associated with a sudden end. For each individual, they foresaw "Continual Progression" in greater "attainments in holiness." Nor was that progress to be confined to some individuals alone. The "diffusion" of "truth and true holiness" would fill "the whole earth." Thus, gradually, "the spread of religion," "peace," "good will," and genuine "knowledge of the Lord" would fulfill the promises of God.[37] Any scheme that foretold an early end to the existing dispensation would barely allow for the preaching of the gospel in all nations, let alone the achievement of the universal prevalence of the gospel, and thus it would come into conflict with God's plan "for the moral renovation of men." "God will not," protested one such critic, "do the work in summary and arbitrary manner"; time had to remain for "the grace of God to flow" through the world, for the gospel to be spread, and for great increases in religious harmony to come.[38] Some anticipated that the progressive changes to come would reach beyond the spread of religion. The diffusion of holiness and increasing knowledge of the Lord would necessarily have ramifications in all realms. One Christian writer looked forward to "the fusing and remoulding of all institutions, religious, political and social, in the furnace of Christian love." The great revivalist Charles Grandison Finney claimed to have instructed William Miller that the "influence of the church of God" would lead to the "overthrow of governments."[39] Whatever the kind of change, it seemed most likely to these opponents of Millerism that it would be generally gradual and progressive.

Not all anti-Millerites were ready to throw out all sense of immediacy, or even all possibility of tumultuous convulsions to come. As one Millerite said of his contemporaries, even those who did not believe in the personal coming of Christ or in the 1843 date "think there must be a revolution." Fred Somkin has noted that many, perhaps even most, Americans living through the "heart-freezing change" of the nineteenth century found the idea of "cataclysmic destruction" compelling.[40] Moreover, the tradition of the jeremiad—warning of judgments and trials to come—remained strong during the antebellum years. Among more orthodox believers, it was still acceptable, perhaps even compelling, to warn that "the church is on the eve of a series of conflicts, such as she has not in our day encountered."[41] For a habitual dissenter like Angelina Grimké Weld, genuine change might begin in the hearts of believers, but could hardly be complete before it resulted in "that great earthquake which is to shake down & whelm forever all organisations, institutions and every social framework of human device."[42]

Nonetheless, the continuing anticipation of imminent change and the recurring images of cataclysm gave way to the predominance of the spirit of progress in the mid-nineteenth century. The challenges presented by the Millerites acted to press forward that change. In response to the threat of a total conflagration in 1843, even those who took the vision of 2 Peter literally tended to push such predicted tribulations off into a distant future. An internal, spiritual improvement, gradually spreading outward, came increasingly into focus.[43]

Millerites posited a radical disjunction between the supernatural and the worldly. God's order defined and encompassed all righteousness; anything that lay outside that order bore a curse. When Millerites spoke of the burning of the world, they referred to the destruction of an ungodly realm by the greatest and holiest of powers. To be precise, adventists did not anticipate the utter destruction of the planet. The physical orb would, in their picture of the future, continue to follow its path. The burning that they foresaw did not destroy, but rather purified. Their image of destruction they put forth in tones of joy as often and as much as with the tones of anger that might have been expected. When the earth melted, the fires would consume the earthly order. A finer earth, cleansed by the burning, would become the home of Christ and his saints.[44]

Some critics of Millerism saw the earthly heaven following the conflagration as an objectionable extension of the focus on the physical that pervaded the peculiar movement. Such opponents contrasted their "celestial" heaven to the anticipation of "no heaven except a residence with Christ on this earth." If the Millerite notion "presents more tangible points for . . . faith and hope" because it "has more of the sensible and of the sensual," it suffered, in this view, from being "less spiritual—less exalted—less glorious." A heaven built upon the mere ashes of the earth, over which Christ would visibly reign—this seemed an impoverished vision to those who glorified an ultimate reality with no more tangible form than the spirit.[45] More often, and sometimes concurrently, those who spoke out against the Milllerites rejected adventist belief in the burned earth because they thought it denigrated their world. "The earth is as fine a one as God could furnish us," protested one writer in an attack on the adventists.[46] If it were God's creation, the earth could not be destined for such horrible destruction. Still, it was not the love of nature so much as the fusing of the natural and the man-made with the supernatural that led the anti-Millerites to cling to their unburned sphere.[47] "The Bible asserts that there is reserved for this earth a more brilliant day than ever yet has dawned," promised a minister in the mid-1840s. "God has great designs concerning this world," and "he has made it for *his glory*," wrote another contemporary of the Millerites. Many Christians were more and more convinced that God's providence was bound to the continued progress of this world. An advent coming soon would therefore be a "cutting short of this economy of things, while the moral plans of God connected with it, remain almost wholly unaccomplished."[48]

Many such antebellum writers saw clearly the goal of "this economy of things" and "the moral plans of God." Like Millerites, they read the prophecies. Unlike Millerites, they found predicted there a better time ahead, growing within the world as it was. They looked forward, that is, to a millennium on an undestroyed earth. They denied that Christ needed to return personally to introduce that new age. Instead, they foretold the spiritual reign of Christ in an era when his influence would invisibly but powerfully come to pervade the world.[49] They maintained consistency in their own view, although they rejected the physical and objective hopes of the Millerites while holding tenaciously to an earthly culmination, by bringing the spiritual to play within and through the worldly. The "Savior's universal reign in that glorious millennium" they expected to consist of "the diffusion over the whole earth of truth and true holiness." Christ would come "upon the hearts of men," and that *"direct providential agency"* would issue in his *"universal reign of grace* on the earth."[50] The image at times became surprisingly earthly, considering that these same writers objected so vehemently to the Millerites' visions. A "Review" of an adventist conference, for example, pictured the true millennium as "a scene of time on earth when all the economy of man . . . is in full operation; such as having families, children, their conversion, uniting with the church, subscribing with their hand, having farms, cattle, . . . horses, and cooking utensils." But this was no merely physical millennium, all of these objects were to have " 'holiness to the Lord' inscribed upon them."[51]

In their concentration on an invisible, spiritual force giving birth to the millennium, evangelical Christians fulfilled, at least in part, the expectations that Silas Hawley expressed when he accused anti-Millerites of going over into the camp of the "errorists."[52] More radical religionists in the antebellum years often accepted the belief that the prophecies applied to the days of Christ.[53] They did not necessarily anticipate any return of Christ—physical or spiritual—in the future. A writer in the *Liberator* scolded that, "so long as [the church's] spiritual teachers inculcate the dogma, that the Second Advent is a future, and not a past event," just so long would beliefs like Millerism be the logical outcome. Another article in the same journal averred, "We do not think that any improvement can be made upon" the first kingdom of Christ "set up 1800 years ago."[54] The radicals implied that the seed of divinity had been sown on earth when Christ first appeared. The divine was, therefore, immanent in the world. Such statements must have struck many evangelicals as heretical. Yet the expectations of the radicals and the more orthodox had become remarkably similar by the 1840s. From a number of points on the religious spectrum came talk of spiritual change and the diffusion of holiness in the hearts of men and throughout the earth.

Similarly, millennium or no millennium, advent or no advent, denigrators of Millerism sang a fairly harmonious chorus of changes to come. Introductory to the millennium, or in continuing fulfillment of the potential of the kingdom of God, religion was to spread through the earth. Among divine promises, these commentators found the extension of the gospel to all nations. If the physical return of Christ were soon to come, there would be no time to accomplish such "moral plans of God" as bringing the "heathen" to Christ "for his inheritance" or the preaching and establishment of the gospel "in all the earth." The object of God's providence was to bring the world to Christ, according to such views. The Christian dispensation on earth had to continue long enough to allow for the fulfillment of that plan.[55] In addition to the prevalence of the Christian religion, the millennium would include a reign of great peace, good will, health, longevity, and knowledge.[56] The changes anticipated for the future were not only religious in a strict and limited sense. The religious change provided the foundation, but it would cause and accompany social and political change. One Christian spoke for many of the orthodox as well as the more radical when he foresaw "the fusing and remoulding of all institutions, religious, political and social, in the furnace of Christian love."[57] Those who remained within the broad center of evangelicalism described that future time in familiar terms and foresaw little turbulence on the road to it. Christianity spreading in the hearts of men would lead to the restoration of "individual rights and privileges." The world would be "governed by men of pure morals"—under civil government, to be sure, but with *"no more oppressive rule"* and *"no more slavery."*[58]

Those closer to the margins of dissent thought that existing structures suffered from more corruption than could be purified without profound disruptions. The Swedenborgian George Bush foresaw great "overturnings." A letter in the *Liberator* claimed that at that very time, in the 1840s, God was "rolling the heavens together" and that that meant the fusing of "churches and other organizations."[59] Even after she gave up Millerism, with its physical cataclysm, Angelina Grimké Weld looked forward to "the downfall of every Earthly throne—the overthrow of every political government—the annihilation of every Ecclesiastical Establishment & the dissolution of every sect and party under the sun."[60] Such radicals and reformers shared with the Millerites a sense of a broad chasm between the demands of ultimate righteousness and the achievements of men. Their anticipation of cataclysm, like that of the Millerites, assumed the existence of a greater order than the apparent one. But they could not go along with Millerites on the location of that higher order. Their standard derived from an immanent divinity that would well up out of human hearts and human action to bring on the earthquakes of ultimate destruction. As a result, their visions of the future, in spite of predictions of impending turmoil, bore striking similarities to those of more orthodox anti-Millerites.

Millerites rejected a millennium—or a developing kingdom on earth—that smacked of the worldly and the political. Perhaps many adventists believed that the earth suffered under a curse so total that only a complete transformation could make it a fit site for a millennium.[61] The glorious age to come was not to be an age of holiness infused through worldly structures, but an era utterly devoid of "carnal things." Henry Jones looked forward to complete peace with Christ, but he believed there could be "no bliss here" in the world as it was.[62] All talk of the universal spread of the gospel and the reign of Christ in the hearts of men was meaningless as long as such hopes were attached to the existing world. The Millerites, careful Bible readers always, accepted that the gospel would be preached to every nation. That did not mean successful preaching in the broad terms proposed by the Millerites' opponents, however. The Gospel was "never to obtain universal dominion and predominant influence." The gradual advance of religion throughout the earth was the delusive vision of a corrupt church that hoped to "deck herself" in "that gay, and gaudy, and frilled, and fimbricated robe, the Millennium," during the latter days.[63] The existing church had emerged "out of the wilderness" and entangled herself with the powers and fancies of the world. The duty of the true church was "to keep themselves unspotted from the world; to be separate, and touch not the unclean thing." And the "unclean thing" was, above all, "the policy of worldly governments" and "a political spirit."[64] The epitome of the worldly, of the accursed order, was the political realm. Miller, Himes, and other adventists saw their religious work in direct contrast to politics. In the last days, they expected to triumph over such worldly spirits and institutions as "crowns, and kings, and kingdoms" came "tumbling to the dust."[65] Only the force of a mighty God and the personal power of Christ could pull down the imposing structures of the existing world, but Millerites anticipated the engagement of just such awesome divine powers in the final task.

THE SALVATION OF MANKIND

"We are not humble enough to believe that God is the

author and finisher of our faith, or that salvation is of God," wrote William Miller. "Are we not saying, not only in our hearts, but also in doctrine, words, and action, that we can do great things?" Of course, Miller believed fully that his contemporaries spoke only of the power of humankind. He rejected this view, and he denied that "the agency of man" would bring about a great "moral change." In place of "that doctrine which gives all power to man," Miller sought to substitute a doctrine that gave all power to God.[66]

Critics of Millerism saw the question in a different light. The work of humanity, they believed, would bring on the millennium or expand the kingdom of God on earth. They refused to believe that their view left God out of the equation: opponents of Millerite supernaturalism they were: opponents of Christianity they were not. They believed, rather, that "God is pleased to employ human agency" in "fulfilling his design to enlighten and reform mankind." Or, as a Methodist had it: *"It is in accordance with the divine economy to save man by human instrumentality."*[67] Miller would have reeled at the arrogance of the evangelical who believed that God, "in employing man as the instrument" for bringing about moral change in the world, "confers honor upon him."[68] Yet many accepted the idea that an honorable role for human beings fit into God's providential plan, since "God works by means to bring his ends to pass," and his chosen means appeared to be works of "human instrumentality." Human means included "prayers, and labors, and self-denials"; another list added "contributions, and combined effort." Bible societies, missionary societies, and other "benevolent" and "moral enterprises" took a central role in this man-made progress toward the millennium.[69] In spite of remaining problems, in spite of opposition to human effort in God's work, the fires of hope kindled high. When human action reached an adequate level, God would bless those efforts. "The church therefore might have the Millenium speedily if she would"; in fact, Finney announced in 1835, "If the church will do her duty the millennium may come in this country in three years."[70]

Acceleration of human effort became both sign of and means to the ushering in of the kingdom on earth. Action and apparent success gave impetus to further work toward God's goals because they demonstrated divine approval and divine intentions.[71] Denial of the efficacy of human effort, therefore, threw up obstacles to the success of God's plan and man's hope. Henry Cowles warned in the pages of the *Oberlin Evangelist* of the "sad, dreadful mistake" of thinking that "God will bring in the Millenium by a sort of miracle, and chiefly without human agency." If people waited for God to "send an angel," Cowles warned, "we should never have a Millenium to the end of time."[72] (To which a Millerite might have replied, "Precisely so!") The "scheme" that denied the hope of the world's conversion and announced the fast-approaching return of Christ in judgment was not only wrong; it was dangerous, as far as many writers were concerned. Millerite visions "operate as a discouragement to effort," said one, and others agreed that anticipation of the imminent advent had to mean withdrawal of support from such laudable measures as Bible and missionary work.[73] By 1842, one such critic was prepared to announce that the Millerites had, in fact, slowed progress toward the millennium.[74]

William Miller insisted that adventists and all Christians were to "do all, and every work, which God in his word has commanded." He included requirements for the church "to spread her banners, send her missionaries, translate and circulate Bibles, educate the rising generation," and "establish her moral societies" among those demands of God.[75] Adventists did not favor such actions because they expected them to succeed in converting the world. They advocated such efforts because they claimed that God required them. Of course, adventist lecturers pursued the spread of their own interpretation of the gospel with vigor, and even Miller once expressed confidence that, through the work of people in conference meetings and protracted meetings, "the truth will prevail."[76] Millerites more often issued a warning against putting "means" before the "First Cause." They favored human effort, but they insisted that all means had power "so far, and no further, than is God's pleasure."[77]

Millerites described a God-centered universe. It was God's pleasure, not man's, that became the ultimate standard for the radical supernaturalist. An opponent could object that the Lord coming "in terror from the flaming sky . . . would not be treating us as we would like to be treated."[78] For Millerites, that was hardly the point. Similarly, the arguments that the earth existed for humanity's use and could not be destroyed when its resources had scarcely been touched, or that the end of God's providence was the happiness "of the whole human family," or that the advent was to be expected when needed and desired—all were arguments that placed humankind at the center.[79] Many Millerites saw the glory of God in his distance from humanity, not in his structuring of a man-centered universe.

Millerites came up against human hopes once again when confronting the question of the availability of salvation. Miller believed in *"Election* particular, personal and certain, governed by the mind, will and plan of God." He expected few to be chosen, and those to be chosen by God for eternity. He lashed out against "the smooth and popular doctrine of the times," Arminianism, and found among the signs of decline in the last days the rise of the *"modern Universalists."*[80] Miller refused to multiply doctrinal tests within his movement, however, and his followers often strayed from his positions on these matters. Henry Jones hoped for "a very sudden, swift and powerful spread of the gospel" in the last days, broadening the offer of salvation to suit his more optimistic temperament. Even Jones objected to any thought of universal salvation, however, and called the idea of the world's conversion "a syren song" of recent origin.[81] Other adventists expected the number of the saved to be far more restricted. One such writer asserted that the end of the world had to come quickly and suddenly to stop the downward course of the world, "lest no flesh should be saved."[82] Like other converts born of the revivals of the 1830s and 1840s, Millerites tended to imply, at least, that people had a role in their own salvation. As time went by, a number of adventists began to see adherence to the second advent doctrine itself as the essential requirement for salvation.[83] Whatever the winnowing principle, Millerites agreed that there would be wheat and chaff at the end—candidates for two resurrections, one of the righteous and one of the wicked.[84]

Universalists sounded the alarm against such limited prospects for human salvation, of course. "Mr. Miller seems to hate, most inveterately, all who believe, that God is the Saviour of the world," cried one.[85] Lydia Maria Child also protested that no one with any common sense could worship a God "who, having filled this world with millions of his children, would finally consign them all to eternal destruction, except a few who could be induced to believe in very difficult and doubtful explanations of prophecies."[86] Even those who did not go so far as to expect universal salvation hoped for a wide influence for the Christian religion and a "great ingathering of the human family."[87] Henry Cowles protested that, if Miller's ideas were true, no more sinners could be redeemed after a very short time. As a result, "The number of our race ultimately lost will immensely exceed the number saved, and the triumphs of Satan will by so much exceed the triumphs of Christ." Cowles expressed dismay at Miller's heaven, peopled by "a little company of us—a mere handful of the race." For Cowles, "one of the richest joys of heaven will grow out of the fact that unnumbered myriads of redeemed sinners will be there with us to enjoy it." Indeed, Cowles expected "almost the entire race" to join him in "the bliss of heaven's benevolence."[88] Cowles measured the triumph of his God in numbers of souls saved.

Millerites did not find the future envisioned in their system "narrow, restricted," or " prison-house more than a heaven."[89] Perhaps the nature of God's triumph was defined by him and known to him alone, or perhaps it was embodied in the culmination of his providence—the return of Christ and the new heaven and new earth to follow. Millerites emphasized the glory they saw in the personal advent. But they could also turn the tables on their adversaries. If their critics chose to raise the question of collective salvation as opposed to a narrow and lonely hope, Millerites could in their turn criticize the harping of their contemporaries on an individual's death as the moment of final account. As far as adventists were concerned, dwelling on an expectation of death rather than an expectation of the coming of Christ "isolates us in our own individuality." If the Millerite vision did not promise universal salvation, at least there could be found in it "no cold and deadening individuality." Among Millerites, contemplation of the imminent second coming "awakened feelings which the anticipation of death had never kindled in their breast."[90] Their sense of collective anticipation seemed to them a greater hope than mass conversions, and they found that sense reinforced when they suspected that the alternative was a solitary moment of judgment at death.

Millerites struck a raw nerve when they accused their opponents of working for the long term and of losing a sense of impending judgment. In response to the Millerite challenge, a number of writers did turn to the theme of preparing to meet one's maker. In 1842, religious papers repeated an anecdote about a Methodist minister who claimed to be "an 1842 man." The minister "preached the great reality of constant exposure to death, AND AFTER DEATH THE JUDGMENT."[91] Another observer of Millerism was supposed to have commented, "Yes, I think the end of the world will come this year—to a good many people."[92] Many of such writings were more defensive than jovial. For those who thought of themselves as orthodox, the recovery of a sense of judgment in the midst of optimistic dreams of progress and in the face of the Millerite challenge often seemed essential. They urged their brethren to "keep in mind that as respects ourselves, our neighbors and our friends individually, the Judge may be standing before the door."[93] For many opponents of Millerism, it was the utility of reminders of death at the door that was most important. The story of the "1842 man" had as its happy ending a flourishing revival inspired by preaching about death. Opponents of Millerism protested that the holy heart and moral life necessary in preparation for judgment were as important in the face of death as they could be on the eve of the second advent.[94] Lydia Maria Child observed that, "liable as we all are to drop into the grave at any moment," there should have been little extra excitement added by the notion that the world was about to end. She, for one, would endeavor "to discharge my duty to God, and with love to my neighbor," whether she expected death or the second advent, but she was very suspicious of the lack of extraordinary morality among believers in the advent near.[95] Americans of many persuasions discovered and revealed, in response to the Millerites, the degree to which they were prepared to interpret their lives in terms of the efforts and hopes of humanity and the prospects of the individual human being. The Puritan forebears the nineteenth-century Americans had stood in awe of a powerful, transcendent God. They had envisioned a divinity that acted directly upon—and often against—sinful humanity. Their hope rested in part in the possibility of individual election, and that state of having been chosen also rested upon a direct action of God, once and forever. The Puritan sense of accountability before God laid burdens not only on the individual but also on the collectivity. God sent warnings and judgments as well as promises not only to his elect one by one but also to his people as a whole.

William Miller was not a Puritan. As a good son of Puritan New England, though, he did hearken back to themes from those earlier generations. His innovations raised to prominence once again words and images that Puritans had viewed as central to understanding the universe and their role in it. When Miller referred to himself as the "Old Man" or "Old Father Miller," he sought to associate himself with that old order.[96] Much of his writing exudes a sense of sorrow over its passing—over the loss of a sense of awe, of the reassuring authority of the Calvinist God, of the subjection of human desires before ultimate standards. In his grief over the passing of Puritanism, Miller mourned, too, the loss of the glory in the promises of God that he found irretrievably connected to divine threats and judgments. Miller's universe rested on a balance of necessary oppositions. If God were great, humanity had to be distantly below God; if some were to be meaningfully saved, many had to be damned; if the desires and demands of God set the true standard of righteousness, the desires of people and the rules of the human order had to count for nil. Miller's supernaturalism encompassed all of these aspects. If his followers did not adhere to his personal beliefs in all their details, they did, at least, share his general sensibilities and assumptions. They, too, sought to retrieve a sense that God really existed, objectively and powerfully, and that his order not only differed from that established by man but also had the force to break up the human stand in its place. Like Miller, they hoped on a grand scale, hoped for a transformation that was total and embracing, and hoped for a salvation that gathered the saints around their savior.

The Puritan commonwealth under the rule of God had already passed—had perhaps passed virtually at its moment of conception. The dominant center of American Protestantism had shifted, beginning in the seventeenth century, moving further in the eighteenth, and continuing to break away from old grounds during the century that saw the Millerites trying to reclaim part of the Pruitan vision. Ideas and experience had chipped away at old orthodoxies. By the 1830s, Americans had begun to find seeds of divinity within individuals, within social processes, and within the nation itself. They had turned reluctantly away from the cohesion of the corporate commonwealth to rely on the tenuous ties growing out of the unleashing of individual energies and interests. They concentrated less on what they hoped to receive from without and more on what they could build themselves, out of resources already existing within and around them. Yet it was not until they were challenged that many of these American Protestants articulated their new beliefs and explicitly reformulated their assumptions. When the Millerites raised the specter of radical supernaturalism, many of their contemporaries responded decisively: of course, they chorused, these alarming visions had no place in the religious systems of respectable and responsible Christians. When they turned to backing up that response, they clarified the positions to which they had gradually shifted, but they formulated those new positions under a strong incentive to distance themselves from the heretics in their midst. If an objective, transcendent God proved to be frightening, or even just out of place in the day of the steam engine, then it was time to imagine a God who worked in and through humanity. Immanence had begun to seem more compelling than transcendence, subjective experience more believable than objective force. If looking to God to act meant anticipating the cutting short of ongoing social, political, and technological change—even the burning of the earth—then it was time to accept that people could act effectively to change the world.

The meaning of supernaturalism, then, actually encompasses two meanings. For Millerites, anticipation of the imminent, personal return of Christ reflected faith in a mighty supernatural being, a God whose nature, means, and demands remained constant and authoritative. It reflected, too, a sense of an immediate necessity to subject oneself to that God. For those who reacted against Millerism, supernaturalism became a foil against which to define and elaborate the true faith of the modern American Christian. Because the supernaturalism of the Millerites took on that second meaning, the study of the process of interaction between Millerites and others opens up an opportunity to view changes in the religious culture of the nineteenth century in categories developed by the participants themselves. The remaining chapters of this book will follow the ramifications of Millerite supernaturalism in several areas of religious and social life—conceptions of the sources of religious knowledge and authority, organization in congregations and denominations, ideals of personal development, demands for social action, and association for the purpose of restriction and control.

CHAPTER III

Revelation and Authority

The Millerites centered their belief on a supernatural power acting beyond human understanding and human means. Like adherents of other faiths, however, they found sources accessible to them through which they might glimpse the transcendent order. Having formulated their positions on access to knowledge and authority, they once again encountered opposition from those who saw new possibilities for faith founded upon an altered set of sources. For both sides in this debate, questions of authority revolved around the roles of the Bible, religious experience, and human and natural history.

Christian history contains a multitude of answers to the question of how to know God and his truth. The Puritan forebears of nineteenth-century Americans had struck a balance among avenues to religious knowledge: divine grace would open the eyes of the believer to apply reason to the truths written in both Bible and nature. Never unchallenged, this balance of religious experience, scripture, and worldly evidence wobbled and tumbled in the eighteenth and nineteenth centuries. The collapse of that order left new generations to choose which mode of authority to emphasize. In the eighteenth century, rationalists glorified Reason while evangelicals focused on Experience. Generations of innovators thereafter selected their own ways of seeking truth, often reacting against the previous generation in the process. For

Transcendentalists, for example, the divine was immanent; neither Bible nor specific religious experience was necessary if the greatest truths held by the universe could be found in nature or within one's breast.

Similarly, by the nineteenth century, the numerous and influential evangelicals slowly divided over the question of authority. Generally, they agreed that a conversion experience was necessary to knowledge of the nature and will of God. Evangelicals maintained a tenuous unity on this point although they differed increasingly on the related questions of the role of human ability in conversion, proofs of valid religious experience, and the proper relationship between conversion and baptism. Evangelicals also agreed on the importance of the Bible. The question of how that Bible should be read did surface repeatedly and more and more insistently. Did the authoritative Bible include the Old Testament as well as the New? Was the authority general and allegorical or specific and literal? Such questions only began to tear away at the evangelical consensus during the antebellum period. The issue of biblical authority was also intimately tied to the problem of the role of history and nature. Historical experience and natural phenomena had happily been used to buttress biblical authority in the past. Now a confusion of priorities arose: Did one accommodate history to the Bible, or the Bible to history? Would signs in the heavens help to give astronomy precedence over scripture, or vice-versa?

Into this arena of confusion stepped the Millerites. They struck against the uneasy evangelical consensus with the weapon of certainty. The Bible, they proclaimed, spoke the truth in all its parts, in all its words, even in all its numbers. The Bible was unquestionably the word of a powerful God. The facts of history and of nature could only support that word. The converted individual could understand this, and had the potential to read the scriptures correctly. Like other antebellum Americans, Millerites teetered back and forth among various forms of religious authority. They began with the Bible, but renewed emphasis on experience—often on a second experience—or on signs in nature and history cropped up among some members of the movement. In any case, they found knowledge of a supernatural order through the direct intervention of a distant but powerful God.

BIBLICAL LITERALISM

William Miller wrote to Truman Hendryx about what he considered most necessary for preachers and teachers: "you must preach *Bible* you must prove all things by *Bible* you must talk *bible*," he admonished, and "You must exhort *bible*, you must pray *Bible*, and Love *Bible*, and do all in your power to make others Love *Bible* too."[1] Attention to the scriptures was a religious duty, but, more, it was a direct and straightforward way of learning about God, his demands, and his providential plans. Reliable to the last, the Bible stood as a final authority and a sure path to truth. It had to be so. Miller hinted at the fearful alternative once in a private letter: "At any rate if the Bible is not true, then who can tell us what is truth?"[2] Miller's religious system centered on the assertion of a truth—the truth of the existence of a transcendent, supernatural order. His distant and powerful God had to be revealed to man somehow, though, and the mighty other chose to reveal himself through the Bible. This, too, had to be so. Man had to know, and the Bible itself testified to its own truth.

Millerites sometimes went to extremes in setting the Bible at the center of their faith. They could occasionally make the simple and straightforward claim that Millerism was the equivalent of "biblism."[3] Miller's interpretation of one of his favorite parables, that of the wise and foolish virgins, also cast the balance of authority far in the direction of the scriptures:

> The Ch[ur]ch[e]s through the instrumentality of Bibles are giving the world the *Lamp* (word) all may trim (read) but all do not have oil (faith) in the lamp (word) therefore to those who have no oil (faith) it can give no light, and he that hath no oil (faith) will be shut out (damned).[4]

In this curious interpretation, the believer was urged to have faith, not in God or Christ, but in the word. Believing the word became a necessity for salvation on a par with faith. Such may not have been Miller's intention when writing this passage, but it is not surprising that he fell easily into the posture of a Bible-worshipper. The certainty of the truth and the totality of the authority of the Bible in Miller's system went hand in hand with the fundamental assumption of the existence and absolute power of an objective divine order. When Miller's God spoke, he did not speak fuzzily or incomprehensibly, but rather finally and with clarity and assurance. The certain and clear authority of the Bible, then, fit into a system defined by radical supernaturalism. The Bible, as a product of the omnipotent God, was virtually a part of him—so great was its truth and so closely bound to the utter reality and final authority of God himself. Thus Miller could come to speak of having saving faith in the word. The word was his lifeline, his evidence, and his token of more and grander intervention to come.

A number of antebellum Christians objected to the Millerite claim to biblical authority. It did not seem possible that Miller was a Bible man; after all, he did not find in the Bible what many religious leaders found. Some were willing to let the differences pass; correct interpretation or no, at least Miller and his advance guard brought the scriptures to the attention of a good many people.[5] Others, especially as 1843 and 1844 approached, refused to follow that line. If Miller's interpretation were wrong, then it was wrong to spread it, even if it seemed to be harmless and to promote study of the scriptures. In the end, the argument ran, faulty interpretation would only bring the whole Bible into disrepute. What was required was a correct understanding of the Bible.[6] But here was the rub: so few had clear ideas and theories on the proper interpretation of the Bible in those decades. They had a multitude of options, to be sure, but the only safe middle ground seemed to be an acceptance of the Bible as true on terms that could not be spelled out.

The "literal" interpretation of the Bible that held sway until the eighteenth century Hans Frei has labeled the "literal-realistic approach."[7] The basic assumption of this approach was that any and all stories in the Bible were literally true and that, as a part of that literal truth, they referred to actual events in history. Just as histories made up a single history, the stories of the Bible made up a single story. All human experience had to fit into the greater narrative. The literal meaning of the words of the scriptures, the historical actuality of the events that they described, and the greater reality of the comprehensive sequence of providence, all came together in a unified Bible. During the eighteenth and early nineteenth centuries, that unity split apart. At the center of that shattering lay a new distinction and distance between the biblical story itself and the "reality" to which it was supposed to correspond. The primary implication of that shattering was that the story itself became secondary. No longer part of a unity, it was forced to refer either to historical events or to a greater reality that was assumed to lie behind or above the narrative itself. Once the story—both the particular story and the aggregate of stories in the sweeping narrative of providence—had contained within itself both the true referent for historical experience and the meaning of both story and experience. Now each story was assumed to describe only a restricted historical reality—if even that—as critics began to ask whether the story as told in the Bible fit what men knew of history. And, insofar as the Bible was assumed to point to a larger, even ultimate meaning, scripture became little more than the pointer that helped to show the way. Throughout the turmoil that accompanied these changes, people continued to think of their own approaches to the Bible as literal—if, indeed, they thought about "approaches" at all.[8] The meaning of the acceptance of an authoritative Bible shifted, while it was hardly clear to those involved that the nature of the authority had been drastically changed.

Frei argues that this change took place among biblical critics. He does not concern himself with popular readings and perceptions of the Bible. The arguments of the Millerites and their opponents indicate that, by the middle decades of the nineteenth century, similar confusions about the nature of biblical meaning and authority had arisen among many groups in the American population. Frei's thesis, therefore, helps to clarify the differences between the radical supernaturalists, who looked for the rapid approach of Christ, and their detractors.

William Miller sought a unity and authority in the scriptures that might have corresponded with Frei's "literal-realistic" approach. He and his followers believed that the truths of scripture were once and always the same. Those truths were elaborated in the unfolding of God's providence, and the sweep of providential history encompassed all earthly events. Moreover, the Bible outlined that providential history. The reader had the responsibility of tracing the connections between that sweeping story and particular events—both of

Bible history and of his own lifetime. Biblical truth, biblical narrative, and history became one, but the last, in practice, had to remain subordinate to the first two. That God's truth was a single and lasting truth was the first point in the supernaturalists' system. That biblical narrative covered a single, coherent story of the playing out of God's plan on earth was the second, indissolubly bound to the first. When people sought to fit what they experienced and saw around them into those larger wholes, the level of human perception and experience remained subordinate. It was no surprise, therefore, that humans erred as often as not in seeking to tie the levels of Bible truth together. There was, nonetheless, no excuse for failing to try. God required people to draw larger truths, the full plan of providence, and specific events of history together in an approximation of the divine unity behind them all. If human beings failed in their efforts, this did not cast doubt on the truths or the course of providence, or even on the unity of those levels with present and past history, but only left them to begin again. Specific connections and interpretations could be wrong; the underlying theory and method of biblical interpretation could not.

Following Miller, adventists generally asserted that they drew together levels of truth into a coherent whole while, in practice, they tended to denigrate recent or present history. Because this kind of reasoning lay behind the Millerite approach to the Bible, Silas Hawley could calmly say that any errors in Miller's lectures could not be "fundamental," since they would relate "to the *time* and *manner* of Christ's coming, and not to the *fact* of his coming."[9] Hawley made that statement just as he was being drawn into the Millerite movement, and later, along with most adventists, he laid much more emphasis on the date. It is significant, however, that he attached himself to Millerism because of the attraction of the unitary truth that he perceived behind the Millerite message and that at first, at any rate, precision in fitting the course of earthly history into the general plan was less important than grasping that truth. Similarly, when Miller confessed his mistake about the fall of the Turks in 1839, he easily put it down to mere human error. He knew that profane history paralleled divine history and that both pointed to the great truths of Christianity. A little waffling on a particular event did no damage to those basic assumptions. He remained optimistic about the possibility of finally establishing the coincidence of all levels of truth and evidence. As he once wrote to his relatives, he believed that "when you have established your posts and pillars," presumably the fundamental truths encompassed by the Bible, then "you will see the filling will come in."[10] Given proper principles—and faith—one could come to grasp the details that fit the course and meaning of providence. Expressions of certainty about the 1843 date represented a change of emphasis within this set of assumptions and not a recasting of fundamental approach.

The unity of meaning, providence, biblical narrative, and history required unity within the Bible itself. That unity within scripture Millerites were pleased to assert. When they expressed the importance of the Bible, they meant one Bible, complete and true in itself and throughout its parts. In order to understand it, one had only to take each passage and fit it into the whole. The Bible, said Miller, was "its own interpreter."[11] One verse became clear through the study of other sections. Thus, for example, if one wanted to determine the truth or falsity of a particular doctrine, the steps were simple: "1st you must believe the Word of God. 2nd you must find two witnesses (or plain texts) in that word to make you, or to cause you, to believe the Doctrine or principle laid down," and finally, "be sure you get one in the old and one in the new testament."[12] Any single passage might be obscure or misleading in itself. Interpretation of the Bible did not proceed, among Millerites, through narrow attention to the precise meaning of specific words.[13] Each passage achieved clarity, rather, through context—through its part in a larger whole. A single scripture passage proved nothing to a Millerite.[14] At least two passages had always to be read together in order to preserve the sense of the whole. In addition, as Miller noted, the coherence had to include both testaments; both meaning and narrative had to encompass Old as well as New.

Adventists connected Old Testament to New and both testaments to history through a system of typology. Individuals portrayed in the Old Testament were viewed as "types," figures, or foreshadowings of people, angels, or saints in the New Testament. Similarly, those described in the Bible found their reflections in ongoing history, at least in the final days. William Miller emphasized the first kind of type, that which connected Old Testament to New, when he considered the unity of the Bible. But his typological approach was intimately bound up with his reading of the prophecies. Just as the literal Michael of the Old Testament symbolized and prefigured the literal Christ of the New, so the symbols and figures of the prophecies in both testaments foretold and foreshadowed their own literal fulfillment in the future. Typology, double meanings, and general interpretation of prophecy all became part of a kind of cosmic seamless web of meaning and authority.[15]

Critics of Millerism often claimed to speak in the name of literalism when they attacked the Millerite approach. One aspect of the changing balance of authority became clear, however, when a perception of history as linear came up against an assumption that biblical meanings overlapped. A Universalist critic said it most clearly: "It is a universal custom in the writing of history, to describe events as they occurred,—not to take up one class, and go through with that, then go back and bring in another class, and so on."[16] That writer referred to Miller's interpretation of the Book of Revelation, but the point was applied more broadly and by many more than a single author. When critics objected to the overlapping of different visions in Miller's chronology, they addressed the same problem. The modern perception of history as linear was thrown back upon the ancient writers. If events unfolded one after another in a progressive development, they implied, then Daniel must have foreseen them that way.[17]

The obverse of this assumption caused problems, however, with what was called the "double sense" of prophecy. The visions of Daniel, for example, were assumed by most of Miller's contemporaries to refer both to historical events of ancient days and to the culminating events of the end of time. If history followed a single line, and if prophecies were supposed to reflect that, however, there was little logical space left for the double sense of prophecy. Most refused to reject the concept, but in their arguments against Miller and his followers, many put new strains on their systems of interpretation.

The place of the Old Testament, therefore, posed special problems for a number of nineteenth-century Christians. Some solved the problem by denying the authority of the Old Testament altogether.[18] Most were unwilling to violate the authority and unity of the Bible to such an extent. A number rejected typology as a means for connecting the testaments, however, since such overlapping meaning obscured and mystified what they thought of as the clear sense of the Bible.[19] In a telling parallel, popular use of typology persisted, but largely in using Old Testament figures as doubles for American leaders: both George Washington and Abraham Lincoln became Moses, for example. Torn out of the context of the unity of truth and experience on a number of levels, typology became yet another way to elevate history—specifically, American experience—to a position of primary importance.[20]

BIBLE BY THE NUMBERS

Millerites, and for that matter a good number of their contemporaries, saw little good and much danger in leaving interpretation of the Bible to the "D.D.s" who concerned themselves with the more obscure points of biblical interpretation. In the aftermath of the American Revolution, religion became more and more a matter for private judgment. No longer were men to be led by a "bigoted priesthood"—or even, in the extreme case, by honest ministers. In the absence of an established church and out of the antiauthoritarian implications of Revolutionary ideology grew a reliance on individual conscience as the only proper place of judgment for religious matters. The American people of the first half of the nineteenth century were also great Bible-readers and Bible-believers, however. Each person, among the majority, checked his or her conscience against the Bible, and, to a remarkable degree, against the Bible alone.[21]

Bible and conscience played off one another. The Bible became the standard by which one could judge the inclinations of private judgment. But individual judgment also became the standard by which one could understand the Bible. The assumption was not that this would lead to a babylon of interpretive voices, although the result sometimes seemed to approach that state. Widespread belief held that the message of the Bible was accessible. Scriptures were not, for the most part, thought to be mysterious and obscure, but open to reading. After all, God gave people the Bible that they might read it. If they were to read it, certainly they could understand it. The general assumption of the perspicuity of the scriptures was buttressed by the psychological and philosophical tenets of the Scottish Common Sense school that was so influential in early America. Basically, the fundamental assertion of Common Sense thinkers was that all men had the faculty of "understanding" necessary to confront and comprehend "facts" in the world. Since all shared that fundamental capacity, all had equal access, in a sense, to knowledge. Moreover, the right use of that common faculty would lead men, ultimately, to similar conclusions, for the understanding could allow the facts to speak for themselves, and the facts always told the same story. Along with facts in nature and in history, antebellum Americans confronted the "facts" of the Bible with that fundamental, shared capacity for understanding.[22]

In middle-class culture, at least, it was an age of democracy and at the same time an age of religious fervor. As the Second Great Awakening and Jacksonian democracy came together in their influence on common Americans, they mingled in a "populist hermeneutic."[23] Millerites, among others, at once inherited and championed this new approach to religious knowledge. Millerites insisted that the Bible was intended for all people.[24] Miller found it necessary to issue frequent warnings against abandoning this principle even within his group. He urged acceptance of the differences of opinion that he thought necessarily followed liberty of conscience, and he threatened that the alternative was a "resort to creeds and [formulas], Bishops and Popes." All were to have their say, he reminded Himes, "especially those who pretend to have bible for what they believe."[25] And Millerites seemed optimistic, as their peers were, about the possibility that unity could arise from the unleashing of individual conscience—under God. With a little help from Miller, Himes was sure that "the people *will see*" the difference between truth and error, and that the people would then naturally leave the misleading D.D.s "to themselves."[26]

Opponents turned similar assumptions and approaches against the Millerites. A former adventist, for example, regretted his earlier "short-sighted and contracted views" and blamed his attachment to Millerism on "my own ignorance and folly in letting others think and read for me."[27] The underlying fault in Millerism, according to this view, was that it was founded on the blind following of the peculiar ideas of a few men rather than a reliance upon the strength of individual consciences working to the same end. The "43 delusion" seemed of a piece with "the artifices, with which the heathen priests frighten their devotees, and the cunningly devised fables, with which the papal hierarchy dupe their votaries."[28] The problem of the individualized approach to the scriptures was that, where any two or more agreed, it could be attributed either to popish power or to agreement reached through the application of the "understanding" to the "facts." The ultimate judge on this question was not individual conscience, but the power of numbers and social influence.[29]

From the beginning, some proved unwilling to throw the judgment of Bible truth into the hands of the common man. They proclaimed in public that "few, save the *uniformed, and illiterate,* embrace Millerism," or that Miller's conclusions were objectionable because Miller did not have the education necessary for a correct reading of the Bible, or that Miller was in error insofar as he did not follow standard authorities—among them those infamous D.D.s.[30] Such sentiments probably hit home among many who feared the multitude of apparently disruptive influences unleashed in the 1830s and 1840s. But their effect had to have been a two-edged sword. For every one who was reassured by the authority of "standard writers" and educated clergy, at least one would have been driven toward sympathy with a group identified with the "people" and the power of their—perhaps uneducated—understanding.

The problem of the perspicuity of scripture and of the ability of the generality of mankind to read and understand emerged in debates over the nature and purpose of those strangely compelling parts of the Bible that Miller and his followers took as their focus—the prophecies. Miller had stated plainly that he believed all the Bible was necessary, important, and comprehensible. He did not read one part of the Bible under one set of rules, and another part under another set—at least as he understood what he was doing. the Christian's duty included study of the prophecies as surely as it included study of the Gospels. Such was the logical conclusion of a man—and a group—who insisted on the unity of the scriptures. All parts of the Bible were related to one another, contained the same system of truth within them, were necessary for a proper understanding of all other parts, and could be read by all people. God gave mankind the whole Bible, and he intended that it should be read and understood. When people read the prophecies, they would gain a deeper understanding of many biblical truths, but they would learn, especially, about the timing of the end.

In spite of the widespread acceptance of ideas about the accessibility of scripture, it was precisely on the points of prophecy and timing that many interpreters balked. It was all well and good, as one reviewer said, to follow what was "plainly revealed"; it was another thing entirely to dwell upon that which was "designedly obscure."[31] Another commentator elaborated on the purpose of the "designed obscurity" of the prophecies. Those portions of the scripture, he said, were certainly meant to prepare people for the coming culmination, but they were "to keep men perpetually on the watch." Uncertainty was necessary, in that writer's view, to inspire constant preparation for what was to come. People would follow their duties more faithfully under such a continuous but unknown plan.[32] The tension of hope and fear before the fulfillment of any given prophecy would be rewarded with confirmation after the event, but no prohecy could be understood until after its fulfillment. Some added that such motivating obscurity showed the great wisdom of God; others rebuked the "idle" and "irreverent curiosity" of those who sought to pry into the secrets of God.[33] All turned to their Bibles to show that, even if one studied the prophecies, one could not know the time of the end. "Of that day and hour knoweth no man," and "It is not for you to know the times or the seasons," they quoted; if all other arguments proved vain, certainly the Bible itself would settle the question.[34]

But the question was not settled. Millerites objected to all of this obscuring of the prophecies. God commanded men and women to study the Bible—the whole Bible. Miller thought his opponents tried to keep people away from an essential portion of the scripture, and he saw behind such action the work of Satan. The devil, he said, sought to destroy faith by raising such arguments against the study of the prophecies as that "they are dark and intricate," "it is presumption to look into futurity," and "it is a sealed book,—not to be understood until it is fulfilled."[35] As good a Bible reader as his opponents, Miller, too, said—at least before the fall of 1844—that the "day and hour" remained hidden. Of course, even to know the "times and seasons"—or the year—was problematic. But the "vision" had been *"closed, shut up,* and *sealed,"* not forever, but until the end. And Millerites knew that their time was the time of the end. They could, therefore, assume for themselves the knowledge reserved for the last days.[36] The reasoning was a bit circular—by knowing that it was then the end of time they could know that it was the end of time—but more compelling for many than the insinuation that there were parts of the Bible too difficult or even too dangerous for the people to approach.

Claiming to have knowledge reserved for certain people and a certain time posed its own problems. Before addressing such problems, we should consider how Miller went about unearthing the timing of the last days. By the early nineteenth century, not only had God supposedly given Americans a readable Bible to study, but he had also apparently given them a peculiar propensity to calculate from "facts—all kinds of facts, including, some would say, the "facts" of the Bible.

Americans in the first half of the nineteenth century glorified their own version of Baconian induction. Francis Bacon had asserted that the surest path to knowledge was not deductive—proceeding from generalizations to the specifics that could be drawn from them—but rather inductive—proceeding from the accumulation of specific facts to the generalizations that could be built up from them. Bacon's ideas had a special appeal to Americans of the post-Revolutionary generations. The individualistic and egalitarian thrust of the experience and ideology of the Revolution left people open to theories of knowledge that made truth accessible to all. The facts that built up to general truths in Baconian induction offered just such access. "Lord Bacon" became a culture hero to generations eager to participate in a democracy of knowledge.

The facts to which Bacon had originally referred included, specificially, the facts of nature. Bacon had urged the observation of physical events in order to build up a body of physical laws. Nineteenth-century American Christians followed the empiricist method of Bacon, but applied it in new directions.

Most important for the present discussion, they applied the method, as they understood it, to the Bible. At a time when a few began to question the Bible because it contradicted the facts of nature and history, others took the stories and doctrines that they found in the Bible and called them facts. The truth attributed to the Bible became a surprisingly concrete and literal truth, and the various aspects of that truth were considered to be facts as clear to perceptions as physical facts.[37]

William Miller joined in the popular assumption that Bible facts, accessible to all, opened the way to Bible truths. He also joined in another trend in the popular culture of the day that joined method to facts. The facts were Bible facts. The method was calculation. By the early nineteenth century, the spread of "numeracy," or the ability to work simple calculations, came together with a growing assumption that number facts and statistics were objective and impartial. Manipulation of numbers was a skill shared by many people, and the facts supposedly spoke for themselves. Such a status for calculating was well suited to the democratic Baconianism of the times. Numbers supplied the facts, and calculating supplied the method for working with the facts. The result would, of course, be access for all the people to great shared truths.[38]

Miller and his assistants played on this trend, not to deceive their audiences, but rather to share their own perception of the possibilities of number facts and Bible calculations. Miller, of course, laid out the basic figures. The 70 weeks as part of the 2,300 days (which began in 457 B.C.) with the year 33 of Christ's death added on, the 1,335 days begun at the end of pagan Rome in 508—columns of additions and subtractions all pointed to the same conclusion, that Christ would return in 1843. Once set off in the right direction, lo and behold, any of the people who tried to track these calculations for themselves could find the same facts right in the Bible. They could apply simple arithmetic to those facts. Millerite lecturers led meeting-halls full of listeners through the prophetic arithmetic, the lecturer referring to his chart while the auditors added up figures on their slates. The same exercise could be repeated by anyone at home.[39] The Millerite method was a triumph of accessible scriptures combined with the democratic possibilities of the Scottish Common Sense school's understanding and Bacon's induction.

Some found biblical arithmetic at least ridiculous and at most presumptuous. One could go to a Millerite tabernacle on Sunday to hear the second advent preached "with mathematical precision," noted the skeptics, or one could do the figuring oneself: "Multiply the wrinkles upon the horns of a five-year old ram by the twelve signs of the zodiac, and that product by the number of seeds in a winter squash; you will then find that Gabriel's going to blow next year."[40] Other critics objected in more serious tones to the presumption of applying humanity's "finite capacity" to follow the rules of arithmetic to the great problem of obscure prophecies; Miller's "egregious egotism," said one writer, seemed to lead him to the conclusion that his arithmetic was a "divine science."[41] And Millerites did not stop with calculations from within the Bible. They ciphered away with all kinds of statistics that might buttress their view of the end—at least such was the opinion of the writer who claimed that a Millerite had concluded that no millennium could come before the resurrection because the resulting population would add up to 18,037,886 per square yard. This, sneered the writer, all based on "figures that cannot lie."[42]

Such additional ciphering was not beneath Miller, at least. At the bottom of a letter asking how the resurrected could all fit on the earth at the same time, he carefully added up population figures and noted his conclusion: "Allow 800,000,000 for 30 years 32 rods to each person *on the globe*."[43] But his detractors were as likely as not to engage in the same sort of figuring. One who called Miller a monomaniac, for example, went on to point out that there could not be a thousand-year judgment at the end of time—such as Millerites had claimed would follow the return of Christ— because the resulting population would add up to 61,062,000,000,000,000,000,000,000,000,000,000 people per square mile. The editors of the *Vermont Chronicle* showed a similar spirit when they pronounced that, if piety were to become universal within the two hundred years that they believed were left before the judgment, people would have to be converted 120 times as fast as they had been since the time of Luther.[44] In "an age of inquiry," said a writer in the *Christian Secretary*, people ask for "evidence."[45] And the best evidence, as far as many in the generation of the 1830s and 1840s could see, was the kind associated with numbers, statistics, and calculations. A statement promoting William R. Weeks' "Essays on the Mistakes of Miller" concluded proudly that the "Essays" contained "proofs abundant, and as simple as that two and two are four."[46] Millerites could not be allowed either accurate facts or proper method. Rather than a "foundation in reason and known facts," Millerites, with the rest of the "ignorant and superstitious," loved to begin with "hypothesis."[47] The adventists were thrown out of the Baconian club, in spite of their attachment to the very assumptions of the modern Baconians, because real facts and correct calculations had always to build up to the same generalizations. Disagreement at the end was evidence of faulty evidence and use of evidence from the beginning.

Millerites and many of their opponents approached the Bible from a similar set of assumptions. Democratic and empirical Baconianism provided a balance of authority that proved very appealing in the first half of the nineteenth century. For all of its proponents, it offered objective truth, existing outside them in hard facts, and equal access to those facts. But the tensions within this view should not be lost sight of. The objective facts of the world and the Bible were, to Millerites, evidences of a greater objective order that sometimes expressed itself in the existing world. An increasing number of others, by contrast, began to see the divine order not as objective, but as subjective—growing out of and existing within the facts and processes of the world as designed once and for all by a God above and outside, and an understanding of Bible facts as infallibly pointing to both knowledge of God and understanding of nature and history. Those who emphasized a different side of that semi-scientific approach to knowledge of God and the godly tended to turn to the organic processes of development that the facts of the world pointed them to, and to call those processes the unfolding of divine truth through and within the world. The first became more and more rigid in their insistence that the facts of both Bible and history had to fit into their conception of an objective, transcendent divine order, while the second became more and more likely to leave the existence or the role of the divine order subordinate to, or at least below, behind, and within, the processes of growth in the world.

HISTORY, NATURE, AND THE SIGNS OF THE TIMES

The problem that divided Millerites from their most vocal opponents was, in part, a difference over the authority and meaning of events in the world around them. The Millerite God existed above and outside the world, but he was ready at any time to intervene directly in the affairs of humankind. In fact, the Millerite God had set up, from the beginning, not only a general plan for worldly history but a very specific plan. Millerites generally believed in "particular providence"—the idea that God directed the details, and not just the overall rules, flow, and purpose, of human and natural history. Because the Millerite God was so great and powerful, and because he existed outside and above the worldly scene, he could take the role of the great chess player, directly choosing every move of every piece on the board. Particular providence, like predestination, seemed increasingly strange to contemporaries of the Millerites, however. They were discovering processes in the world that seemed to work independently of direct divine intervention, and many of them gloried in the vision of a God who set off or embodied himself in worldly processes that could work toward his ends without the disruption of direct interference. They did not give up belief in God's providential plan as often as they embraced the idea of a general providence that was to be worked out through human action in the natural and social world.

Millerites sought in every action or event in the world the precise meaning that had to accompany particular providence. Everything had to join together and fit into the more general plan and the meaning behind it. In addition, all significant events had to fit into the plan as God had told humanity about it in the Bible. Once again, the unity of levels of meaning defined the thrust of Millerite interpretation. Overall meaning and providence had to fit together finally and absolutely with specific narratives in the Bible and with things that happened in the world. In a proper reading of all the evidence available, then, one was required to line up what the Bible said with the train of human and natural history in order to place both accurately within the broader scheme. At any given moment in history, one could look around to discern the signs that located one's period within the chronological plan that God had laid out.

Miller and his fellow leaders and spokesmen understood that this approach required a careful balance. No single event could be elevated above others in directing the understanding of the whole course of providence. As was the case with Bible-reading, consideration of events and signs had always to be fit into context, with different events and levels of meaning brought together and made coherent as a whole. The intent of the leaders at least was to leave interpretations of historical and natural events secondary to the larger principles and to the primary sources of knowledge—faith and Bible. Although it did not stop them from making a go of it, they knew that trying to figure out where certain events fit into the prophetic scheme was a dangerous business. They were required to seek such a fit, but the Millerite leaders generally tried to emphasize the overall chronological scheme and to downplay any particular case of matching event to Bible. This balance was a difficult one to hold, of course. They sought to hold tight to certain historical landmarks upon which they hung their entire dating of the end in the 1840s. Without such matchings, their system lost one of its strongest supports. They also believed that all events fit into the larger scheme, and that knowledge of such coincidences were accessible to all. But they exercised caution about giving too much authority to signs in the heavens, for example. Although the general course of history seemed to match safely with the narrative and intentions of God, too much focus on comets and shooting stars and dark skies seemed, to the leadership, to smack of superstition, magic, and fanatical inspiration.

Miller's chronology rested upon certain parallels between biblical prophecies and historical events. The fourth kingdom foreseen by Daniel meant, according to Miller, the Roman kingdom. The little horn of the seventh chapter of Daniel that arose after the fourth kingdom meant the papacy. The little horn of the eighth chapter referred to Rome itself. Through these equations, Daniel's basic visions took concrete shape within history. Miller and his followers went on to examine the time periods mentioned, as they read it, in the Book of Daniel. The 70 weeks began with the decree of Artaxerxes Longimanus in 457 B.C.; this was, in the Millerite reckoning, the date of the decree to rebuild Jerusalem. The 70 weeks made up the first portion of the 2,300 days, which would end only with the resurrection of the saints. Finally, persons, places, and dates came together in the decision that the little horn of Daniel 7—the papacy—arose in 533 A.D. with the decree of Justinian. A slight adjustment put that event into full effect in 538 A.D. Another 1,260 days were to pass before the end of the civil reign of the papal power, and that left 45 days to the resurrection. All of this put in the context of taking a prophetic day to mean a historical year—an approach known as the "year-day" principle—left the essential pieces in place. When the Bible and history were brought together, they pointed to 1843 as the year when the end might be expected.[48]

If 1843 were to bring the end of the existing world, then the years before 1843 had to be the "time of the end" or the "last days." As Miller cast his history, the last days included the 45 years between 1798 and 1843. During that final phase, the meshing of history and prophecy was to be reinforced with special "signs of the times." Those signs would appear in both the human and the natural worlds. The times of the end, according to Miller, had begun with the end of the civil power of the papacy brought about by Napoleon in 1798. The final days were associated with the Laodicean church of Revelation. During those years, the church would be rich in the estimation of the world, while being lukewarm in reality. When the world drove out the false church under the papacy, it embraced the true church, which came out of the wilderness. The successes of the church were obvious on the surface; Miller and others pointed to the proliferation of Bible and mission societies and the spread of the gospel to all corners of the globe. But Miller saw a darker story under the apparent successes. The external strength of the church was matched by the lack of piety at its heart. This, too, Miller saw around him, among Christians dead to revival fires, ministers more interested in learning and in salaries than in heart religion, and attention to the show of empty morality. In the religious world, too, the last days were to be known by the proliferation of sects, the numbers of false teachers and false prophets, a parallel unwillingness to hear sound doctrine, and the shouts and guffaws of scoffers at true religion. These Miller could easily find in infinitely divisible denominationalism, Arminian preachers and Mormon prophets, and, of course, increasingly vocal, and even physical, opposition to Millerism itself. As people departed from the faith and followed such "seducing spirits" as Roman Catholics, Shakers, Pilgrims, Fanny Wright, and Robert Owen, they would also increase in worldly knowledge and run "to and fro" across the physical terrain. The hustle and bustle, the educational and reforming attainments, the religious push of the antebellum years—all masked the reality of continuing alienation from the great and distant God upon whom Miller pinned his hopes.[49]

The Bible also pointed to signs in the natural world. Miller dutifully followed the word. Signs in the sun, moon, and stars, he said, added further proof that the final days had come. Miller himself was less comfortable in this field; he had been a student of history, not of the stars, before his conversion. He tended to avoid elaboration on these points, perhaps because he could foresee the danger in every person's reading signs in the skies, perhaps because his rationalism fit poorly with the magicalness of stars infused with divine purposed. Many of his followers found the signs of the natural world much more compelling. They dwelt upon the "dark day" of May 19, 1780, when the sky was so darkened—perhaps by ash and soot from great fires—that daylight did not show through. They contemplated the possible divine message behind the blood-red moon that shone the following night. They pondered both the comets and the wondrous shower of meteors of the 1830s.[50] As J. F. C. Harrison has reminded us, many people in the early nineteenth century lived in a world where nature carried messages and omens; they combined the necessary attention of an agricultural population to the clues that nature provided with a continuing belief in the magical properties of events in nature.[51] Miller himself was more the calculator than the diviner, more the student of history than the student of magic. Nonetheless, his interpretation appealed to many who were less rationalistic than himself and who found meaning in the symbols Miller presented because they meshed with a more magical as well as miraculous sense of the unity between human and natural events and Christian truth.[52] The power of the Millerite movement depended on such multiple appeals. Had the leadership come down hard against attention to signs in the heavens, they would very likely have lost a good number of their adherents—a possibility that seems not to have been lost on Himes and others.[53] On the other hand, to let the focus on signs and wonders go too far would have been to lose the balance that the movement depended on to maintain its stability and force—a balance defined by the preferences and sensibilities of the leadership more than by those of the rank and file.[54]

Millerites turned to history and to signs in the heavens to buttress their assumptions about the nature and course of divine providence. Opponents of Millerism castigated the advents on both of those fields of evidence. For the critics, the first—history—became more authoritative, while the second—heavenly signs—became less so. The dominant culture was moving toward a history-based, not just history-buttressed, faith and toward an immanent, not intervening, infusion of the divine in nature.

According to his detractors, Miller not only "falsifies the language of the Bible" but also "makes equally wild work with profane history."[55] Critics displayed their erudition, whether deep or superficial, in analyzing the errors in Miller's history. Sometimes it was the application of history to Bible, and vice-versa, that bothered such opponents. Was the second little horn of Daniel really Popery, or was it Mohammedanism?[56] By questioning Miller's correlations, critics denied the major guideposts of his chronology. But it was Miller's understanding of history in itself that brought down more criticism. The laying out of the course of history was being standardized by students of history and the Bible, and Miller deviated from the standard. Miller did not, according to William Weeks, in his exhaustive rebuttal of adventism, agree with "common chronology." At least eighteen of Weeks' 160 points explicitly challenged Miller's understanding of history, and many of the other 142 points actually did the same. The student of history could reconcile the events recounted in Judges with those recounted in Kings without resorting to allegorizing and overlapping; Roman history held no evidence that pagan Rome fell in 508 A.D.[57] Other critics took the same approach. Kittredge Haven claimed that Miller was only guessing when he set up his main points of correlation between Bible and history, and he went on to deny Miller's history, too: Rome fell in 476, not 508; the civil power of the Pope could not be dated specifically from 538 to 1798. Dowling added his voice to the chorus. Connections between Bible and history were wrong: Jeremiah and Ezekiel could not have prophesied about the captivity of Manasseh if the prophetic books were written after the captivity. And Miller knew nothing of history as it was then understood: Miller did not even know, apparently, that Christ was really born in 4 B.C.[58]

Miller gave his critics an opportunity to flex their intellectual muscles. In refuting Miller, religious spokesmen refined and elaborated their picture of historical development. If their purpose was really to refute Miller, however, they missed the point. Miller understood the big picture; his task was to make historical events fit into it. His opponents often elevated history above the sweeping narrative of providence, and they sought, unlike Miller, to build the historical picture and then compare the Bible to it. The two sides talked past one another because they believed that they were engaged in the same enterprise while they were not. Opponents were not entirely wrong when they accused Miller of taking his date—1843—and counting backwards from it to fit history to Bible and both to his end-point.[59] Miller did, in fact, begin with his general conclusion and work outward from there. He knew, because of his religious experience and his reading of the Bible, of the nature of God and Christ. He knew, similarly, of the plan and purpose of the transcendent divine order. The details and history, he was sure, would add up to a conclusion that was consistent with those assumptions. That was, in Miller's way of thinking, the nature of the universe. One did not need to fear the facts, because the facts would always agree with first principles.

If opponents of Millerism were adamant about placing evidence before floating general assumptions when it came to history, they took a different tack when it came to a consideration of the signs of the times. On signs in the human order, they simple disagreed, for the most part, with Miller and his followers. The great progress in spreading the Bible and pursuing missionary labors was no deception to most anti-Millerites; it was, rather, what it seemed to be—evidence of success and progress. "The signs of the times all indicate," said Dowling, not the horrors imagined by Miller, but "the gradual, though certain approach of the millenium."[60] There was cause for concern certainly—they were "portentous times" that indicated approaching crises—and it was imperative to keep working toward greater progress.[61] But there was not, according to the dominant view, a hidden layer of corruption at the core of all of the great work of the day. Historical fact was historical fact, it proved its own truth, and the historical truth of the time was a continuing upward course. That trend and the evidence for it were general, of course. Those who disagreed with Miller had little patience for the precision of particular providence. Carefully picking through "the most ordinary events" and seeking to invest them with ultimate meaning was not for them.[62]

The broad picture of activity in the human world gave added force to inclination toward belief in progress. Signs in the natural world, on the other hand, were rejected altogether. Seeking deep meaning in the dark day, in earthquakes, and in meteors seemed to many "the highest grade of modern credulity."[63] To "shut God out of his own world, and ground . . . predictions of woe on the 'signs of heaven' was a "'heathenish' custom."[64] Superstition was supposed to have been replaced by human reason, and yet there were those living anachronisms, the Millerites, finding divine magic in every event of earth, sea, or sky. The only possible conclusion was that they were crazy throwbacks to another age—an age of superstition and ignorance.[65] The idea that natural events held transcendent meaning seemed so silly that the Millerites became the butt of a string of jibes and jokes. "The Millerites recently discovered the planet Venus in the daytime," snickered one writer who knew very well that this was "no uncommon occurrence." Another suggested that a February that passed with no new moon was certainly singular enough to deserve the status of a sign.[66] The comet that passed overhead in 1843 arrived at a propitious moment both for Millerites and for their detractors. One paper ridiculed Millerites who were "foolishly frightened" by its appearance; another, who apparently could find no Millerites to observe on the occasion, simply predicted that the comet would take its place in their system of signs and portents.[67] One report, with the authority of Brown University behind it, pictured the belated inheritors of the superstitions of other ages—"incorrigibly bent upon making reason and common sense subordinate to the most childish fears and the most whimsical and preposterous fancies"—predicting "martyrdom at the tail of a comet." On the other side, the report set out its version of the truth. Comets were "a part of the creation which God made. They pursue their respective and appointed courses with as much order and harmony with respect to the great laws of planetary motion, as do the members of our own little system."[68] The contrast was plain, and the distinction thus expressed was, in fact, not far off base.

Millerites believed in an objective, transcendent order that stood outside both history and nature. The power of that order was expressed in part, however, in its continuous and intimate involvement in, or, better, rule over, both of those areas. God was so powerful that he controlled every event in the world. For those with eyes to see, that control was also revelation; if one could properly interpret the signs, one would know what God intended his people to know. Both control and signs always referred back to overarching purpose. To see God at work in the world was to catch one more clue about the unified truth behind all divine action. Both history and nature, then, tied into the grandest plans and purposes of God. But the key was that they tied into something larger; if they did not seem to fit, that was due to the limitations of human vision. If they did fit, it could never be on their own terms, but only in terms of the greater order and purpose of God. The heart of the Millerite approach to nature and history—indeed, to all sources of knowledge and authority—was radical supernaturalism. But the manifestation of radical supernaturalism in adventist interpretation of history and of signs of the times did not seem to others to be the product of faith in the real Christian God, only a peculiar expression of ignorance and superstition.

SPECIAL KNOWLEDGE

Millerites expressed an annoying certainty about the Bible. They had a peculiar penchant for seeking signs in the world around them. Both of these approaches to knowledge struck many contemporaries as strange, irritating, or even threatening. Yet the real problem of access to knowledge was perhaps one that seemed to lie behind Millerite readings of the Bible, history, and nature. Critics suspected—and with good reason—that at the end of the logical path that supernaturalism would follow lay a claim to a special religious experience or direct revelation that would bring special knowledge to a select few.

Generally Millerites, like other evangelicals, struck a balance between faith and scripture. As one convert confessed, he had become an adventist "by the united influence of the

Word and the Spirit."[69] One of Miller's "Rules of Interpretation" of the Bible—the one he called the "most important rule of all"—was that "you must have faith."[70] The converted Christian could read the Bible literally and find God's truth. So far, Millerites fit into an orthodox frame of authority. But there remained, first of all, the problem of knowing what other generations did not know—the manner and, especially, the time of the end. The Book of Daniel said that the vision was shut up until the last days. Millerites claimed that they lived in the last days and that it was therefore no surprise that the vision should be opened up to them. But this posed anew the problem of balance among authorities within the movement. The transcendent God of the Millerites had to be the same for all time. His objective existence beyond the vicissitudes of history was a central tenet for adventists. The revelation that that sturdily omnipresent God gave to man in the Bible was also supposed to be a single, unchanging truth for all time. Yet the Millerites had to claim that somehow they could read that truth better or more fully than believers had in the past. To know as much about the end as they claimed to know, they had to know more than others had known. At first it was sufficient for Miller simply to assert that the all-powerful divinity had unsealed the vision—the vision that had remained the same, though hidden, through history—and that the vision could be correctly read for the first time since Daniel's own day. That answer did not satisfy all critics, however, nor was it sufficient for a number of believers as the fervor of the end increased.

Most American Protestants in the middle decades of the nineteenth century experienced and interpreted conversion as a receiving of the grace of God in the heart. Regeneration through conversion was the one thing essential to salvation; all other requirements went along with or supported that central point of experience and belief. Conversion was not direct revelation; the experience of grace turned the individual toward a correct reading of scripture and other evidences of God's truth, but it was not a passing on of specific truths itself. The psychology of conversion—the sense of alienation followed by the assurance of reconciliation—became very important to the understanding not only of the self but also of the processes of history and providence for many sons and daughters of the Second Great Awakening. One of the major problems of conversion in terms of personal experience was that it promised more than it could deliver. Conversion was supposed to result in a true reconciliation, in a turning toward a good and moral life, and in possibilities for growth in knowledge and grace. Many inevitably found that the reality fell far short of their expectations. They continued to feel distant from God, they continued to do things they knew they should not, or perhaps they did not feel that they grew closer to true gospel knowledge and greater grace fast enough.

Just as the experience of conversion spread rapidly through the American population during the Second Great Awakening, the experience of disappointment after conversion spread, too. One of the results of that widespread disjunction between promise and reality was an increase in the number of individuals and in the number of movements that focused on a second religious experience. The Methodists had held to the possibility of a second blessing—an experience of "sanctification"—since the century before. The general acceptance of the centrality of conversion induced people to believe that spiritual life could, and maybe even should, proceed through a line of datable experiences. When these factors combined with discomfort over the imperfections of conversion, many turned to some variety of additional religious experience to renew their commitment and perhaps to try again to achieve the level of grace that had remained out of reach after conversion. Methodists returned to the notion of the second blessing. Oberlin Perfectionists developed a similar concept of sanctification. The holiness movement, which put a second experience at the center of a religious system, arose. In a similar vein, abolitionists said that they had datable experiences of turning to a commitment to immediate abolition.

A number of Millerites followed the path of a second experience as well. In their accounts of those experiences, they tended not to distinguish, or else to see strong parallels, between receiving sanctification—perfect holiness or the potential for perfecting holiness—and receiving the doctrine of the second advent. The account of the Millerite Mrs. E. J. Marden is revealing in this respect. Having once been converted, she later had a second blessing and dedicated her life to "the cause of holiness." The continuing attachment of her church "to the spirit and customs of the world" did not cease, and the problem was not solved by her own commitment to and influence for holiness. Then "it was plainly shown" to Marden "that the belief of the immediate coming of Christ was needed to break off the strong attachment of the world." Neither conversion nor sanctification had proved strong enough to tear loose the tight grip of worldliness. Something again more powerful was required. That which was more powerful than the Holy Spirit working through people was the power of Jesus Christ himself, in the flesh. As Marden told her story, it was the preaching of the time that finally brought her around: "I joyfully received the evidence my mind could grasp, that in 1843, I should see Jesus and be made like him." She "received" evidence of 1843 as she had once received the grace of God in conversion. And this third experience—the experience of the second advent doctrine—took her to a new level of grace and knowledge. "The increase of light and love in my soul," she said, "was superior and more abundant than any thing I ever experienced before, as was the blessing of holiness superior to all former blessings."[71]

Marden said she "received" the doctrine of the second advent in 1843 "by Faith."[72] Other adventists spoke of "conversion to the Second Advent doctrine" or of a "heart" that "received the doctrine of the speedy coming of Christ."[73] Millerites believed in an objective sacred order that made ultimate demands upon people and also broke through into history at certain times and places. They sought to assert the great power and final authority of that other order while also becoming personally reconciled to it through their own submission to demands and receipt of mercy. The yearning for the absolute at the heart of the Millerite supernaturalism could not be satisfied by a commonplace conversion followed by a dreary, upright, and unexceptional life. It is not surprising, then, that Millerites sought religious experiences that would raise them to a higher level of grace and knowledge. But the nature of their second—and even third—experiences proved troublesome in terms of the orthodox assumptions of their day.

To begin with, any second religious experience was suspicious, no matter who went through it, when, or how. If conversion were the one thing necessary to salvation, then a second experience was unnecessary. If it was unnecessary, it might also, some reasoned, be misleading or even heretical. If some had a second blessing, then they claimed to have a superior religious experience, but it should not have been possible to have an experience superior to that which offered salvation. And if some did have a superior experience, they made themselves a religious elite—something unacceptable to the godly democrats of the 1840s. The second blessing, then, posed a whole set of problems for Americans of the antebellum years, and it remained suspect even where, as among the Methodists, it had the force of tradition behind it.

The additional religious experience claimed by the Millerites did not resemble that of Methodists or that of Oberlin Perfectionists, however. The latter groups saw the second experience as an empowerment to or an infusion of perfectibility in grace. Their experiences did not have specific doctrinal content. The additional experience of a Millerite was not just an experience of holiness. It was an experience of the second advent doctrine. When that kind of substance entered into religious experience, it no longer resembled an orthodox receipt or nurturing of grace, but rather resembled a direct revelation from God.

All of these problems and implications were clear to critics of Millerism. The Rochester Methodist Samuel Luckey included an extended attack of these points in his lengthy complaint against Millerism. To speak of an expectation of the end of the world in 1843 as the "hope within them," said Luckey, was a "wretchedly perverted use of the Scripture language." While claiming to rely on the "facts" of the Bible, Millerites also "set themselves to praying *for evidence* of the truth, and profess to *receive* it" as they would "their personal *state of grace!*" This, Luckey pronounced, revealed the adventists' "secret infidelity respecting the truth of the Bible." Bible truth clearly showed Luckey and other evangelicals that conversion was sufficient for salvation, and if that were true then belief in "1843" could not also be necessary.[74] A correspondent to the *Signs of the Times* accused the Millerites of substituting belief in the imminent second coming for regeneration as the point on which salvation turned, and of a "reliance upon dreams and individual revelations, and vague impressions made upon the imagination."[75]

Once again, the God of the Millerites was pictured muscling

in and meddling with the world. To Millerites, that seemed to be for the best. They organized their belief around a God who stood apart and was all-powerful but who also took a precise and direct interest and role in the affairs of the world. The God of the adventists had to be distant and omnipotent, but also accessible—or rather, less accessible to people than having access to them whenever he chose. To opponents of Millerism, this picture of divine power and activity ran against the grain. Most who spoke out against the Millerites sought to reduce the direct relationship between man and God to the single, brief moment of conversion—if they retained belief in the necessity of conversion at all. Otherwise, they knew God and saw God acting through processes in nature and history. Their authority, unlike that of the Millerites, revealed itself in the human heart, the human world, and in human processes of change.

CHAPTER IV

Out of Babylon

When William Miller first announced his conclusion that the world would end "on or before 1843," little excitement ensued in the Low Hampton area. Perhaps his neighbors put his calculations down to an eccentricity. More likely, many of his contemporaries acknowledged that, since it was an orthodox expectation, it was a real possibility that Christ would return in the clouds of heaven. A sense of anticipation was certainly common to a majority of Americans in the new republic. When Miller began to take his message into a broader arena in the early 1830s, there was similarly little hostility. He received invitations, he spoke, he led people to acceptance of Christ, and he moved on, while the local churches reaped the benefits of his inspiration. As the 1830s went on, however, the place of millennial expectation in the culture changed. A number of people tried to objectify their hopes—John Humphrey Noyes in Putney and Oneida, Joseph Smith in Ohio, Missouri, and Illinois, and Albert Brisbane in his Fourierist phalanxes. Others pressed their expectations into the service of increasingly radical causes—Lyman Beecher and the total abstinence forces, the New England Non-Resistance Society in their version of peace, the Grimké sisters through escalating demands for women's rights, and, of course, William Lloyd Garrison most famously and eclectically. Millennial dreams not only could buttress the cause of the developing nation, but also could disrupt the smooth working of the republican experiment. At the same time that many had second thoughts about the virtues of ultraism, of course, a number of people were identifying with the radical and utopian causes. By the late 1830s, William Miller had joined those who benefited from this polarization. Invitations poured in at a swiftly accelerating pace. Audiences throughout the Northeast clamored to hear the news of the impending glorious day. While increasing in number, Millerites engaged in a flurry of organization; periodicals and conferences, for example, gave structure to the adventist impulse.

Little wonder, then, that a profound ambivalence toward the Millerite movement replaced the earlier tolerance. Between about 1839 and 1843, while tremendous numbers of converts and sympathizers were enlisted to the advent cause, some who remained aloof continued to view the movement with calm acceptance. A growing number, on the other hand, began to react to the anticipation of the imminent return of Christ with hostility. During the early 1840s, opponents developed a critique, if not entirely consistent, at least fairly thorough, of the Millerite system as they understood it. That critique drew force from, and in return gave impetus to, changes in behavior on both the Millerite and anti-Millerite sides. There is little point in concentrating on who rejected whom first. Developments within the adventist movement led the followers precariously close to, and then over, the line between criticism from within and withdrawal from the churches. Both in response to Millerite behavior and as a part of a larger process of polarization, those who did not adhere to second adventism first sought to check and in some cases finally resorted to eliminating those associated with the doctrine from their religious organizations.

COME-OUTERS

American Protestants by the early nineteenth century had become firmly committed to the principle of private, individual conscience. The sense of having founded a new order committed to a democratic spirit took deep root during and after the Revolution.[1] This attachment to the principle of individual judgment gained force from the assumptions of Scottish Common Sense philosophy and from widespread belief in a simplified Baconianism. Truth was accessible to all men equally; application of the "understanding" to "facts" uncovered the truth.[2] Such reverence for individual perspicacity—if ritualized in worship, preaching, and self-definition—did not necessarily lead to wholesale rejection of hierarchical structures. It was, after all, the Methodist Church, with its bishops and levels of conferences, that achieved the greatest victory among American Protestant denominations by 1850. Methodist individualism paralleled that of all faiths that embraced emphasis on private judgment; it was a consistent undercurrent beneath waves of denominational growth. Periodically, too, that current would swell up and break into schism, creating new denominations that altered the surface of American religious life between the Revolution and the Civil War.[3]

Insistence on the primacy of individual conscience took more specific form in anti-creedalism and anti-institutionalism. Both of these tendencies took force from a suspicion of any human authority beyond the individual, who in his or her conversion and commitment was the irreducible locus of the "plan of salvation." "No creed but the Bible" was not only the clarion call of the new Christian/Disciples of Christ movement but also an affirmation reaching across denominations that a person alone with his Bible had access, indeed the clearest access, to all necessary truth. Similarly, many antebellum Americans were suspicious of any structure or institution that claimed authority apart from and therefore antagonistic to legitimate sources of values and norms—the person, his Bible, or the republic itself.[4] These people lived in a world of institutions and creeds, however. "No creed" Christians had standards of belief, although they carefully avoided calling them creeds, and "antipartyism" was a force behind the emergence of more than one political party.[5] The initial stage of the formulation of many a new denomination, party, or other structure was, in the parlance of the time, "Come-Outerism." The continual quest for greater purity, for more room for conscience, for greater commitment to a particular truth, for less imposition of structure, was a natural concomitant of the millennial fervor of the age. Infractions and encroachments were perceived not just as errors or adjustments, but as sins, conspiracies, threats to the republic, or even the workings of the Antichrist.[6] Compromise with such treacheries was unacceptable. Efforts to set guidelines for belief or action or to assert authority often met with the biblical injunction "Come out of her my people."

"Come-Outerism" formed part of the social and cultural context in which Millerism flourished. Tendencies within the movement reinforced those broader influences. Miller himself had long expressed ambivalence toward the churches of his day. The church had come "out of the wilderness," said Miller, but he had a peculiar interpretation of that phrase from the Revelation of John. He chided his longtime correspondent Truman Hendryx for assuming that the church's being out of the wilderness "meant something good." No, replied Miller, as long as the church was in the wilderness, it remained pure, uncorrupted by the lusts and organizational distractions of the world. Coming out of the wilderness meant gaining the approval of the world and being seduced by its ways. The inevitable result was corruption.[7] Miller granted that the church worked with tremendous freedom in the nineteenth century, and that organizations such as Bible and missionary societies spread light further than ever before. Such successes were part of a paradox, however, for in the midst of such liberty and growth, the church had "departed from her Lord." Given her pride and haughtiness in this state, the church "must be humbled."[8] The church, according to Miller, had by the first half of the nineteenth century become very much like the seventh church of Revelation 3, the last, Laodicean church. The Laodicean church, as Miller saw it, would be "making great calculations for the outward or worldly concerns of the church," displaying "theological writings and publications" and hiding, behind its "pride, popularity, and self-righeousness," a dearth of piety.[9] Glorious in externals, the existing church was rotten at its core.

All of the organized churches and denominations bore an alarming similarity to the sick church of the last days. The Millerites, for their part, insisted that they had no intention of forming a "sect." The corresponding secretary of the Philadelphia Second Advent Association protested that the Association had "no constitution, bye-laws, or anything bearing the stamp of organization." Rather than "forming a new sect," Millerites were associating for the purpose of furthering "advent missionary labors"—and so, presumably, spreading pure Christianity.[10] Miller often issued similar protestations and warnings. In his public lectures, he associated the rise of sectarianism with the struggle of the dragon of Revelation to gain ascendancy in the last days and with the trials anticipated under the pouring out of the seventh vial. The seemingly endless divisions among Christians presaged the chaos that would reign before Christ appeared.[11] In spite of such interpretations hostile to schism and sect-building, the work of organizing went on. Millerites did not passively await the end of the world in isolated bands, but dispatched lecturers, published periodicals, convened conferences, and gathered meetings to proclaim that the end was near. An alternative social and institutional base developed for adventists outside the previously organized churches. While they continued to claim that they had no intention of leaving the denominations or setting up one of their own, Millerites established a set of structures that would make it easier to "come out" when the time came.[12]

In the 1840s, Millerites moved toward an insistence on the 1843 date as an integral part of their belief. In place of the generalized, though fervent, expectation of the return of Christ that characterized the Millerism of the 1830s and the beginning of the new decade, they edged into place a more rigid standard of belief. As their focus narrowed, they pressed their ministers and fellow congregants to give more emphasis to the approaching millennium and even to their particular vision of the introduction of that great day. Simultaneously, tales of harassment against those holding to second adventism came to the attention of the advent press. As Millerites pushed for a wider hearing, pressure increased against public pronouncement of their doctrine. The logical conclusion of this escalating conflict burst forth in July 1843, when Charles Fitch gave a sermon on Revelation 18:4, "Come out of her my people."[13]

How many people had quietly withdrawn from regular church meetings before Fitch's call is not clear. The 1843 sermon opened the floodgates. The removal of a Methodist minister from his post in Chicopee, Maine, occasioned the establishment of alternative preaching for the local Millerite group.[14] In New Ipswich, Massachusetts, a Brother Spaulding and his wife joined a group of adventists in setting up "separate meetings." Later, the Spauldings saw it as their duty to withdraw formally from the Baptist church.[15] A resolution passed by the First Baptist Church of Eden, New York, in January of 1844 warned against missing two or more covenant meetings and communion seasons without an adequate excuse. Millerites may well have been the intended target of this warning. It may also have been directed at a more general group of dissenters, including abolitionists as well as Millerites, who protested by their absence insufficient commitment to their principles in church meetings. That the Millerites could at least be caught up by such a ruling became clear when a member came before the Eden church charged with both "going after the Miller heresy" and "refusing to walk with the church."[16]

Such cases multiplied. One by one, family by family, or in large groups, Millerites chose not to attend services, meetings, and communions after 1843. Secession, as they saw it, followed logically from their most fundamental principles when those principles came up against the proud and self-serving natures of men organized in institutions. A Methodist, for example, posed the tyrannies of majority rule and proceduralism against "Bible arguments" and *"God's eternal truths."* When he withdrew from the Methodist Church, this preacher associated his action with a commitment to those truths.[17] The source of authority was all-powerful, uncompromising. The choice was clear. The doctrine first asserted as an integral part of Christianity had become the defining tenet of true Christianity. Those who would not uphold the second advent doctrine stood outside the fold, and many adventists feared for the purity of their faith as well as the freedom of their consciences should they stay in congregations or church bodies in which the doctrine did not hold sway.

EXCOMMUNICATION

Unresolvable crises within the churches precipitated by the presence of Millerism sometimes resulted in the adventists' withdrawal and at other times led to their excommunication. As often as not, excommunication followed withdrawal in any given case. It is possible, nonetheless, to distinguish between the two processes for the purpose of analysis.

In the scattered examples of excommunication across the northeastern United States, existing forms of church discipline combined with mounting pressure for the exercise of discipline to deprive Millerites of their formal standing in their churches.[18] Evangelical churches of the 1840s exercised careful scrutiny over the belief and behavior of their members. Churches tended to have general statements of faith and codes of behavior that served as guidelines. The codes included procedures for dealing with infractions that required adherence to certain steps, from confronting the accused through gathering evidence to establishing a verdict. Each denomination followed a particular pattern that it justified as biblical. Baptists, in keeping with their congregational polity, resolved most disputes locally. An aggrieved individual, following accepted procedure, met with the person or people suspected of stepping out of line. If he did not find satisfaction in such meetings, he took his complaint to the congregation. A committee then took over, again working first with the accused in private. If the subject of the investigation proved intransigent, if evidence of a wrong existed and evidence of repentance did not, the case came to trial before the congregation. Witnesses appeared for both sides, gave statements, and answered questions. A vote finished the procedure. The accused then returned to full fellowship, suffered suspension, or was set outside the fellowship of the congregation. Similarly, a Baptist minister suspected of wrongdoing—or wrong thinking—was subject first to the decision of the congregation. If disputes proved irreconcilable at the local level neighboring churches might be asked to send ministers and other prominent members to work with the divided church.

This pattern was reflected in other evangelical churches, with accommodations made for differences in polity. Among Presbyterians, the first resort was to the Session, which included the minister and representatives of the congregation known as elders. The court of appeal for members and the seat of judgment for ministers lay in the Presbytery. The Methodists dealt with problems first within the class—again a local, personal arena for settlement. The Quarterly Conference could also be called in to investigate differences. Methodist ministers were subject to the authority of the Annual Conference, which consisted entirely of clergymen.

The grievances covered by discipline in the evangelical churches spanned a broad range. First, a number of accusations pointed to doctrinal or theological deviance. The statement of faith of a church was likely to be general, covering such points as the divinity of Christ, the authority of the Bible, and the final judgment of all people.[19] In some cases, as among the Methodists, an appeal to the "standard writers" of the denomination gave more content to such broad outlines. In any case, it usually fell to disciplinary councils—congregations, Presbyteries, or Conferences—to make the final judgment as to whether a certain belief fell within or stood outside the acceptable range of the denomination. The churches were not inclined to make fine distinctions. The cases that came to trial tended to point to rather obvious disagreements—acceptance of universal salvation, for example, or "imbrasing the *Morman heresy*."[20]

The range of behavioral questions raised before the churches, on the other hand, almost astonishes the modern reader. A church might inquire into a question as private as a husband's fears of his wife's infidelity. Actual adultery was, of course, not an uncommon accusation. A Baptist minister was "guilty of imprudences" because he repeated a conversation "which had a tendency to produce Jealousies among our members." Actions outside the church and the home also fell under the purview of discipline. Most evangelicals opposed working on Sunday. Congregations insisted that their members make good their debts. A favorite accusation covered a range of grievances, some specific and some extremely vague: this was the condemnation for "disorderly walk" or "walking disorderly."[21] Ministers and other officers of the churches faced an additional set of potential charges. A number of Methodist ministers came up before Conferences for "bad administration." One responded to accusations of "secularity" and "inefficiency."[22] Finally, the exercise of discipline itself occasioned a number of further cases. One Methodist minister was called to account for improper discipline, another for the less concrete failing of conducting a case "without charity." Members, too, could find themselves on the opposite side of the bar from that on which they had begun. When a Brother G[?] of the Baptist Church in Pompey, New York, said that his minister was involved in a "combination" to put down a former minister, it was Brother G[?] who suffered the withdrawal of fellowship.[23]

Clearly the purpose of discipline was to maintain the integrity of the church. If it meant anything to be a Baptist, say, it meant upholding certain standards of experience, belief, and behavior. But demarcating the "ins" from the "outs" was only one side of the function of disciplinary proceedings. Investigations and trials were used to reintegrate the wayward and to provide a kind of ritual reinforcement of the unity of the church. Congregations turned to the trial as a last resort. The steps leading up to a trial gave substantial opportunities for smoothing over the difficulty in question. The time lapsed between original accusation and final vote left room for the subject of the inquiry to reconsider his or her position and for the investigating committee and the community to exercise pressure to conform. Ideally, no disciplinary procedures would be necessary. Once the procedure was set in motion, there remained hope for the reconciliation of the individual to the congregation before the trial stage. If a trial did take place, it became an occasion for the group to come together and affirm their common values. Even if exclusion from the fellowship of the church followed, congregations frequently proved willing to readmit the errant individual and give him another chance.[24] These were, after all, evangelical churches. Their purpose was to extend the evangelical way, to hold the ground they had attained, and to gain more converts to the Lord and his presumed requirements. Moreover, as has often been noted, American churches in the nineteenth century tended to count their successes in numbers. Without some exclusivity, their existence lost part of its meaning. With too much exclusivity, they lost power, prestige, and the sense that they were forwarding the work of the Lord.

From this perspective, the triumphs of revivals cut two ways. The intensity and the accession of church members that came to a locality with the revival were measures of success. The very intensity of the revival tended also to carry with it an increased degree of scrupulosity—an escalation of demands for purity placed on oneself, one's fellow congregants, and the church as a whole. Before the First Baptist Church of Palmyra, New York, Ann Wigglesworth declared her "opinion that she is unworthy to participate in the Privileges of the *church,* and still refuses to walk with us, believing herself not to be a Christian," and Abner Crandall, too, said he was no Christian and "unworthy."[25] Thus, in one of those ironies with which history is replete, the Millerites promoted the conditions that led to their exclusion. The Millerites receive substantial credit for whipping up the revival fires that raced through the northern states in 1843 and 1844. As might be expected, the revivals of those years were followed by increased attention to orthodoxy in both belief and behavior and by the initiation of a large number of disciplinary proceedings. The same revival that gained so many converts for Millerism set the stage for the later trials of those converts.

The evangelical churches did not lose all caution in the heat of the revivals. Congregations moved slowly toward bringing complaints against Millerites. Churches first put on a good deal of pressure to silence adventist views.[26] Most disciplinary actions did not arise until the Millerites, in large part in reaction to that pressure, had stopped attending church services. Even then, most Millerites were not charged with Millerism. Discipline for heretical views, as mentioned above, was used rarely and with caution. The charge that brought about the formal separation of adventists from their churches was in most cases "neglect of the church," "neglect of covenant duties," or "refusal to walk [or travel] with the church."[27] In a number of cases, even these charges were not raised until well after the Disappointment of October 1844. Perhaps church leaders thought that if they waited until the excitement died down, the dissenters could be persuaded to return to the fold.

INDIVIDUAL DISSENT

Case studies of Millerites who left their churches reflect a number of themes revolving around come-outerism, church discipline, and the roles played by Millerite supernaturalism in communities. A look at local examples demonstrates the variety in the drama of social divisions played out in association with the Millerite excitement.

Millerites sometimes stood alone, or formed a small minority, within their churches. Although adventism took form as a broad and organized social movement on a large scale, its adherents sometimes faced the consequences of their convictions in relative isolation. Such was the case in the First Presbyterian Church of Palmyra, New York, which received Marshall B. Sherwin as a member on April 8, 1838. Religious dissent was not unknown in Palmyra; it was in this neighborhood that Joseph Smith had founded Mormonism around 1830. Yet the local Presbyterian church maintained a remarkable calm in the late 1830s and 1840s. Suspensions and excommunications were few and far between—one case in each of the years 1839, 1842, 1845, and 1848, and Sherwin's in 1844. Members did move in and out, but for the most part peaceably and in small numbers. In 1843, however, the number received into the church surged to twenty-three. And in 1846, the number dismissed by letter—that is, leaving in good standing—jumped from the usual one, two, or three to nine.[28]

The evidence indicates, then, that the Presbyterian Church of Palmyra took part in the wave of revivals that crossed the northeastern states in 1843 and 1844. It is not clear who led the revival in Palmyra—the local minister or ministers, a traveling revivalist, perhaps even a Millerite lecturer. In any case, the congregation presumably participated in the fervor of the revival that had struck other areas. And under the influence of that fervor, a few individuals took "ultraist" stands.

Marshall B. Sherwin belonged to the Palmyra church before the 1843 revival. Perhaps he had long held sentiments sympathetic to adventism. It is likely that the revival either inspired his conversion to the second advent doctrine or led him to be more insistent and single-minded in his Millerite stance. By the winter of 1844, he was not meeting with the church.

In March of 1844, the church received a written statement from Sherwin affirming his adventist views. As the church clerk paraphrased that letter, Sherwin stated his belief in "the speedy coming of Christ according to the doctrine taught by William Miller," and he expressed "a desire to spread this doctrine in a manner inconsistent with his convenent engagements." Sherwin may have insisted that the church make room for the teaching of second adventism. He probably set up special lectures or meetings to promote Millerite doctrine that appeared to contradict or compete with the authority of the church. Sherwin also said he had "other reasons" for withdrawing from the church; he chose not to state them but rather simply to make known his desire to secede.

The church set the letter aside for some months while a committee conferred with Sherwin. The majority probably held some hope that the delusion would simply pass. But, in July, after no sign of repentance from the wayward brother, the church gave its formal attention to Sherwin's communication. Sherwin was now called before the church in Session. At this meeting, he went beyond the letter's statement of belief in the imminent return of Christ. Church organizations with "Confessions of Faith and Covenants" were "entirely unscriptural and wrong" went the substance of his testimony. Each Christian's "immediate duty" was therefore "to come out from among them." As with many another Millerite, increasing rigor and certainty led him to condemn those who did not agree with him and so seemed insufficiently pure. Accused of acting contrary to the requirements of scripture, the church was not likely to go on carefully ignoring Sherwin's dissenting fervor. As if his fate were not sealed already, Sherwin went even further and made jibes at Presbyterian doctrine. Infant baptism, he proclaimed, was "unauthorized by the word of God." The wicked, he added, faced not eternal suffering, but annihilation. Just so is deviance likely to build on itself. Having begun by thinking dissent, Sherwin had finished by talking heresy.

Even when confronted by such heresy, the church still waited. It heard Sherwin's statement in early July but not until late August did it take a vote. Then the body "unanimously Resolved" that Sherwin be excommunicated. The sentence was proclaimed in public on September 1, 1844. Sherwin was reluctantly but firmly removed from the orthodox evangelical fold.

Sherwin seems to have trod alone down the path to heresy. In other cases, dissent tore through congregations in a number of guises, of which Millerism was but one. The individual was more likely to turn to the peculiarity of Millerism if he or she had already taken on unorthodox beliefs and behavior. The context of a congregation that would produce deviant belief and behavior might prove fertile ground for second adventism. Such was the case in the story of Eleanor Lum of the First Presbyterian Church of Seneca Falls. Hers was not a peaceful congregation in the 1830s and 1840s. In 1832, 21 of between 150 and 200 members left to join the Free Congregational Church. A number of cases arose in the thirties over questionable behavior, such as intoxication, lying, and cheating in business. Nor was the theology of the congregation utterly uniform. One member faced charges of perfectionism in 1837. A resolution "that no minister shall be admitted to the use of the pulpit without the consent of the majority of the Session" passed in 1838 and pointed to the ongoing tensions within the church.[29]

A number of the difficulties in the Presbyterian church

came to a head in 1843–1844 with the trial of Rhoda Bement. Bement had attended an abolition lecture by a woman on a Sunday, thus offending her more conservative peers in several ways at once. In addition, because of scruples about the kind of wine offered, she had for some time refused the communion cup. Finally, she was said to have publicly accused the minister, Horace Bogue, of intentionally ignoring the notices of an abolition lecture that she left for him to read from the pulpit. In a single case, a whole range of questions over which there were differences in the church forced their way to public notice. Abolition, woman's rights, temperance, the authority of the minister—all were debated, explicitly or implicitly, in the course of the trial.[30] Rhoda Bement left the Presbyterians for the Wesleyan Methodist Church, as did her fellow abolitionist Daniel W. Forman. The ferment that underlay the Bement uproar did not disappear immediately, however.

Eleanor Lum, like Rhoda Bement, had doubts about the wine passed to her at communion. Moreover, Lum also attended Abby Kelley's abolition lecture. During the Bement trial, her testimony on Kelley's talk is revealing:

[Session] Did you hear the Presbyterian Church denounced there as corrupt?

[Lum] This nation was guilty of slavery & the Presbyterian Church was also guilty as being connected with them.[31]

Later, this exchange ensued:

[Judicatory] Will you state what you have heard Miss Kelly say or advise members of this church in regard to leaving it.

[Lum] Ans: She said, if you can remain in the church & do any good there, I should advise you to remain where you can do the most good.[32]

Come-outerism was not restricted to Millerites; abolitionists, too, found the churches suspiciously like Babylon.[33] Kelley did not actually advise coming out of the church. But she did imply that one should remain in the church only on the condition that one could promote abolitionist views there. The traditional authority of the church took second place to the demands of conscience or to the demands of an all-powerful, transcendent deity. As the testimony went on, Lum replied that Kelley had traduced the minister, Bogue, by pointing to his supposed ties to the slaveholding South.[34] Throughout her participation in the Bement trial, Lum exercised great caution and avoided outright denunciation of the power of the church or the principles of the minister. Nonetheless, it is clear that the convictions associated with abolitionism easily became mingled with resistance to authority. If individual judgment were to reign, neither the pastor nor his church could take deference for granted.

In 1846, two years after the Bement trial, the First Presbyterian Church of Seneca Falls excommunicated Eleanor Lum. She had become a Millerite. For Lum, perhaps, adherence to second adventism was a logical extension of the views that she shared with Abby Kelley and Rhoda Bement. These women had accepted dissenting views, as indicated by their interest in abolitionism. Lum and Bement exhibited a scrupulosity beyond that of their peers in regard to the communion wine. And all three were associated with a religious culture that could tend to elevate private judgment above community and institutional rules, even to the point of condemning community values and institutional authority. In the end, such women stretched the conciliatory power of church disciplinary procedures beyond the breaking point.

SCHISM

Eleanor Lum was the only convicted Millerite in the Seneca

Falls Presbyterian congregation. She was not entirely alone in her beliefs, however. William Miller himself had lectured in the town; other Millerite lecturers passed through occasionally. The First Baptist Church of Seneca Falls proved fairly hospitable to adventist belief. The Baptist pastor, E. R. Pinney, was "much Engaged in the Sentiment of Christ Jesus coming in 1843." Although the clerk associated the fact of "some of the members of the church Embracing the doctrine" with a "verry low time in the church," a sizeable number disagreed. When Pinney tried to resign in January of 1844, the church voted that he should continue as pastor. Such divisions within the church continued to reverberate through the town.[35]

The First Baptist Church of Williamson, New York, saw a similar pattern of disagreement and hostile alignments. Located just east of Rochester, in a county bordering Lake Ontario on the north and reaching almost to the Finger Lakes on the south, Williamson lay deep in the burned-over district. With no claim to reknown, Williamson and its First Baptist Church nonetheless took part in the ferment that inflamed and ravaged the society of the county and of the local Baptist Association.

The troubles in the Williamson church focused on Elijah G. Greenfield, pastor from 1841 until 1844. Greenfield first appears in the records of the area in the minutes of the Second Baptist Church in nearby Walworth. Greenfield and his wife became members of the Walworth church in March of 1840; in April he was ordained. It seems that Greenfield had the kind of personality that exacerbated tensions in a community. In any case, by June of 1840 the Walworth church confessed the need to "reconsile some unpleasant feelings." In February of 1841, less than a year after his ordination, Greenfield received a letter of dismission and recommendation. He moved to Williamson with letter in hand but without full remuneration for his services in Walworth.[36]

Williamson had experienced the wave of revivals that had earned the burned-over district its name. The Baptist church had inherited the increased membership, the intensity, and also the contradictory impulses that the revival so often left in its wake. By the early 1840s, the rumblings of differences within the congregation began to sound. Questions arose about the role of the minister, the propriety of close communion, and other matters. Onto this brittle kindling fell sparks from the irascible temperament of Elder Greenfield.[37]

The substance and timing of Greenfield's first confrontation with his new congregation remain obscure. In June of 1842 the church lost its first member to attribute her difficulties entirely to Greenfield. From that point on the troubles did not cease.[38] The pastor sought dismissal from the church. A resolution proclaiming the church satisfied with his performance convinced him—or met the conditions on which he would agree—to stay. A dispute over the lot line between Greenfield's property and that of his neighbor arose at the same time that the issue of slavery came before the church. Personal irritations and principles reinforced one another. The congregation began to take sides.

The year 1843 found the First Baptist Church of Williamson in a state of confusion that continued unabated through 1844. The troubles opened with "hard and unpleasant remarks" spoken about Greenfield by Brother Gilbert. A Mr. Austin took the occasion to affirm that he believed he had done no wrong in withdrawing from and censuring the church, a pronouncement that met with a grumbled retort from the abrasive Greenfield himself. Differences heated up over the issue of slavery. The church passed resolutions against both the "unholy" institution and communion with slaveholders, but the objections that followed made it clear that the sentiments behind the resolutions were not held unanimously. In the new year, 1844, Greenfield finally received and accepted a letter of dismission from the Williamson church. Once again he moved on while his pay was in arrears, and the problem of settling with him continued to haunt the church. In a climactic move, a number of dissenters left the church *en masse* in the last month of 1844.

Greenfield came to trial for acting as "the procuring cause of the main or principal trouble or division" in the Williamson church in February of 1845.[39] The first substantiating charge against him pointed to his "persisting in preaching the second advent doctrine." The record had not mentioned this peculiarity previously, and the charges did not indicate how long Greenfield had spoken from a Millerite perspective.[40] His attachment to second adventism alone had never caused him to be brought to trial. When held to account, he was accused because he had extended his Millerite convictions in ways that directly challenged the authority and stability of the church. The second charge focused on Greenfield's "denying that the church was organized on the gospel plan and comparing it to Babylon." The third claimed that Greenfield had established meetings separate from the church where, he was supposed to have said, the people could go and hear "the truth preached." The competition engendered by the come-outer spirit added to adventist belief was more than the church would bear. While adding up the charges, the church raised two more related to divisions in the church but not so directly associated with Millerism: the "pursuing" of "a dishonest and unchristian course" with regard to his salary, and the "influencing" of members "to subscribe to several resolutions [presumably antislavery resolutions] which tend directly to divide the church."[41]

The Williamson church sustained the charges against Greenfield, but judging him guilty could not in itself calm the turbulent waters. A council of local churches gathered to confer with the parties involved—the Williamson church, the Parma church, where Greenfield had gone upon his departure from Williamson, and, interestingly enough, the "Williamson Conference." The Conference was the body of adventists that had originally gathered in Greenfield's meetings outside the churches. In calling together the council, the local Baptist churches chose—or felt themselves forced—to treat this Millerite association as a legitimate religious body. Of course, the proceedings might well have made the Millerites, in their turn, squirm. Being dealt with alongside Baptist churches must have smacked of organization—of sect-building—of becoming part of babylon. Whatever the discomforts, the council pursued its business, tried to settle outstanding financial problems, urged all toward "mutual reconciliation and union," found Greenfield guilty once again, and advised the troublesome pastor "to desist, at once, from all stated ministerial labors" in the vicinity.[42]

It took the Williamson church into 1846 to sort out the confusion left by the Millerite schism. Two groups had, for opposite reasons, come to "neglect their covenant obligations" and to "refuse to walk with the church"—those who left because they could not tolerate Greenfield and those who joined Greenfield in setting up the Williamson Conference. The church followed up each individual case, seeking to find out who wished to travel with the church and who was lost to the Conference and hoping to draw some back into the fold. A few successes came to them: the Graham family chose church over Conference; Brother Twadel had joined the Conference but later recognized that that organization "had no gospel rule" and returned to the church. The losses were many, however. Most of the Pulman family, the Hoaglands, the Gibbses, the Kenyons, the Smiths, Widow Eddy and her daughter, Albert Polhamos—the list goes on of those who followed the Conference rather than the church. The discouragement of others drove them away from both camps: Sister McCagg (or Macagg) refused to join either group; Brother Clark considered rejoining the church, but in the meantime he communed with the Methodists. And a number suffered exclusion for "neglect" whose destination remains unknown.[43]

The examples of Millerism in Palmyra, Seneca Falls, and Williamson illustrate the impact of radical supernaturalism on the local level. The demands of God, as perceived by individual Millerites, took precedence over subjection to the community of the church. The escalation of Millerite fervor did not take place in a vacuum, however. Intolerance of Millerism drew from an altered perception of the requirements of true Christianity as well as from a reaction against the claim for absolute and immediate subjection to a higher order. Theoretically, the Millerites had the option of remaining within the churches. They could have done so had they remained silent about their convictions, never asked for their opinions to be aired, and agreed not to meet even outside regular church assemblies to discuss and spread their beliefs. Conditions were ripe for withdrawal from the churches, but a primary catalyst for the final break came from within evangelical orthodoxy itself, in the refusal to take a broad view of acceptable interpretations of doctrine and hopes for the future. Shifting assumptions within evangelicalism, and the denial of the alternative ethos symbolized by Millerism, were not matters for mere speculation. The result of the confrontation over Millerism was social disruption in churches and towns across the northern states.[44]

CHAPTER V

The Individual: Ideals and Control

In the 1820s and 1830s, Joseph Smith went digging in the hills of upstate New York and uncovered, he claimed, golden plates that could be read only through special lenses. In the years that followed, many Americans reoriented their lives because they believed that the golden plates contained a new Bible. In 1842, P. T. Barnum opened his museum of oddities in New York. In the days after that opening, many Americans went to gawk at those peculiarities that they suspected were, or hoped to be, real. Phrenologists claimed that the minds of men could be probed through the bumps on their heads. Fourierists promised a new age built on the precise structure of the phalanstery. Robert Matthews called himself the prophet Matthias and claimed to hold within himself the spirit of Jesus Christ. Soon a movement seeking contact with the spirits of the dead would be set off by two girls cracking knucles in Rochester. The decades of the thirties and forties seemed, to many an observer, rife with humbug. It should hardly have been surprising, in that time of humbuggery, to find Americans believing that Jesus Christ was about to descend out of the clouds.[1]

Humbug it was to share adventist expectations—from the perspective of many a non-believer, at least. But humbugs of the sort of Millerism—and Mormonism, to note another example—did not deserve only ridicule. After all, there was the problem of all those people who took the new religious beliefs seriously. Humbug—even Barnum's humbug—always had its serious side. In the America of Jackson and his successors, it became increasingly difficult to distinguish the genuine from the fake, the sincere man from the confidence man. The confusion proved all the more serious because of the new conceptions of the proper and necessary foundations for social order that were taking hold. Americans of the Victorian age believed that character was the first of those foundations. Character could not develop and flouirsh in a world in which one could not judge the character of another. Influence from others—first the mother, but later other acquaintances—molded character. In the age of humbug, it was very hard to tell whose influence deserved trust.

Millerites, like their contemporaries, were concerned about the development of inner strength, about the expression of inner qualities in proper behavior, and about the stability of the contexts in which good qualities and habits might grow. Many observers of Millerism refused to believe that those concerns were genuine, however. Millerite supernaturalism seemed so peculiar that commentators generally thought there had to be, somewhere in the adventist movement, a core of unadulterated humbug. They did not believe that the deception could safely be left to the category of innocent fooleries. This kind of humbug, many believed, posed a direct threat to foundations of social order, including personal character, work, self-mastery, and self-discipline. Supernaturalism was not just a religious problem. As critics of Millerism responsed to the new movement and told tales and elaborated arguments against it, they defined Millerism as a social problem.

CHARACTER

By the 1830s, religious Americans had come increasingly to view a subjective change of heart and an objective self-discipline as central to a righteous life. The transition to "inner-directedness" was not restricted to specifically religious culture, however, As the nation entered the Victorian age, the belief that external restraints were breaking down spread widely. In reaction, and in part because of the pervasive influence of the changing religious culture, a subtle but far-reaching change took place as people were encouraged to make "character" the foundation for social order.[2]

The fundamental requirement for the individual in the Puritan order had been piety. Having been chosen by God, some were brought to a life that focused on the divine. No matter what activity the pious person engaged in, he or she was expected to act for and remain conscious of the greater glory of God. Certainly, piety was expected to issue in moral behavior, and desirable behavior was reinforced by the vigilant rule of the commonwealth. Yet the individual returned always to an introspective self-examination and a desire to humble the self before the ever-present Other. Character, by contrast, was a self-creating act of man. In the ideal it, too, required a certain quality of inner states, but those of a fixity requiring no vigilant, recurrent introspection. Its legitimation came not through constant humbling of the self before God, but through continual moral and dutiful action before humanity.

Character was, in the words of one author of advice manuals, "the revelation that we make to the world of our inward forces, virtues, and principles."[3] Character was two sided. First, it meant the development of inner qualities of fixed principles and moral purpose. Second, it meant the outward extension of those qualities in self-control, right behavior, and fulfillment of duty. Each side depended on both. When Emerson defined character as "moral order through the medium of individual nature," he summed up the connection made by many more than Transcendentalists.[4] The virtue of the self-governing individual formed the proper basis for an order both moral and social.

Americans by the mid-nineteenth century defined deviance against the developing ideal of character. If the ideal required internalized strength of purpose and discipline on the part of the individual, then those who gave evidence of a lack of fixed principles of self-control were subject to accusations of nonconformity and, through nonconformity, of threatening the foundations of society. Conversely, those who were viewed as outsiders were accused, *ipso facto*, of lacking in necessary character. In the context of the emerging inner-directed ideal, the supposed fanaticism of the Millerites became a touchstone for much that opposed the ideal of character and the order that it was presumed to uphold.

An obituary of Charles Fitch spoke of his "unbalanced" and "undisciplined" mind, "easily led astray by the wild, the powerful influences which operated upon it." Similarly, the abolitionist and Millerite Elon Galusha, accoring to one account, "inherits a peculiarity of temperament that plunges him into every new excitement"; like Fitch's, Galusha's mind was "unbalanced."[5] Fitch and Galusha lacked the internal gyroscope necessary to do orderly, acceptable work in the confusing world of the 1830s and 1840s. Observers considered the lack of stable purpose and standing principles of these men characteristic of Millerites and their ilk. Because they had no deeply held sense of purpose to guide them, individuals who were attracted to Millerism were likely to bounce from "ism" to "ism," latching onto each new idea as it passed.[6] Opponents saw Millerism as one manifestation of the "unbalanced" and "undisciplined" mind all too common in a world of rapid change and instability. The outward result of the careening will without a moral center was action that indicated a loss of the all-important self-control. Millerites' "hallooing and wailing until midnight and past," the "wild delirium" of their meetings—such rumored chaos bespoke a lack of self-government that posed a threat to stable progress.[7] The "monstrous excesses" and "shameful extremes" to which this lack of self-discipline led even extended to physical endangerment; at one meeting where believers would "struggle" and have "pretended visions on the floor," a preacher kicked a man so hard that "his life was despaired of for several days."[8]

Millerite spokesmen tried to distance the movement from such disorderly behavior. They emphasized the "great regularity and good order" at Millerite meetings and quickly renounced any connection with those known to have engaged in raving, rolling about, or wreaking "waste and havoc."[9] Silas Hawley averred simply: "We repudiate all fanaticism."[10] Another Millerite writer counted "DECISION OF CHARACTER AND CONDUCT," "*self-control,*" and other attributes contributing to a fully developed sense of responsibility among the practical effects of the second advent doctrine.[11] The fact that Millerites claimed the same values and goals as did their opponents did little to disarm the skeptics, however.

Spokesmen for the new Victorian values listed a number of dangers threatening the development of character and thus of moral and social order. Opportunity and ambitions, mobility and instability, and a myriad of specific temptations worked against the growth of steady principles and self-control. Against such forces, secular as well as religious spokespersons set the power of "influence." The personal, constant pressure of example and persuasion defined the direction that an individual would take. Reliance on influence for the development of character helped to define both the hopes and the fears most common in the culture of the mid-nineteenth century.

When people deviated from the right and proper path, many observers sought the reason that they assumed lay behind such suspicious nonconformity. A number of commentators thought they could easily put their fingers upon that malevolent force behind Millerism. The adventist leaders—including Miller himself, and most of all Joshua Himes—bore accusations of leading pushing their followers astray.

The mass of Millerites seemed to their contemporaries to be suffering under a "delusion." The leaders, on the other hand, were often suspected of perpetrating a "humbug" that made "dupes" of thousands.[12] One writer dramatized the role of the leaders as that of "vampyres sucking life-blood of society," drawing all they could from "those whom they dupe." Each one a "hypocrite," the leaders acted more specifically as "impious perverters of divine truth," "ignorant pretenders," and "selfish, weak men."[13] The torrent of accusations pictured those at the forefront of adventism as fully aware of their deception, wilfully playing on their victims, and seeking to make something of themselves at the expense of individuals and of society as a whole.

Such critics evinced as proof of their claims two major categories of evidence: tales of profits amassed from deluded Millerites and stories of preparations made for a future beyond 1843 or 1844. A favorite in the latter category was a report that William Miller had had a stone wall erected on his farm. Such a substantial earthly structure showed a commitment to this world and anticipation of a continuing life here—or so the anecdotes implied.[14] Other small but supposedly telling examples buttressed the image of Millerites preparing, not for the end, but for ongoing prosperity on the unburned earth. In some versions, improvements to Miller's home included a well and a stove in addition to a stone wall. Charles Fitch, too, took an unseemly interest in his surroundings, and wanted to rent a house through the year 1843—or so went the story. The *Signs of the Times*, a New England paper reported, took subscriptions for a full year in advance even as the appointed time approached. And Miller's copyright for his lectures ran for ten years beyond 1843.[15]

In addition to such evidence that Millerite leaders did not believe their own predictions, critics tallied up the profits that they believed adventist leaders to have amassed. A number of prominent adventists were supposed to be "gorging and fattening on what they extort." Occasionally, Miller was singled out as a "money-hunting impostor." But it was Joshua Himes, above all, who came in for scathing attacks on his "base and low motives" for stirring up a religious excitement as an "extensive and lucrative business."[16] Himes took on the business end of adventism as his bailiwick, and he established the enterprises that extended the Millerite message and built the foundation for a large-scale movement. He became the obvious target for those who doubted that Millerism depend on a concern for raising the sights to Jesus Christ. His publication and sale of periodicals and pamphlets, for example, seemed as much greedy peddling as dissemination of divine truth.[17]

Stories of the lust for gain attributed to Himes and other Millerite leaders focused not only on the greed of those individuals but also on the relationship between the prominent few and the gullible many. The profit-seeking of the leading adventists demonstrated their hypocrisy. The success of their money-gathering schemes showed, as some critics saw it, the power of the perverse use of influence. The editor of the *Christian Watchman* could "hardly conceive of a character more entirely depraved, more completely lost to every obligation of justice and honesty" than one who would "receive the spoils of his fellow-men by bringing them under the influence of a delusion so destructive and pernicious." Yet this, according to the *Watchman,* was the character of Himes, whose spoils consisted of large sums of money.[18] Himes and other "pretenders" could prevail upon "weak-minded and ignorant, but in many instances well-disposed and pious persons" to "part with their little savings, their worldly all," under the pressure of assurances that the end was imminent.[19] Thus attachment to the things of this world, profit-seeking, and the destruction of the character of innocents came together in the image of Millerite leaders, and especially of the wicked Mr. Himes.

Critics did not speak with a single voice on the matter of the character and influence of those at the forefront of adventism. A number of spokespersons dissented from such attacks, and their disagreements highlight the diversity and confusion of the culture of the 1840s. Americans were not faced with the simple choice of becoming Millerites or denouncing them in tones determined by the loudest of critics. The careful balance of some writers between these two poles revealed some hesitation in embracing the increasingly popular ideal of character, conformity, and order.

Some wrote in the popular press in defense of Millerites and of freedom of expression. One paper pronounced Himes an "honest and upright, though a deluded man" who may have brought "great mischief" in his wake, but was not, on that account, to be "needlessly slandered."[20] The Rochester *Evening Post* applauded the "active benevolence" of "respected citizens" who helped to erect the Millerites' "Great Tent" after it had blown down. People should listen and balance the arguments on Millerism, as on all issues, "calmly and attentively," opined the *Post*. "All mankind," after all, "do not think alike—nor reason alike—and it is difficult to ascertain whose opinion is correct," the article went on, "particularly on mysterious subjects connected with religion."[21] The few voices raised in favor of a fair hearing for Millerism, free of groundless slander, spoke for an individualism and a reliance on internalized conscience and restraint unusual even in an age that supposedly glorified such ideals. Although they implicitly accepted the notion of personal character as the basis for social order, these writers were unwilling to require conformity as the hallmark of character. In a sense, they took on one aspect of the emerging Victorian ideal with a vengeance: the internal gyroscope was elevated above the order in which it was meant to issue, and individual principle and self-reliance were to be accepted in good faith and allowed to complete in the intellectual and moral marketplace. That allies of this position could take on the ideal of character with a vengeance against an alternative as well was spelled out by the writer who praised Miller's "independence of mind, and . . . integrity of character" and contrasted these to the "indiscriminate denunciation" of the father of adventism by "the haughty kingdom of the clergy."[22]

A few others defended the integrity of Millerites in the name of religion. These writers thought Miller "honest" and "candid in his belief" and Himes "an amiable, excellent man, and a man of considerable talent." The widespread questioning of the characters of such men and the popular ridicule aimed at their beliefs seemed to these commentators to redirect the course of the argument down a dangerous gulley. "Interest in such a prediction as Mr. Miller's," one such spokesman pointed out, "indicates nothing weak—nothing ridiculous or absurd." Another added that to repeat the common anecdotes aimed against Miller was to "trifle with solemn things." Resorting to "infidel scurrility, and blasphemous witticisms" seemed as dangerous to this group as anything the adventists themselves did or proposed. These writers sought to bring the focus of discussion back to the Bible, to the prophecies of Daniel, to the doctrine and word of God—back, in short, to "solemn things" of a clearly religious nature.[23] The weakness of this chorus next to the thunderous denunciations of the full choir of anti-Millerites only serves to underline the degree to which American culture had shifted its focus. First, the source and locus of religious discipline moved to an internal, private realm, and that discipline was understood increasingly in terms of character rather than piety. Next, the glorification of the strong principles and self-control of the inner-directed person was pushed aside in favor of a concentration upon the external, behavioral conformity that came to be taken as evidence of deep-seated character.

The dominant ethic of mid-nineteenth century America held that the outward manifestations of character both suggested desirable inner, personal qualities and established stability and made possible improvement in the broader social order. The inner life had not lost all importance, but subjective religious experience was equated less with subjection to God's will and more with willed cultivation of character. Whatever the nature and source of valued inner qualities, they received legitimation through the behavior in which they resulted. That apparent self-control, duty, and activity would take prominence over experience as well as doctrine, and that those important areas of concern would come under social rather than strictly religious authority became clear in, for example, the profusion of etiquette books in the later Victorian era. The lines of emphasis and of authority were not yet so clearly drawn by the 1840s. In that decade, the confusion of ideals and demands broke forth in crises that served to introduce Victorianism.

The patterns of behavior that signaled adherence to accepted norms and participation in the common cause included restraint from immorality in general and from specific immoralities. As enemies of the new order, Millerites were often accused of both—of having "become immoral" as well as of "smoking with a vengeance," encouraging theatrical entertainments, and engaging in promiscuity.[24] Yet the danger represented by the Millerites seemed less one of immoral acts than of passivity, less a problem of "thou shalt not" than of "thou shall." Opponents reminded themselves time and again through their own diatribes against adventists that what really mattered was action, and that action had to be oriented toward the future. In spite of their jeremiads, critics generally looked forward to continuing progress. They saw in their own portraits of the Millerites a rejection of the essentials of the new and improving order, and for many of the critics and their contemporaries, work counted high among those essentials.

WORK

The "momentous act of transvaluation" that turned the "inescapable" burden of work into "an act of virtue" had reached its first pinnacle of success by the 1830s and 1840s. The America—at least the North—of the mid-nineteenth century celebrated an "unequaled commitment to the moral primacy of work."[25] Work had once been a secondary piece of moral order, more an expression of piety than a pious act in itself. By the nineteenth century, the modified "Puritan ethic" divided work from the subjection before God that had once been the essential reason behind work. Action became an end in itself—the evidence and even the substance of morality.

Anxieties about work brought to the surface by the Miller excitement served less to introduce than to reinforce, extend, and reorient the ideal. The problem was no longer to tie work to virtue—or, as mid-century spokespersons would have it, to character—although the occasion was taken to tighten that bond. The problem, in the 1840s, and in the face of Millerite predictions, was to turn the package of virtue or character and work toward a discipline for and an acceleration into the future. If work was a moral act, then it could hold its legitimation within itself. In the nineteenth century, however, the legitimation of work came to lie not only in present behavior but also in the results of that behavior stretching out into the future. In the manipulable and changing world of the modern age, work not only reinforced an existing order but also defined the order of the future. Individual and collective human action determined the continuing course of inward principles taking outward form. Hope for a better order depended on the energetic and ambitious action of all individuals every day.

John Humphrey Noyes spoke for his age when he noted that fanaticism or "evil spiritual influences" always produced "stupidity, a listlessness, inertia, and *indolence in reference to worldly business,*" while good spiritual influences produced "activity and a wide-awake interest in everything profitable; energy in business, as well as in every other direction."[26] Millerites generally agreed that one of the virtues of the "*active* Christian" was "DILIGENCE IN THE USE OF TALENTS."[27] Although an adventist might have discovered this attribute among the fruits of his doctrine, critics expected anything but productive activity and diligent work from end of the world men. Perhaps they perceived a real difference behind the advocacy of similar behavior. To most Americans, that diligence and energy seemed necessary because the great possibilities for the future on earth could be opened up only through such means. For Millerites, perhaps, all work and all action became necessary not because of the demands of future progress, but because of the demands of God. Or, since a Christian perspective pervaded both of these attitudes, it might be more accurate to say that the majority pressed for action to facilitate the spreading of the power of an immanent God. Millerites, on the other hand, favored dutiful work in spite of the fact that it bore no promise of efficacy and because it was required of those who had been blessed with a direct experience of a powerful and distant divinity.

By 1840, opponents of Millerism stated their expectation that those who adhered to a belief in the approaching end would "forsake their business" and "abandon their several employments." These critics turned to history and found there evidence of the past, and presumably typical, behavior of millenarians.[28] By the winter of 1843, observers claimed to have confirmation that Millerites acted true to form. Stories confidently told of Millerites who had "relinquished their business" or given up "their ordinary occupations to wander the country." Others assumed that Millerites had habits of "idleness and *profligacy*" and admonished the errant to "go to work you sanctimonious rascals." Commentators took the occasion provided by the Miller excitement to preach a bit on the importance of acting always as if the judgment approached by fulfilling duties in all areas of life while, of course, preparing for the world to go on and, presumably, not believing for a moment that the final day might actually have arrived.[29]

Even the Millerites themselves did not deny that some among them had stopped working when the final moment in October of 1844 had drawn near.[30] Opponents jumped at the chance to tell the tale: a brickmaker did not work for two or three weeks, a farmer thought it was not his duty to harvest his crop, guardians were appointed to protect the businesses of some who had left them to go to waste, and a sign on a store supposedly read: "This shop is closed in honor of the King of Kings, who will appear about the 20th of Oct. Get ready, friends, to crown him Lord of all."[31] Any given story of passivity and neglect by Millerites might have been only baseless ridicule. In this case, on the other hand, strong evidence that some adventists did stop working added to the powerful evidence of the non-event of October 22 to lend legitimacy to the arguments of the anti-Millerites. Not only did adventists seem to be peculiarly unable to focus on what was going on and what was needed in this world. Sometimes they acted upon, not an inability to focus on this world, but rather a refusal to do so. Some Millerites followed the logic that detractors had already traced out: if what counted most was a transcendent God who was about to break into history and stop everything short, then there was no point in going on engaging in the efforts of this world. In fact, from the perspective of some adventists, it seemed sinful to do so. It is important to remember, however, that those adventists who traveled this road broke away from the original Millerite position on work during the last days. Passivity was not an inevitable part of anticipation of the advent. It was just as compelling for some to say that the expectation that God was about to return in judgment provided the strongest possible incentive to dutiful behavior. Nonetheless, the critics who said that adventism had to imply passivity and laziness had numbers and time on their side, and helped to confirm that stereotype for years to come.[32]

Association of radical supernaturalism with passivity, laziness, and waste was not the only point of the tales told, however. Critics elaborated on an ethic of saving, delayed gratification, and concentration on the future that went along with the basic element of work as virtue and duty. They objected to the refusal—real or rumored—by Millerites to "lay up treasures upon the earth." In story after story, an adventist gave away goods—the fruits and cakes from an apple-stall, the shoes of a shoemaker, the whole stock of a store, and entire households of personal belongings.[33] One of the more fanatical was even portrayed burning his money and notes to the tune of four hundred dollars.[34] As the Reverend John Dowling had pointed out as early as 1840, "the enjoyments, the hopes, the fears, and the prospects of the whole human family" were "most deeply involved" in such belief and action. Dowling himself admitted that, if he believed that Christ was going to return within a few years, he would exclaim, "Build no more houses! plant no more fields and gardens! FORSAKE YOUR SHOPS, AND FARMS, AND ALL SECULAR PURSUITS," and he would go out to publish the truth to the world. But Dowling, of course, did not believe in the second advent doctrine. He had a different vision of "the prospects of the whole human family," and he worried more about neglect of business, property, family circumstances, and personal savings than about neglect of sounding an alarm about impending judgment.[35]

A Universalist writer added his note of dismay about a whole generation:

Hundreds, yes thousands of young men, once enterprising and imbued with a laudable ambition to obtain rank and influence among their fellow men, where they might have been instrumental of doing much good . . . have through the blighting influence of this new scheme [Millerism], suddenly become spiritless misanthropes—neglecting their temporal concerns,—wholly given up to their wild dreams of approaching bliss.[36]

The Millerites seemed impatient and so uncontrolled; their

"wild dreams" demanded immediate bliss. The Millerites' present was a present without a future. Glory today left no time or reason for preparing for tomorrow. And when the young men who were the hope of the future became infected by Millerism, the loss of their competitive upward scramble was a loss to society as a whole. As one student of Victorian culture has noted, most mid-nineteenth-century Americans agreed that the "individual self-assertion" of the "hard working and conscientious," serious and inner-directed man "would be the most effective way to promote the general material welfare."[37] Remove the self-assertion, the Victorians would have said, and the potential for general good would be correspondingly damaged.

The punching of a time-clock had not yet become a common experience among Americans in the 1840s. Conspicuous by its absence in complaints about Millerite refusals to work was any reference to the new experiment in production, factory labor. Millerites, said their opponents, neglected shops and farms, and such stories serve as a reminder of how far Millerites and their contemporaries both stood from the triumph of industrialism. Yet the problem of work and time that would be played out again and again in restructuring communities and population groups around industrial time and work discipline had its earlier counterpart in the years when artisans and small businessmen first lived in the world with the modern factory. In confrontation with the Millerites, spokespersons for the emerging order reaffirmed the link between work and character and helped to forge the link between the morality of labor and the necessity for work as a guarantee for the future. Virtue in work was not its own reward, but would be rewarded in the future of the individual, in future generations, and in the future of the republic. The restatement and reaffirmation of this complex version of the work ethic laid the foundation for the infusion of that ethic into the new industrial order. With the Great Disappointment, the Millerite vision of work and time lost the competition to provide a cultural interpretation of the emerging system. Critics of Millerism, and their fellow spokespersons for a work ethic legitimized in ongoing social processes in this world, emerged triumphant in this crisis as they would in later instances as industrial work-time took hold.[38]

In religious terms, the culture of the mid-nineteenth century had moved far in the direction of assumptions of divine immanence and human ability. When opponents of Millerism turned their attention to adventism as a social problem, they produced arguments parallel to those that emerged in the religious sphere. Just as the ultimate source of religious values and hopes existed within and worked through the human and the social, so the final justification for social norms was pinned to needs and desires within the realm of people and their actions. When critics accused Millerites of passivity in a world that demanded action, they did not necessarily present a true picture of how adventists behaved. Most of the time most Millerites worked, and worked hard. Behind the accusations of the critics lay a certain insight, however. Millerites did not work because they shared the work ethic of their contemporaries. They did not value action in the world for itself, nor for its future results. They valued work because they believed it satisfied a demand from God. Their God was not immanent in this world—in nature, in men, in society, or in social processes. Millerites, therefore, did not work because work was an expression of a divinity within them. They did not work because work was legitimized in itself or through its results. They worked—when they did—because work was an act of submission before a powerful and transcendent God.

Millerites, among others, seemed to threaten the peaceful

continuation and perpetuation of the ideals of character and work. An individual believer in the advent near had the potential to disrupt those important bases for order and progress. During the 1830s and 1840s, a new kind of institution flourished on the American landscape that embodied new assumptions about how to deal with those who did not fit or who threatened jsut such social foundations. That institution was the asylum or hospital for the insane. Millerites were among the most prominent deviants at the very time the popular assumption that such misfits could generally be assumed to be insane and fit for institutionalization took hold in the general culture.

THE ASYLUM

Reports of Millerite insanity poured out in the 1840s, especially in the climactic years 1843 and 1844. The stories came out of virtually every corner of the northern United States. From New Hampshire and Vermont on the north: the asylum at Concord held twelve "victims" in early 1843, the Brattleboro Asylum twenty-six ("not so many there as should be") in 1844. As far south as Baltimore: Millerites who sold property at a "nominal price" in anticipation of the end were almost certain to be declared under "mental delusion." At least to Ohio on the west: the wife of Captain Chase became a "raving maniac" because "the errors of that one idea," the approaching advent, "took possession of her mind," and she ended by trying to take the lives of her children.[39] All kinds of papers repeated the stories—the Rochester *Daily Democrat* and the Springfield *Republican, Zion's Herald* and the *Christian Reflector,* the *Liberator* and *Niles National Register.*[40] Individuals of all stripes promoted the identification of Millerism and insanity. William Lloyd Garrison, hardly a stranger to accusations of lunacy himself, asserted that the effect of Millerism was, "in many instances, to produce insanity." Samuel Woodward, superintendent of the Worcester, Massachusetts, Asylum, perceived an increase in insanity caused by religion in 1843 and pointed to fifteen cases attributed to Millerism. One bona fide lunatic in the Brattleboro, Vermont, Asylum added his own voice to the chorus: a peaceful life in the Green Mountains was shattered when "the destroyer came. He entered paradise in the form of a serpent and—all know the rest. He appeared in the form of a false prophet, Miller." The town fell for Miller's "fearful belief" and neglected their crops. As the winter settled in, they suffered "cold, hunger, and deprivation," their "fair daughters were pining away, and dropping one after another into the cold grave," their sons became "wan, pale, and timid," the "demon, suicide," took victims daily. But all of this "mattered not" to those who believed that "'the end of things was at hand!'" This convalescent finished with a solemn warning against "the worst of all madness—THE MADNESS OF THE SOUL!"[41]

High drama, this—individuals led astray by deceivers or madmen, become raving maniacs, pacified, or at least prevented from doing harm, behind the solid doors of the hospital for the insane. The stories and the actual incarceration of Millerites make sense only when viewed in context. What did it mean, in the 1840s, to pronounce a person insane? What were these havens—these asylums—that were presented as the appropriate homes for the religiously deluded lunatic?

Europeans invented the insane asylum, as a specialized institution, in the seventeenth century. Americans, too, began to look to hospitals for lunatics to solve the problem of the restriction and care of the mad. In the years between 1818 and 1850, American society as a whole "discovered" the asylum. Private hospitals for the insane appeared first in this cycle, beginning with the McLean Hospital in Massachusetts and the Friends' Asylum in Pennsylvania. The first modern state hospital for the insane opened at Worcester, Massachusetts, in 1833. Although public support did not rise high enough to build institutions funded by states alone in most cases, a mixture of state and private money stood behind the opening of a raft of hospitals in the northern states in the 1830s and 1840s: in Vermont in 1836, in Ohio in 1838, in New Hampshire, Maine, and Boston in 1840, in Utica, New York, in 1843, in Indiana in 1845, in Rhode Island and Illinois in 1847, in New Jersey in 1848. After 1850, the asylum moved west with the nation. Even before 1850, however, hospitals for the insane began to carve out a niche as an accepted social institution in the new republic.[42]

In the first half of the nineteenth century, too, a group of doctors took upon themselves the special task of understanding and treating insanity under the rubric of medical science. Benjamin Rush, the prominent physician of the generation of the founding fathers, had taken a particular interest in madness. A later generation probed more deeply and systematically into the causes of mental disease and put their findings to a practical test. These men were the first generation of psychiatrists—often called alienists at the time—and their leaders took on the professional role of superintendents of hospitals for the insane.

Samuel Woodward, Pliny Earle, Edward Jarvis, Amariah Brigham, Isaac Ray, and others believed that insanity stemmed from a variety of factors. These superintendents and students of lunacy sought both predisposing and precipitating causes. Heredity, environment, and trauma, both physical and psychological, took their places among the complex origins of mental aberration. In spite of their interest in underlying factors and in the multiplicity of influences that produced insanity, these men concentrated most heavily on short-term causes, and they very often settled on a single cause per case. The Bloomingdale Asylum in New York issued a fairly typical report on the causes of the insanity of its 219 patients in 1842. One factor was singled out to account for each case. Although heredity took the lead as the single most common cause, it covered only 26 of those 219 cases. Close contenders included "puerperal" (15), masturbation (15), "disappointed affection" (14), and "domestic troubles" (13). Also high on the list was religious excitement, with 14 cases to its credit.[43]

The medical superintendents sometimes suspected that organic lesions were associated with insanity, but organic damage became both cause and effect in association with more important factors. Although a bump on the head could precipitate lunacy, actions out of line with behavioral norms could also lead to physical damage, in the prevailing view. Questions of individual behavior became the more important concern for the early psychiatrists—a focus that suited the widespread concern about the emerging social order among antebellum Americans as a whole. The individual took steps that led to his descent into madness, but the mobility, scrambling competition, fever for liberty, and lack of restraints that characterized the new republic formed the setting and offered the temptation for the person's incautious pursuits. It was, finally, the spirit and structure—or lack of structure—in the country at large that took the blame for the insane.

If the perversion of the individual will under pressure from widespread instability lay behind the persistence of insanity in the American experiment, it was fitting that the effort to cure insanity focused on efforts to remove the afflicted from the dangerous social environment. The presentation of the asylum as an almost utopian solution to the problems associated with liberty, competition, and civilization promised a remedy perfectly suited to the dominant interpretation of the disease. The ideal asylum offered a haven of cleanliness and order. It restricted contacts with the presumed sources of the inmates' lunacy, including their families. It afforded opportunities for a peaceful regimen of rest and, especially, productive labor. The regulation of the physical structure and of a schedule by the clock promised, according to the superintendents' claims, a quick cure for all sufferers who were institutionalized at an early stage.

The problem of distinguishing the genuine sufferer, the lunatic, from the sane received less attention from the medical superintendents and others than did questions of cause and cure. The experts did work toward categorization of varieties of mental illness; mania, for example, was distinguished from dementia, and both were set apart from depression. The founders of psychiatry also described symptoms manifested by the insane—refusal to eat, auditory hallucinations, delusions, violent behavior, and so on. Nowhere did they draw a distinct line between sanity and insanity, however; nor did they systematically delineate sets of symptoms that defined mental illness. The diagnosis of insanity remained broad, vague, and largely intuitive. One of the few definitions of insanity from the 1840s read: "a chronic disease of the brain, producing either derangement of the intellectual faculties, or prolonged change of the feelings, affections, and habits of an individual."[44] If behavior seemed odd enough, if the individual deviated from former patterns of belief and action enough, these indications led to a conclusion that madness reigned.

Imprecise definitions of insanity went hand in hand with practice in the decision to institutionalize a suspected lunatic. Relatives or friends carried the unfortunate to the hospital, where the superintendent confirmed—or disagreed with—the lay diagnosis. The medical men tended to go along with placing the responsibility for that initial decision in the hands of the untrained. Such a division of labor suited both their emphasis on causes and cures, not diagnoses, and their assumption that the presence of madness was intuitively obvious. The superintendents frowned upon requirements for legal procedures and second opinions prior to incarceration. Madness was a disease, not a crime, and it was a disease that could be recognized by any one man as well as by all (sane) men.

Medical superintendents and their supporters were engaged in setting this system in place when the Millerites burst upon the national scene. The Millerites—perhaps most unfortunately for them—gained attention just in time to take a part in the redefinition of insanity on a popular level and in the campaign to raise popular support for the new asylums. As a result, the Millerites reflected another aspect of change in the religious culture of the mid-nineteenth century—the restriction of the sphere of religious authority through infringement by other professions, institutions, and systems of thought about human behavior.

Tradition attributed numerous cases of insanity to excessive religious excitement. Accusations abounded that John Wesley and George Whitefield drove people mad; in America, too, the fervor of the Methodists had aroused suspicions of lunacy. Psychiatrists expressed and reinforced the prejudices of many American Protestants when they pronounced Irish Catholics to be monomaniacs.[45] The medical superintendents did not reject the connection between religion and insanity, but rather gave it the stamp of scientific legitimacy.

Not all cases of religious insanity were tied to religious causes. The insane expressed their mania or melancholia in religious terms often, the theory had it, because insanity took on the coloration of dominant influences in the surrounding culture. The superintendents found the cause, in many cases, in illness or disappointment. The delusions in which the insanity was sometimes expressed, on the other hand, took religious form because religious images were common fare in antebellum America.

In many cases, nonetheless, superintendents of asylums attributed a patient's lunacy to religious causes. The excitements of the revival, especially, stimulated the passions of the susceptible individual beyond the breaking point. Alternatively, too much concentration on sin, damnation, and depravity could drag a person to the depths of melancholy. Time and again, reports issued by the asylums listed religion prominently among the causes of sufferers' insanity.[46]

Medical superintendents could not alone prescribe broad popular assumptions about insanity, its causes and cures. Other authorities—the clergy still prominent among them—competed for the ear of the public on questions of mental health. The people at large, too, heard stories of lunatics and promotions of hospital cures through perceptions attuned to preexisting categories and assumptions. Inevitably, all of these sources interacted in the 1830s and 1840s and influenced one another in ways determined, in part, by the events of the time.

It is quite likely that significant numbers of Americans in the 1830s had not shaken off beliefs that tied insanity to diabolic possession. Millerites themselves drew on a broad set of assumptions that attributed phenomena to mysterious forces, and in an age of persisting religiosity, those forces took on aspects of faith and anti-faith, Christ and anti-Christ, agents of God and agents of Satan. Yet Americans in the second quarter of the nineteenth century also took pride in their rationalism and in their openness to persuasion by sound, factual evidence. Scientific explanations of insanity, therefore, appealed to many side by side with demonic explanations.

Whether a manifestation of the devil's work or the result of an organic lesion, insanity was not to be attributed to the true religion that the great majority refused to deny. Medical superintendents may have found religious experience suspect, but a large and influential number of clergy and laypersons saw in the revival and the new birth the best defense against madness. Nonetheless, many evangelicals repudiated the excesses associated with revivalism. While maintaining the value of true religion, they hedged in the sphere of respectability by denying manifestations of excitement that went too far. Many religious people, then, could easily accept the argument that religious fervor tinged with fanaticism might lead to insanity. For some—the more "liberal"—of the evangelicals, too, as for their Unitarian cousins, dwelling on hell and damnation seemed surely calculated to throw a mind off course.

Superintendents of hospitals for the insane could ill afford to ignore popular opinion about lunacy. These medical men were charged not only with treating patients and administering the daily routines of their asylums but also with establishing and ensuring the survival of the institutions. By the 1840s, to be sure, the wave of asylum-building was well on its course, but the continuation of that trend as well as the supply of funds to maintain existing hospitals depended on the sympathies of many outside the medical fraternity. It was not clear that the asylum would endure as the primary structure for care of the insane. The superintendents, aided by publicists such as Dorothea Dix and Samuel Gridley Howe, faced the job of persuading state legislators and private benefactors to keep their experiments alive and functional.

The *Journal of Insanity,* chief organ of the early psychiatrists, not only facilitated communication among experts but also performed a publicizing function. The first volume of the *Journal* included an article on "Millerism." Rather than raising the problem of the association of Millerism with insanity to the level of scientific analysis, the author chose to begin by quoting from newspapers. "The evil results" of Millerism "are known to all," reads the article, "for we have scarcely seen a newspaper for some months past but contains accounts of suicides and insanity produced by it." The expert gives whatever legitimacy he has to lend to the popular accounts of Millerite insanity. The most suspicious reader might even say that the author sounds as though he might have received his own education on religious insanity from such stories. In any case, no complicated analysis follows, but only a firm acceptance of Millerism as the (single) cause of insanity in a number of cases, a cheery note on the possibilities for recovery, and the bestowing of a medical title upon the Millerite disease: *"epidemic or contagious monomanias."* In keeping with the assumption that his audience was composed primarily of lay persons—potential supporters, or even potential patients—and not only experts, he goes on to give advice for avoiding such monomanias. With a good bit of apology, he concludes that staying away from protracted meetings is the key. He walks a careful balance between his condemnation of religious preaching that would excite, agitate, and wear out its audience—of doctrines "not unfrequently productive of disease, madness, and death"—and his bow to the importance of acceptable religion. He "would carefully avoid saying any thing that might hinder the spread of the truths of the Bible, or the conversion of a single soul," he protests. The superintendents dared not offend the religious sensibilities of their contemporaries, but they did play on popular fears of religious "fanaticism" in the process of explaining and promoting their own work in the asylums.[47]

In fact, the newspaper stories to which the *Journal* referred helped to give form to popular conceptions of insanity, of Millerism, and of the two as one and the same. Accounts in paper after paper throughout the northern states gave brief pictures of the horrible effects of the advent delusion. There was nothing subtle about the lunacy so pictured. Even the superintendents tended to believe that the presence of mental disease was easily detectable; the popular accounts reinforced such an assumption. The (reputedly) insane Millerite was most often described as a "raving maniac."[48] In case readers had any doubt about the wildness that made up such "raving," some stories gave more dramatic detail. A female whose "insanity was occasioned by the influence of the doctrines of Millerism" had to be taken out of a railroad car and "required four persons to hold her."[49] It might seem anticlimactic, in contrast to such stories, for another writer to sum up a case of supposed Millerite madness by saying that "reason was ousted from her throne." Yet the essence of the mental disease brought on by Millerism, as these accounts held it, was that "imagination, under the maddening influence of this belief, ran riot with reason." And in spite of the careful distinctions of theologians on this point, the press were not loathe to equate reason with the soul.[50] Beyond the assumption that wild, disruptive behavior characterized the Millerite lunatic, newspapers made little effort to distinguish that what supposed insanity was. They slipped easily from calling advent belief a "delusion" into portraying adherence to that delusion as insanity. The distinction between false belief and outright lunacy was vague at best; if this line of definition eluded the experts, how much more easily the casual observer slipped over it. Occasional apparent distinctions contributed more to an appearance of scientific categorization than to any genuine effort to mark the point at which aberration ended and madness began. One report on the "fatal" delusion, for example, thought it "calculated to make those who embrace it, completely monomaniacal, and not a few absolutely insane." Another pictured the objects of the delusion "with minds weakened, and in not a few cases, insane, and even demented."[51] The effect of such passages was hardly to clarify the meaning of monomania or dementia or to distinguish them from insanity. The impression left was one of a horrifying descent through levels of loss of reason, and the peppering of the commentary with light portions of seemingly scientific vocabulary lent a note of authority to the voice of scandal.

Anecdotes in the press left little doubt about the effects of having such religiously deluded lunatics at large. A "young man named Tiehonor" had the good fortune to be saved from a suicide attempt made while he was insane from the influence of Millerism. On the other hand, a man only "partially deranged" went so far as to cut his wife's throat. Sometimes only the Millerite himself was in immediate danger, as in the cases of Moses Clark and Mr. Kulp, both Millerites who were supposed to have done away with themselves by drowning. The safety of entire families could be endangered by the terrors resulting from Millerism; at least it was assumed that Moses Butterfield, who killed his wife and children, must have been a Millerite. Even the instincts of motherhood could be perverted to the point of opening the door to infanticide, as in the cases of Mrs. Chase of Ohio, who was said to have failed to kill her children, and of a Mrs. Garrison in Newark, New Jersey, who did away with herself and her two youngest children by administering arsenic.[52]

If lunatics threatened the lives of themselves and others, the question remained what was to be done to restrain or cure them. The press made suggestions for those with ears to hear—and, given the horrors pictured as the result of leaving the insane at large, many may have been ready to hear. One story laid out three alternatives: "Four females, living within a short distance from each other in Somerset, have within a few weeks become deranged in consequence of the preaching of the Millerites. One is since *dead* one has been sent to the Insane Asylum at Worcester, and two remain with their friends."[53] The mad person could be left to die, put under the care of associates or relatives, or put away in a hospital for the insane. The first alternative was hardly to be recommended. The second became less viable as time went on, both because changing social and economic patterns made it more difficult to care for the sick and deviant at home and because the public were encouraged to fear for their own safety if they lived with lunatics. Consequently, the third option became the favored choice. While medical superintendents, Dorothea Dix, and some others advertised the asylum as the humane and medically sound choice, the press portrayed the insane hospital as the standard solution. In 1843, papers reported twelve insane Millerites in the asylum at Concord, New Hampshire, eleven at Worcester, Massachusetts, and at least four in Maine. In 1844, the press published counts of twenty-six Millerites in the Brattleboro, Vermont, Asylum, fifteen in Worcester, and twenty-eight—or perhaps fifteen—or pehaps seven—in the Utica, New York, hospital.[54]

Stories sometimes reflected the optimistic and humanitarian view of asylums that the superintendents sought to promote. The Worcester Hospital was "a noble monument of Christian philanthropy"; hospitals for the insane deserved the favor of the public, inmates of the hospitals their sympathy; allowing the insane some of the niceties of civilized life and according them respect, as the administrators of the new asylums intended to do, was calculated to raise the unfortunates out of savagery and induce them to act as "reasonable beings."[55] Yet the popular view encouraged by the press reflected more ambivalence than the writings of the superintendents or the reports of Dix.

Especially when referring to insanity associated with Millerism, stories often emphasized containment more than cure as the primary function of the lunatic hospital. Certainly, restraint was implicitly demanded by the tales of violence attendant upon Millerite madness. By 1843 or 1844, when articles on Millerism and insanity, and also commitment of Millerites in asylums, became common, the call for action to roll back adventist fervor and influence had reached the level of a dull roar punctuated by hysterical shrieks. As one commentator noted, the lunacy associated with the Miller excitement made it imperative to "consider what may be proper . . . to arrest the further progress of such an abominable and dangerous delusion." Another observer was more certain of "what may be proper": he recommended confining Joshua Himes "as they would confine any other maniac." The most advanced medical opinion may have promoted a stay in an asylum as a restful cure; more broadly disseminated opinion emphasized the incarceration of dangerous elements.[56]

In the popular mind, Millerites became madmen, madmen fit for institutionalization, and thus candidates for the asylum. It was not always and inevitably so; the redefinition of popular religious culture and the reassignment of responsibility for supervision of deviants came together in the 1840s to issue in that result. Perhaps the religious extremist would once have been labeled a witch; perhaps, more to the point, the relogous extremist of 1843 would once have been called a saint.[57] The fanatic, if he were understood as such, would once have been subject to the authority of the clergy and church, the family and community. Although these social groups had by no means lost all authority by the 1840s, one aspect of the problem of religious deviance was being handed over to medical experts and the institutions they supervised.

It is worth noting that before the routinization and condensing of the conversion experience in the Second Great Awakening, manifestations that later became evidence of insanity had been accepted elements of an individual's religious journey. Auditory hallucinations, in the eyes of psychiatrists, helped to mark the presence of madness. The hopeful believer, before the nineteenth century—and even later, though not in respectable circles—heard the voice of God demanding his love and subjection. A range of behaviors set the melancholy or depressed apart, as the medical men saw it—refusal to eat or sleep, brooding on the state of the soul, even temptations to suicide. Yet here, again, was a condition that earlier generations might well have understood in religious terms—the state of conviction of sin. After Finney, the accepted model of religious transformation put the convert through the paces—hearing God's call to repentance, bending under the weight of a crushing sense of inadequacy and alienation, and reemerging a triumphant child of Christ—all in a day or two, and preferably during a single revival meeting. Evidences of depression remained acceptable religious behavior in this context. This initiate might ignore bodily functions, give in to despair, hear and see things, as long as he got through it all quickly and got on about his daily business. In other days, this process might have taken months, or even years, to complete. Family, minister, and congregation would have labored with the person undergoing the long process of conversion, offering prayers, advice, and the understanding that this was the work of God. In the 1840s, on the other hand, such an extended religious experience was increasingly likely to land its subject in an asylum, where the rather different labors of the medical superintendent and his assistants would issue, ideally, not in conversion, but in cure.[58]

Even if one interprets Millerism not as a throwback to a distinct and scrupulous religiosity, but as a recurrence of a deviant fanaticism that would have been as unacceptable to the seventeenth century as to the nineteenth, the lessons of social function and cultural context remain, essentially, the same. Church and state worked together in seventeenth-century Massachusetts, for example, to condemn the deviant (the witch) and the fanatical (the Quaker) to death or exile. Although the state moved slowly out of the business of defining unacceptable religious excesses, by the end of the eighteenth century the churches were left, for the most part, to their own devices in dealing with the heterodox and the fanatical. As the evangelical empire extended its grasp in the first half of the nineteenth century, more and more Americans came under the disciplinary strictures of the denominations. Yet the religious freedom of the new nation and the centrifugal force of denominationalism sapped the restraining power of the churches. By 1843, the impatient and the forward-looking could refuse to wait to see if the churches could hold back the Millerite whirlwind. They turned eagerly, instead, to the asylum, in hopes that incarceration, or the threat of it, would make for a quick and effective and to disruptive religious enthusiasm.

Millerites would have confessed happily to the charge that something outside themselves had a grip on their souls. Commitment to an objective, transcendent God was, indeed, something akin to possession—except that, in this case, Millerites hoped that they were "possessed" by the power of ultimate righteousness. Their contemporaries were less prone to see the distinction. People who believed in the existence of objective—even embodied—supernatural powers belonged to another age, as far as the forces of cultural orthodoxy were concerned. Theirs was supposed to be an age of enlightened order and scientific rationality. Those who challenged the order and questioned the rationality could be threatned with incarceration where those forces supposedly reigned. Family, community, church—none of the traditional institutions seemed capable of restraining the fanatical, the deviant, or the dangerous any longer. Through a coincidence in time, Millerism arrived on the American scene at an appropriate moment to become unwitting and unwilling participants in the selling of a new means to order—the asylum. Asylum superintendents and their allies played on the prejudices of their contemporaries and promised to relieve the churches of an impossible burden when they pronounced Millerites insane. Other opponents of Millerism gave the asylum an unsolicited boast in public opinion by portraying the dangers supposedly inherent in radical supernaturalism.

Some Millerites may have been crazy. Perhaps every Millerite confined to an asylum in the 1840s would have been judged fit for institutionalization by a twentieth-century psychiatrist. Neither of these possibilities negates one point. The fact remains that conceptions of what constituted insanity and of the proper action toward the insane changed in the nineteenth century. What had been a religious and social problem became a social and medical problem. In the popular mind, a conflict of religious liberty versus religious oppression became a conflict between sanity and madness. Where church, family, and community had once held sway, the asylum came to reign.

Character, self-control, and hope for the future faced an ultimate denial in the loss of reason and especially in the suicide that was closely associated with insanity. In anticipating the sudden return of Christ, Millerites were often perceived as both cutting loose all restraints on behavior and cutting off all hope for the future. Subjection to a transcendent God meant the annihilation of the individual. Such was the message of many anecdotes about Millerites. It had not been so for the Puritans. Meaning and righteousness for the individual had once been inseparably tied to that subjection. By the 1840s, however, Puritan piety was no longer perceived as a sound basis for social order. In fact, keeping one's eye on a distant, transcendent God, especially as expressed in the anticipation of the imminent return of his Son, focused attention and energies in the wrong direction. What counted now was the perseverance of the individual—perseverance in principles and perseverance in moral, dutiful behavior. Such reinforcement as remained for individual obligation shifted from church and godly commonwealth to influence in social interaction, especially within the family.

CHAPTER VI

The Society:
Ideals and Control

Problems and concerns raised by Millerism about ideals for and control of the individual were matched on a number of fronts by excitement over the relationship of Millerism to broader social institutions and social ideals. By the mid-nineteenth century, the social institution considered to be most critical by spokespersons for American orthodoxy was the family, specifically under the tutelage of the ideal of Victorian motherhood. Another set of institutions considered through the medium of attacks on Millerites was the congeries of voluntary and reform societies—groups among which Millerites found themselves caught by the vituperative barbs equally of conservatives and dissidents. And just as Millerites faced at least the threat of action on an individual basis in the possibility of incarceration, they faced off group against group in confrontations and attacks that sometimes culminated in violence. Finally, the divergent points at which Millerism became defined as a threat to social order and social change generally pointed to a common goal in collective hopes for the American nation.

FAMILY

Character may have been endangered by the wrongful influence of "confidence men" in the wider world, but Victorians found a safe haven for the exercise of benevolent influence. The temptations and turbulent competition of public life led to a person's downfall only if he were unprepared by nurture and moral force to face those challenges. Conscience, principles, discipline, and restraint raised formidable barriers against the threats posed by opportunity and immortality, according to the new Victorians. By mid-century, those adherents to a nascent set of modern values had discovered the perfect environment for nurturing good character in the bosom of the family. The family, in turn, could fulfill its office in building the foundation for the social order only under the watchful direction of that paragon of purity, piety, submissiveness, and domesticity, the ideal Victorian woman.[1]

Once again, critics found in the Millerites a compact version of almost all that threatened the stability envisioned as an inevitable counterpart to emerging Victorian values. Once again, as opponents vented their fears in rage against adventism, they articulated a new position defined in contrast to the perceived enemy. Once again, then, the use of Millerites as a foil not only provided an opportunity for openly defining the values toward which so many antebellum Americans turned but also ensured that those new values would be carefully distanced from the attitudes and beliefs for which the Millerites were presumed to stand.

The widespread assumption that Millerism upset the stability of the family sometimes surfaced in vague claims against the new movement. Opponents counted among the evils attendant upon the adventist delusion "family peace destroyed," "domestic concerns . . . disturbed," and the "happiness" of families ruined.[2] More specific charges surfaced as well. One Millerite Methodist, for example, appeared in the newspapers as one who deserted his family and went west to indulge in polygamy.[3] Another husband and father killed his wife and children, "we presume," said the teller of the tale, as "another fruit of the Miller humbug."[4]

Showers of tales of woe fell less upon husbands and fathers, however, than upon wives and mothers. Women stood as the great bastion of nurturing influence on whose moral strength the whole society had to depend, according to the spokespersons for the new middle-class Victorians. Questions of where and how woman exercised her influence, and whether she would persevere in her role, took on tremendous significance in this scheme. If women "under the influence of fanaticism" at a Millerite camp meeting were seen—or imagined—"who tore out their hair," the scene struck chords of anxiety in those who accepted the vision of a society with pure womanhood at its base.[5] Nor is it surprising that the Millerites, who apparently counted but a few women among their lecturers, were caught up in the furor of the time over women speaking in public before mixed audiences. One observer spoke for many when he complained of having "to take another dose of Millerism" from a woman—probably Olive Maria Rice—who "would better be discharging her duty & more becoming the dignity of her sex in the private walks of life in the domesticated circle." The speaker had stepped out of her proper role and into a morass of immorality. Such, at least, was clear to the correspondent, who went on to report that two men from the neighborhood "flipped a cent to see which should go home with her the last *night*."[6]

Of course, those who perceived the perversion of women's proper place and behavior among the Millerites foresaw spreading ramifications of such deviance. The family, especially, would have been expected to suffer when those who gave it its heart and foundation went astray in the forests of fanaticism. Many found it easy to believe that such a strange group as the Millerites would give up "marrying or giving in marriage" or turn to the concept of "spiritual wives." Such threats had their most dramatic effect when ties to tales of women deserting their homes and so breaking up that fundamental social institution, the family.[7] But the family was not safe from the horrors of fanaticism if the woman infected with adventism kept her children with her; the result in such cases could be the death of the young through exposure and neglect, or even murder.[8]

The family became the resort not of a people who had given up religion, but of a people redefining their religion in a way that emphasized private, subjective experience and morality defined by worldly order. In a sense, family and church came into conflict because the isolated, nurturing nature of the new religious sensibility could find a suitable home within the domestic unit as easily as in the denominational one. Family and church did not come out fighting, however, to wage a war to determine which would hold primary authority over spiritual and moral concerns. Instead, they formed an alliance.

The clergy began to promote a version of Protestant Christianity that revolved around the values and attitudes increasingly associated with women and the family. The rigor of the Calvinist God was giving way to the sentimentality of the Victorian deity; obedience to divine will found its replacement in the soft holiness of a good heart and the nice propriety of good behavior. The turn to Christianity began to come more often not in a dramatic encounter with a transcendent Other, but through a long process of nurture. The development of the Christian, in short, held a striking resemblance to the growth of a person of character.

As character and Christianity mingled, clergymen joined with women working in the family to promote the new ideal and to establish a new base of authority. Religious writers emphasized the important role of woman and family in the development of that happy internal state that fit the young person for responsible life in society and also fulfilled the requirements of a benevolent, personal God.[9] Given the importance of the moral and religious role of women, the following handbill could only have been met with shocked amusement:

THE JOE MILLER PROPHET.—It is reported of this Infernal Fool, that he is to figure on the *gullism* order, in Cambridgeport [Mass.], for the especial benefit of the female sex, proving to a dead certainty, that no *women* will go to heaven—as the Book nowhere says to such effect—but that at the close of the year 1843, the shrieks of the women will be of such thundering effect, that the moon will turn to blood, the stars fall, and the sun recede from existence, and the end of the world come. Joey says he will then be found on the top of the highest mountain, sounding a tin conk-shell to drown hell of its horrors!

BILLY HIMES, *Scribe*[10]

This far-fetched parody went beyond the usual criticism of Millerism, but it represented in caricature the point behind much anti-Millerite propaganda. Those odd supernaturalists turned assumptions about religion and society askew, according to their opponents. If women held the key to religion and morality, Millerites would damn them all. If proper ladies behaved in a dignified and pious manner, Millerites would send them shrieking. If the female sex worked its influence appropriately and beneficently within the domestic sphere, Millerites would have them out of doors, loudly calling down the wrath of the heavens. If the safest and noblest course for society called its people to retreat to the private security and strengthening influences of the home, Millerites would flaunt all such decency and perch atop mountains, gleefully hailing the thunderous retribution they hoped to bring down around them.[11]

REFORM

Character was to be molded within the family, but for many mid-nineteenth-century Americans, character expressed itself in action, and action gave energy to unfolding social development. For most, action meant, above all, work, and their ethic focused on the cluster of values surrounding work. But there were others for whom the demand for action pointed to a different kind of work—work directed specifically toward changing the social and moral structure of the nation. The reformers demanded character on both the internal and external sides, but they put character to work toward a different, more rapidly approaching future order than that envisioned by most of their contemporaries.

Americans in the northern states during the nineteenth century were, as a group, reformers: they organized in voluntary associations toward a wide variety of ends, and they held in common the sense that it was both possible and right to change things for the better. The most popular reform movements of the day were the movements for religious and moral reform. Antebellum Protestants pressed diligently forward in the causes to share the Bible, send our missionaries, and bring behavior into line with what they understood to be basic moral values. To many, Millerism seemed contrary to this tradition of ongoing organization and continuing change. Outsiders did not believe that Millerites favored the energetic extension of the gospel to all men. They were wrong, but—as in the case of the problem of Millerites and work—they were also right. Miller and his adherents favored evangelization, they believed that the gospel had to be spread, and they often went forth themselves on campaigns to share the word—at least their interpretation of it. Once again, however, the basis for their action differed from that of most of their contemporaries. They did not expect their efforts to issue in an overwhelming acceptance of the gospel. They pursued their course because it was required of them, not because it would produce glorious results. They acted, again, in submission to a distant God. The result was left to God, and it was separable from any human effort or process of change in the world.

If Millerites clearly differed from the majority of their contemporaries, there was one group with whom they might rightfully have claimed kinship. Radical reformers—centered in the abolitionist movement, but involved a host of causes—shared cultural background, psychology, and status as deviants with Millerites. Yet the reformers refused to recognize the kinship, and they often condemned second adventism with as much vehemence as any anti-Millerite group.

Millerite leaders were as likely as not to emerge from the ranks of abolitionists. Henry Jones, at the time a temperance agent, had already entered into correspondence with William Miller when his mind became "enlightened & awakened on the subject of *'abolition'* or *'Anti-Slavery'!"* Joseph Bates, too, traveled the path of temperance, antislavery, and Millerism. Charles Fitch published his *Slaveholding Weighed in the Balance of Truth and Its Comparative Guilt* right before he began a three-year struggle over committing himself to adventism. These men were joined by others who held antislavery sentiments—the former Methodist preacher George Storrs, the editor Nathaniel Southard, the businessman Ezekiel Hale, Jr. Prominent among this group, of course, stood Joshua Himes. That organizer *par excellence* participated in the founding of the Massachusetts Anti-Slavery Society and figured prominently in the New England Anti-Slavery and Non-Resistance Societies well into 1843. Although apparently distracted by the impending end in the year of the Great Disappointment, Himes came back in full force in time to attend the Evangelical Alliance meeting in London in 1846.[12]

Antislavery may or may not have been as prevalent among the rank and file as among the leaders. Certainly the prominence of abolitionists among Millerite leaders opened doors and attracted attention among antislavery sympathizers. Miller himself opposed slavery, and from his position as the embodiment of second adventism, he advertised the movement as consistent with his convictions.[13] It is not surprising, then, to find evidence that antislavery, and strong antislavery at that, took its place among the shared assumptions of many Millerites.[14]

The affinity between abolitionism and Millerism should elicit little surprise. The two movements arose from the same culture and followed essentially the same dynamic. As Whitney Cross has pointed out, the revivalistic religion of the sons and daughters of New England lent itself to the development of "ultraisms." Out of their common heritage, abolitionists and Millerites drew commitments to a "higher law" than that which ruled existing institutions. Among both groups there arose immediatist demands for a commitment that set the righteous apart from the unjust, immoral, or ungodly. That second conversion that opened the way for the perfection of the individual also pointed to the perfection of the larger order—introduced by the spread of abolitionist sentiments or by the personal appearance of Jesus Christ. The psychology of both groups demanded more than the conversion of the prevalent evangelicalism and the comfortable holiness of everyday morality. It demanded an immediate commitment to radical transformation.[15]

Just as many abolitionists thought that their cause extended true Christianity, many Millerites believed that adventism was a fuller version of the principles at the core of abolitionism. Abolitionists-become-Millerites such as Luther Boutelle looked forward to the rapid freeing of the slave, not by the spread of "moral truth," but by "physical Omnipotence." In the kingdom to come, one such reformer pointed out, "pains and groans, and the slaveholder's scourge" would be "felt no more." The antislavery agitation had not been raised for nought just because it could not succeed on its own power. It had, rather, appeared to accomplish a "sifting," a sorting out of the real adherents to the truth from professed Christians. Consistent with the psychology of immediatist abolitionism, these Millerite reformers emphasized not only the freeing of the slave but also the purification, or salvation, of the reformer through his commitment to the truth. Millerites proposed a "sifting" beyond that accomplished by abolitionism, however. Although many asserted that no true adventist rejected abolitionism, they suspected that not all abolitionists would accept adventism. The final separation of sheep from goats would be accomplished by raising the issue of the Lord's appearing. Those who looked for the second advent would be among the chosen. This did not mean that all antislavery activity should cease in the meantime. In the face of imminent judgment there was all the more reason to carry out God's commands, and for Millerite abolitionists, those commands included the requirement to "do all in our power to ameliorate the condition of our fellow men," slave and free.[16]

When Millerites first began to gain more attention and more converts after 1839, abolitionists who did not join the ranks took the new quirk of their peers quite calmly. The *Liberator* advertised Miller's lectures in the expectation that they would be "of a salutary character." The reformers expected Miller "to give much truth" on abolitionism, non-resistance, and temperance in spite of his "computation of the end of the world."[17] The Garrisonian abolitionists did not, as a group, take on Millerism as they did women's rights and non-resistance, as a necessary extension of their principles. For a time, however, the radicals accepted the adventists as a group who seemed to do little harm and had the potential to do some good. From 1840 on, in fact, even as they grew increasingly hostile, abolitionists used incidents of intolerance of Millerism to plead their own case; they complained that churches closed doors to Miller that were "swung wide open for the entrance of slaveholding clergymen," for example.[18]

Non-Millerite abolitionists began to shift their ground very soon. Although they continued to make jabs at churches and lecture halls that would close out Millerites while letting in proslavery men and slaveholders, they emphasized their disapproval of adventism more.[19] The sheer number of abolitionists who took an interest in Millerism might well have inspired the skeptical attention of their peers. Besides the Millerism of abolitionists already mentioned, for example, Garrison soon found Millerism running rampant among the group in Groton, Massachusetts, to whom he had recently sent his fond regards—Silas Hawley, Luther Boutelle, and Benjamin Hall.[20] Garrison and other non-Millerite abolitionists did not accept the addition of the second advent doctrine to the list of convictions that many antislavery people shared. Garrison had met opposition when he had introduced "extraneous" issues such as women's rights to abolitionist platforms. Now Garrison, in turn, set a limit to the extension of the principles undergirding antislavery. It was true, in part, that such abolitionists became more hostile to Millerism because the advent cause represented competition for people, time, and money. The truth is not so simple, however; some issues that could have been defined as competitive were defined, instead, as complementary, while Millerism was not.

The *Liberator* expressed the ambivalence of at least one branch of the antislavery movement toward Millerism. Attacks on adventism in that reform journal often took the same form that they did in a variety of religious and secular papers—scurrilous anecdotes portraying the fanaticism and dangerousness of Millerites. By 1842, the *Liberator* began printing tales of insanity among adventists; in 1843 and 1844 it repeated stories of suicides, murders, and the ubiquitous ascension robes.[21] In reprinting such pieces, the abolitionists drew on the common store of information—and of certain assumptions—of their day.

In their more direct conflict with Millerites, abolitionists expressed dismay at the passivity that they associated with the watchers for the end. Garrison worried privately to Henry Clarke Wright over the "considerable number of worthy abolitionists . . . carried away" by Millerism and so "rendered completely useless" to the cause of antislavery.[22] One correspondent to the *Liberator* expressed pleasure that Miller had become "particularly odious to the selfish conservatism of the day" through his espousal of temperance, antislavery, moral reform, and non-resistance, but regretfully concluded that Miller's views were ultimately "pernicious." The same writer spoke up for Himes, who had been "true to his convictions of duty" and "a faithful supporter of the antislavery movement," but was grieved again to report that the reformer had "become the victim of an absurd theory."[23] A commentator in 1844 reflected the growing rift between the two causes. Himes had reported that, through Miller's lectures, "the whole city" of Baltimore was "moved." The writer in the *Liberator* responded scathingly:

If there be any meaning in these statements, . . . we are to understand, of course, that a great change has been wrought in the minds of the people of Baltimore, on the subject of slavery; for the reception of any dogma or doctrine, in regard to the "Second Coming," which does not relieve the oppressed, is good for nothing. Could Mr. Miller deliver eleven lectures against slavery in that city, without being driven beyond its precincts, or lynched? We are quite certain that he could not; and our inference is, that Satan and his minions are incomparably less excited in view of the burning of the world by material fire, than they would be if the proposition to abolish the slave system were enforced upon them with equal boldness and fidelity.[24]

This reporter did not find any implication of reform sentiments inherent in Millerite propaganda. Unlike abolitionists of a few years before, the writer was not willing simply to discount the advent message as long as he knew that Miller also favored antislavery. By 1844, both Millerites and abolitionists had escalated their demands; this alone could account for the growing hostility between the two groups. In addition, the abolitionists had taken up the general objections to Millerism that implied that second adventism threatened discipline for action. By 1844, even other dissenters agreed that millenarian anticipation distracted from duty.

Action and duty were the keys. Promoters of reform, like propagandists for work, sought justification in doing. The abolitionist quoted above found no virtue in a doctrine that did not issue in action for the betterment of humanity. Similarly, Theodore Weld once insisted on the importance of being "fully prepared to *act out* my belief."[25] Abolitionists, like the proponents of character, were unwilling to ignore the problem of internal states. They often stressed the importance of conversion to immediatism in the heart. But though commitment to immediatism was a purifying act, it had to be played out, ultimately, in behavior. Millerites insisted on the primacy of awed subjection to a present God. They promoted reform in the name of a higher law, but that law was handed down from a distinct and distant power. The demand for action did not mean that action was efficacious—either for salvation or for results in the world. The radical reformers responded to a higher law that lay within the world—in the hearts of people if not in existing institutions. Action in concert with that immanent law, they believed, unleashed its potential within the world. Process and result were one to the radical reformers, and they rejected the Millerite division between process—change within a world that could not rise above the sinful state of man—and result—a final culmination achieved by God alone.

THREATS, VIOLENCE, AND THE MOB

Millerites and abolitionists shared a cultural heritage. They also shared the dubious distinction of being singled out by their peers for ridicule, opposition, and even physical attack. Just as the churches took action to silence and expel the Millerites, so individuals and groups working outside the churches went beyond words in their opposition. Certainly, the Millerite subculture seemed peculiar, even threatening. The degree of seriousness with which adventist deviance was taken finds its measure not only in argument but also in action. The strenuous efforts of the churches to contain dissent gave evidence of the disruption caused by the emergence of Millerism. Those efforts failed to issue in total victory for the existing congregations and denominations. Similarly, violent and disruptive acts demonstrated the virulent force of anti-Millerite sentiment in the broader community. Again, the success of the opposition was mixed at best, but again, too, the event tells much about the cultural context of the Millerite excitement.

In 1834, William Miller received a threatening letter "from some bullies and black guards." The inhospitable group of some ten men made it plain "that if I did not clear out of the State they would put me where the dogs could never find me."[26] This incident in the first decade of Millerite evangelism foreshadowed a phase of opposition after 1840 when "bullies and black guards" would take a prominent part in seeking to put down the new movement.

The organization and outreach of the Millerite movement stepped up considerably after 1839. What had once seemed a boon to the churches and a manageable difference of opinion in society came to threaten disruption. It is perhaps not surprising to find that the redoubling of Millerite successes and expectations met with new and more intense opposition.

An early outbreak of action against the Millerites occurred in Nashua, New Hampshire, late in 1841. Resistance to adventism had already penetrated the town; when Calvin French came to lecture, no meeting house opened its doors to him. Millerites, their sympathizers, and the curious gathered in a hall to hear French's message. But the meetings were not destined to run smoothly. During the first evening of French's stay in Nashua, the Millerite gathering was "well nigh broken up by twelve or fifteen fellows" characterized by a Millerite as "of the baser sort." The disrupters resorted to "swearing, shouting, clapping of hands, stamping of feet, breaking down seats, &c. &c." During the second evening, their number augmented, the opponents started by throwing nuts and making noise, and finally managed to break up the meeting "by throwing it into confusion, some running one way and some another, and others crying." Although they may have threatened that they would not leave until they "got hold of brother French," the intruders stopped short of violent acts.[27]

The rowdy crowd in Nashua might have been rather small as mobs go, but the Millerite T. M. Preble was not far off base when he characterized the incident as a "disgraceful and wicked affair." Expression of adventist views had caused some people discomfort in the 1830s; when the Millerites became numerous and influential enough, discomfort verged on anger and fear and verbal assaults were accompanied by active opposition. From the distance of more than a century, observers might be tempted to put resistance to Millerism down as "ridicule."[28] The targets of even so feeble an attack might at any time be less generous in their assessment.

Actual attacks on Millerites occurred only sporadically at first, and incidents generally stopped short of serious violence through 1842 and even into 1843. Just as the churches attempted to silence Millerism without resorting to trials in these years, groups acting outside of the churches first turned to more subtle, if hardly friendly, persuasion. Angry critics issued threats against the mayor of Albany for allowing the Millerites to hold tent meetings in that city, against Joshua Himes personally, and against the offices of the *Signs of the Times*. One man disturbed a Rochester meeting by throwing ink on a Millerite chart; "a horde of scoffing professors and non professors" caused "some trouble" at Boylston, Massachusetts.[29] Such incidents, if expressive of intolerance, threatened neither life nor limb. The very ineffectiveness of such persuasion may have added to the continually mounting success and fervor of Millerism in turning the most extreme opposition to violence and mobbing.

The mob was, by the 1840s, a time-honored institution, not unfamiliar to the course of American history. Usually viewed as an instrument of social control, the mob pictured by historians drew from widely varied segments of the population, reacted to diverse actions and perceived threats, and sought a wide range of goals. The "common people" rose up to force members of the ruling elite to adhere to traditional responsibilities. "Gentlemen of property and standing" came together into angry crowds to stop the overturning of traditional distinctions and the encroachment of cosmopolitan organization on the territory of local elites. One study has found a high tide in the number of mobs in the 1830s with an ebbing, still far above a low-water mark, in the 1840s. Certainly, Americans perceived a high level of violence in the 1830s. As a result of the long history and recent flourishing of the mob, such crowd action must have had a peculiar status in the early 1840s—customary, yet extreme, familiar, yet frightening.[30]

Anti-Millerite mobs appeared as early as 1841 in Nashua and 1842 in Newburyport, Massachusetts. The peak of such opposition did not come until 1844. The spring of 1844 witnessed mobs in West Troy, New York, and in Philadelphia, as well as an explosion in the Old South Church of Portsmouth, New Hampshire, during a lecture by the Millerite and abolitionist George Storrs. Relative peace reigned through the summer. In October, as the "final day" approached, mobs came out in force. Boston, Philadelphia, and New York were sites of anti-Millerite crowd action. Incidents also occurred in smaller cities and towns; Rochester, Scottsville, and Dansville, New York, all reported some degree of disruption of Millerite gatherings. The passing of October 22 may have ushered in another period of calm. Just as the Great Disappointment did not signal the end of adventist belief, however, the passing of the established day of the end did not completely pacify the critics. The years 1845 and 1846 saw a retreat to the level and frequency of violence of 1842, but active resistance to Millerism was by no means dead.[31]

The timing of anti-Millerite mobs and violent incidents, then, fits into a general pattern. The outlines of the opposition appeared, as with other forms of opposition, between about 1840 and 1842. Active resistance peaked during the same period when Millerism reached its highest level in numbers and influence—a period marked by violence and mob action against a variety of dissenters. Finally, violence tapered off after the Great Disappointment. In terms of specific reactions to Millerite successes, the pattern was not consistent. Opposition may have reached an initial high in April of 1844, after the first predicted time for the end had passed. The greatest outburst against the Millerites, on the other hand, came in the two weeks before October 22, 1844. In the first instance, violence followed after a period of intense evangelization, heightened fervor, and great success—at a time, in fact, when Millerism was lapsing into temporary confusion. In the second instance, mobs and other disruptions struck before and at the appointed time for the end, when excitement was high, loyalty great, and the number of converts probably at a maximum.[32] If levels of violence did not consistently correlate with seasons of increased Millerite activity or success, then a consideration of the context—more specifically, of the rioters themselves—would seem to be all the more important.

In the face of mounting Millerite strength, who incited and who participated in the riotous behavior? One can assume that active opponents drew on the assumptions and believed the criticism discussed in earlier chapters. But most anti-Millerites never resorted to violence. Who were members of the mobs? How did they differ from other opponents of adventism? Unfortunately, it is extremely difficult to locate participants in anti-Millerite actions. William Miller dismissed the crowds as "rabble." Although T. M. Preble characterized the mob at Nashua as "fellows of the baser sort," he saw behind them the directing hand of the clergy. William Peabody of Scottsville, New York, the site of incidents in 1844 and 1846, also pointed to the support of "those professing to walk in the high-way of holiness" behind the "wicked" crowd. But the clergy were not the only powers suspected of instigating violent opposition to Millerism. Apollos Hale envisioned "republican office holders" associating with "desperadoes," "gentlemen of property and standing" destroying "every maxim of decency," and "civil officers" disturbing the peace that they were sworn to uphold.[33] The Millerites thought they were under attack from combinations of men of all stations.

If the actual planners and participants in anti-Millerite actions cannot be identified, at least attitudes may be inferred, to some degree, from responses to outbreaks of violence. In Philadelphia in the winter of 1843, the disruption of Millerite meetings by a crowd led the owners of the building to close the series of lectures early. The next year, as the twenty-second of October approached, it was the Philadelphia police who closed down Millerite services "in consequence of a large gathering of persons outside of the [Julianna Street] chapel." In New York City, too, meeting places closed their doors and services were canceled in the face of mobs. Except for an offer of aid from the mayor of New York, these histories give no sign of official support for the Millerites. Rather than protecting the adventists, the preferred solution was to silence them. In Boston, the police did break up a mob that broke into the Tabernacle, reflecting perhaps respect for the rights of speech, assembly, and private property, and perhaps the experience of that city's force with mob violence. Even in this case, reports outside Boston lay the blame for the disturbance on the Millerites themselves.[34]

It seems, then, that attitudes toward Millerites were mixed at best. The "powers that be" rarely stopped mob action in time to protect peace and property, and when violence was cut off it was either through or in tandem with restrictions on the Millerite message. The individuals and groups who chose which citizens were worthy to receive full protection placed the Millerites among a second class. Even in Boston, the influential were probably split—some favoring support for the rights of the Millerites, as evidenced by the action of the police, and others willing to pull the rug of civil liberties out from under the peculiar group, as demonstrated by the emergence and persistence of the mob over two days. The very fact of continued outbursts of crowd violence through 1843, 1844, and into 1845 and 1846 attests to a good degree of both popular and elite support for anti-Millerites. Even if the mob had, to a great extent, returned to a position of acceptability in the 1830s and 1840s, the institution was sufficiently marginal that its persistence had to be backed up by a broad base of sympathy.

In spite of wide support, however, the anti-Millerite mobs could hardly be said to have achieved their goals. Those goals probably included terrorizing individuals out of their association with the movement, warning new converts away, making the spread of Millerite doctrines difficult or impossible, and setting up adventists for ridicule. Among some groups, however, angry opposition to Millerism became cause for supporting the adventists. Abolitionists, especially—familiar as they were with physical abuse and the fury of the crowd—often sympathized with the end of the world men because of the persecution they themselves had suffered. A writer in the

Liberator who viewed second adventism as an "absurd theory" and a "delusion," Millerism as "pernicious and untenable," confessed: "The most conclusive argument that I have seen in favor of the soundness of Mr. Miller's theory, is the bitterness with which it is assailed by a benighted and corrupt priesthood, and the scoffs and jeers which it elicits from the profane rabble."[35] Millerism produced no conversions in such cases, but it still reaped public sympathy among those concerned about the rights of dissenting Americans, including even the absurd and deluded.[36] Moreover, abolitionists were pleased to use tales of anti-Millerite violence, as when Millerite lecturers were "hooted at, pelted, and dragged from the stage" by a mob in St. Louis, as lessons in the true nature of slaveholding societies.[37] Spreading sympathies through association with the issues of antislavery and civil liberties built up a broad base of support beyond the committed adventist membership and also a wider and more fertile field for conversions.

Violent action did lead to both new conversions and renewed commitment by earlier converts. "The mobs in Philadelphia," wrote Himes to Miller in the spring of 1844, "have produced much conviction that we are right." The result of the threatening crowds, as Himes saw it, was that "the people want to hear [Miller] there very much."[38] Lydia Maria Child thought the Millerites only became more firm in their fanatical self-righteousness because of threats and attacks. She claimed that Millerite preachers in New York began, in the midst of the uproar of October 1844, to claim that their people needed no worldly protection, because "four angels" were "stationed at the four corners of the earth" who had "sealed the foreheads of all the saints" so that "no harm can come to them."[39] But if, as Himes and Child suspected, attacks only strengthened the Millerite movement, the threatening and mobbing also contributed to the shift in the appeal of the adventist group that took place between about 1842 and 1844.

William Miller had been, for most of his life, as "mainstream" as he was "marginal." His youthful diversion into deism may have shocked a number of his contemporaries, but was actually a common enough step in his generation. His positions in the towns where he took up residence implied that he held a position of some respect among his neighbors. Nor were Miller's early converts exceptional. More than seeking a different path, they seem to have been embracing a new understanding that made sense within the dominant strains of their culture and yet provided a focus for their new, intense anticipation. Even in the 1830s, however, signs appeared that those who rejected identification with the majority in their culture could easily find a home in the new movement. Henry Jones had repeated run-ins with his fellow clergymen before he gave up a full-time ministry, and when he chose a new career it was on the outer edge of reform, beyond the crusades acceptable to the mass of his contemporaries in causes that, as the majority saw them, mixed threat with promise.

The recruitment of Joshua Himes to the movement marks a turning point in many ways, including the beginning of the shift in appeal from primarily mainline evangelicals toward marginal individuals. Himes himself had a heavy investment in defining himself as an outsider. His commitment to the radical edge of reforms signaled this. In addition, he focused insistently on persecution. Although Himes stopped short of craving martyrdom, he cultivated enough opposition to give him a sense of the righteousness of his cause. As he committed himself to adventism, Himes repeatedly implied that this was the coloration that he would bring to the movement.

"The opposition is on the increase," he wrote to Miller with apparent eagerness. "You will drive the clergy to do something—I don't know what." Later in the same year: "I am in the midst of enemies—but I *fear not.*" And later still: "Although I have made myself of no reputation, by associating myself with you, yet I feel that I have gained a thousand times more than I have lost."[40] Under Himes' direction, the movement chalked up both converts and enemies at an unprecedented rate. And the two results were not unrelated.

By 1843, Miller spoke in tones of Christian humility that may well have taken their inspiration from Himes. "I rejoice that I am counted worthy to receive persecution and slander for the truth's sake," he said.[41] For many Millerites who felt the same way, mobs could only strengthen their resolve. Perhaps the angry crowds were even necessary; were not scoffers in the last days among the signs of the end?[42] Mobs encouraged those who saw themselves as exemplars of persecuted Christianity. New converts, in turn, emerged more and more from among those who considered themselves to be different, to be outside the mainstream of American life. In perfect circular fashion, these people were most likely to court and thrive on the kinds of resistance presented by the mob.

Threats and violence, then, became self-fulfilling prophecies in action. Opponents attacked the Millerites as fanatics, and in the process made Millerism more attractive to the fanatical. Critics pictured Millerites as the kind of people who deviated from norms in work and family, for example, and thus they advertised Millerism as a refuge for the deviant. Anti-Millerites, finally, attributed to the adventists the power to tear deep into the fabric of society, and through violent attacks, as much as anything, they contributed to that power.

Emerging from within the bounds of evangelical orthodoxy, Millerism expressed a reaffirmation of faith in a powerful and transcendent God. In placing the supernatural firmly at the center of their lives and—as expressed in their expectation of the imminent return of Christ—of history, they pulled away from some of the dominant tendencies within the religious culture of their times. They did not just remind people of the existence of a God above but made a radical commitment to the centrality of the supernatural order. Many of their contemporaries found Millerites amusing or irritating. Some found them threatening or even frightening. The measure of the alarm raised by Millerism can perhaps best be taken by considering not only the number of words written but also the extremity of action taken against them. Certainly, Millerites were subjected to abuse, and especially to violence, in association with other dissenters—especially abolitionists. They probably did not suffer the level of persecution experienced by Roman Catholics or Mormons. But it was precisely the context of the clamping down on a variety of dissenters that pulled the marginal Millerites into the center of some of the major processes of change in the 1840s.

In a sense, we can look at the mob as the second traditional institution that failed to restrain the growth of Millerism. The first was the church, with its established forms of discipline. These controls were not tried serially, or course, nor was there a conscious perception that these were old and potentially complementary modes of control. Opposition to Millerism followed no such orderly and premeditated path. Nonetheless, opposition in all its varieties hit a peak in the final days of 1843 and 1844 and can fairly be said to have suffered failure in its immediate goal of discrediting and silencing Millerites. Time itself was the opponent strong enough to defeat—or perhaps only to reorient—the adventists' hopes. The passage of time swept Millerites aside so that opponents could turn again to building for the future of the existing world, and especially of the American nation.

AMERICAN PROGRESS

All of the required activity demanded by so many antebellum spokespersons—whether moral behavior, work, or reform—moved Americans toward a grander future. The question most "expressive of the spirit of these times," as one writer put it, was not *"What is?"* but rather *"What next?"*[43] Principled action rolled out along the path of time in an accelerating motion. For most Americans by the mid-nineteenth century, the future seemed destined to play out two themes. First, the time ahead would witness unprecedented progress. Second, in that progressing scheme of things, America would find a peculiar and central role. All of the developing ideals and assumptions discussed earlier fed into this final vision of the future, according to the mode of understanding that dominated by mid-century. When Millerites challenged—or seemed to challenge—subjective religious experience, accepted religious authority, ideals of character and family, and demands for action in this world, they implicitly challenged the possibilities envisioned by so many.

If action gave evidence of character, action also gave impetus to progress. Ideally, one writer noted, Americans would hold onto old principles—to the system of morals he believed to derive from original Christianity. He went on to indicate where people needed to go with those principles. "The work of this age," he said, "has been to apply these principles—to carry then out—to translate them into action. This," he concluded, "is human progress." An evangelical paper quoted a Unitarian approvingly on the point that God intended humanity "for effort, conflict, and progress."[44] The association was clear; action and progress came together in a system oriented toward the future. A person's duty was to do, and what he did was to press toward improvement reaching out through time.

The anticipation that there was "reserved for this world a more brilliant day than ever yet has dawned" was tied to the notion that the United States had a central role in the new dawning. The great influence of the new nation, both actual and potential, put it in a position to lead the world into a better future. In fact, God had chosen this nation, many believed, to be "the instrument in the hands of Divine Providence for re-modeling the visible condition of the world."[45]

The idea was not wholly new. From John Winthrop's "City on a Hill," through Jonathan Edwards' hope that the millennium would dawn in Northampton, through the Revolutionary generation's religious and political rhetoric, many had posited a unique role for the new land in the greater scheme of things. One aspect of the dream of the redeemer nation that was new in the nineteenth century, however, was the extent to which the hope for America's special destiny was tied to—even defined by—political and technological realities.[46] The rhetoric of the antebellum years had the providential plan unfolding within social processes. "In this age of steam," as one observer of the 1840s noted, "progress is more rapid than formerly." Technology provided evidence against Millerite arguments; people could not believe the end was so near, said the anti-Millerite Luther Dimmick, when such innovations as the printing press and the steam engine had so recently appeared. Another opponent confidently stated that "while our commerce is stretching over every sea, . . . it is hardly to be expected that many of our citizens will believe in Mr. Miller's views."[47] Indeed, some found sufficient argument against Millerites in their supposed indifference to "far-reaching schemes of national improvement." As an example, one writer asserted that Himes opposed the expansion of the

Erie Canal and all public works as well as the researches and inventions of scientists, and that the Millerite leader thought "the next Presidential election, the Sub-Treasury, and the northeastern boundary" in addition to the "general bankrupt law" unimportant or "of trifling consequence."[48] With reference to potential for progress, then, Millerites were cast against hopes very much within this world. Opponents of adventism found their ammunition in technological and political developments set in contrast to any reference to the supernatural.

Americans in the 1830s and 1840s did not necessarily anticipate smooth, linear progress. A sense of crisis pervaded the mood of the republic.[49] Yet the "afflictive model of progress," which posited advancement through trial and conflict, underwent a shift in the nineteenth century.[50] American Jeremiahs continued to warn of the corruption on the dark underside of apparent progress.[51] Because of the impurities buried deep in the nation, America was, as one Methodist spokesman put it, "in the furnace of affliction." Yet that same writer still saw the world's hope in this nation, and he looked forward to the day when "every vestige of error and corruption shall be swept from the face of the earth."[52] It was in this world that redemption would be found, and efforts to speed that redemption were to focus on the processes of this world more than on otherworldly demands. The progress that was to follow inevitably upon the resolution of the existing crisis would be built on religion, certainly—although it was to be a "practical religion" disseminated by human effort. That upward movement was also to be built upon relationships and institutions defined by American norms, however. The hope of the future had reference to the spread of republican political institutions, the "progress of free principles," the "discoveries of modern navigators," commercial relations, and the actions of the American Congress at least as much as to the transcendent demands of a living God. Many felt assurance that the crisis would pass and leave open the way to continual progress. They saw both the promise and the means to that progress within the American system.[53]

Millerites shared neither the hope nor the faith in worldly solutions of so many of their contemporaries. They did share the sense of crisis. They shared the sense, too, that the passing of that crisis would issue in a more glorious future. Their hope was immediate rather than progressive, however, and they refused to shift the locus of the greater purpose into mediating agents and processes. Their point of reference hovered above in a supernatural order, and even so great a cause as the destiny of the United States finally remained under the judgment of a transcendent power. Millerites sometimes went so far as to foretell the destruction of the nation at the end of a precipitous downward course.[54] In any case, they had little room for a special destiny for America. The divine power was about to break through the heavens and set the whole world ablaze. Not the United States, but the believers in the advent near were brands to be plucked from the burning.

CHAPTER VII

Epilogue

The Great Disappointment left Millerites in disarray while reinforcing the legitimacy of their opponents. Neither for the individuals involved in the dissenting movement, nor for the culture in which they acted, did the story end on October 22, 1844, however. Only speculative connections can be drawn between Millerism and long-term changes in American culture. More direct evidence allows a summary of what happened to Millerites and Millerism after the fall of 1844.

MILLERITES AFTER THE END

No percentage breakdown is available to show what proportion of Millerites gave up and went home, or held fast in the faith, or followed some other route, after the Great Disappointment. Presumably, some—the most recently convinced, the least thoroughly committed—gave up on anticipation of an immediate return of Christ, repudiated all connection with Millerites, and returned to unextraordinary lives. Not all former believers in the advent near took that route, however. Some moved from one deviant position, as Millerites, to other roles as outsiders, in other groups or with other faiths. Those who held closest to the adventist tradition took part in long-term divisions and realignments that issued in the appearance of new sects on the American religious scene.[1]

Miller and other adventists gathered in Albany, New York, in 1845 in a final effort to unify the Millerite movement. Disagreement proved stronger than the forces binding the group together, however. Proponents of the "shut door" theory—the idea that no more could be saved who had not entered the fold in 1844—refused to compromise with those who believed that opportunities for salvation remained open. Other controversies also divided the conference. This final attempt to hold Millerite adventists in a single movement and to build a loose organization for that movement ended in disarray.[2]

William Miller himself offered no further points around which a resurgent movement might gather. In his *Apology and Defence*, published in 1845, he reaffirmed his belief in the approaching personal return of Christ. This point he clung to until the end; he died in December 1849, and his tombstone echoed the remains of his message: "At the time appointed the end shall be."[3]

While Miller retreated to his home during his last days, a number of his former followers struck out in a variety of directions in search of a new religious formulation that might replace the Millerite anticipation of the coming event. Some continued to set dates for the imminent end, but this approach had lost its power to inspire the imaginations of many. Others deemphasized the question of the timing of the advent and focused on other theological issues such as whether the wicked would be annihilated at the return of Christ. The origins of several minor adventist sects can be traced to this "scattering time": the Church of God (Seventh Day), the American Evangelical Adventist Conference, the Advent Christian Church, and others.

The most obvious and prominent legacy of the Millerite movement took form out of the interpretation of Hiram

Edson, a Millerite from Port Gibson, New York. It was Edson who insisted that the October date had not been an error. A dramatic event had in fact taken place on that day. Edson believed that what had happened was not an event in the physical world, however, but rather an event in the spiritual realm. The "cleansing of the sanctuary," he stated, meant that Christ had entered the heavenly Holy of Holies, there to preside over the "investigative judgment" of men. When this work was done, Christ would return as predicted, suddenly and personally. At first but one of many attempts to make sense out of the Great Disappointment, Edson's interpretation would, in the long run, become a central basis for the Seventh-day Adventists.

Edson's reinterpretation did not alone give birth to that successful sect. It gave new life to adventism in association with a new practice and a new leadership. The new practice that ritualized the community, and the separateness, of the adventists was the celebration of the seventh day sabbath. Association with Seventh-day Baptists introduced this innovation among certain adventists who thereafter set themselves apart from the majority of their contemporaries by worshipping on Saturday. The leadership giving new force to adventist ideas and adventist practice centered in Ellen Gould Harmon White. White had converted to Millerism in 1842, married Millerite adventist James White in 1846, and began during that period to have the visions and to issue the prophecies through which Seventh-day Adventist teachings would be filled out over the years. The eventual success of the new group could hardly have been foreseen in the turmoil of the 1840s, however; the denomination itself did not take organizational form or add its distinctive emphasis on health until the 1860s.[4]

Association with Seventh Day Baptists indicates a second

route for Millerites after the Great Disappointment. Some who had waited for the advent of Christ moved into existing religious groups on the fringes of respectable religious life. A dramatic example of this took place in Ohio, where a number of Millerites joined the Shakers, at least temporarily, in 1845 and 1846. Lawrence Foster has speculated that this switch appealed to disappointed adventists for a number of reasons. First, following J. Gordon Melton, he notes that the "spiritualization" of prophecy is a common mode of reinterpretation that allows a group to maintain its tenets but remove what outsiders see as the failure of the group's predictions. Shakers, like Millerites, emphasized the return of Christ, but their conception of the return was, indeed, spiritualized; Shakers viewed Mother Ann Lee as the second incarnation of the spirit of Christ. Foster also points out that Shakers represented social success, in contrast to adventist disarray. Shakers had successfully built communities and put their principles into practice.[5] The appeal or appeals seem to have been persuasive, in any case. At the Shaker settlement at Whitewater, Ohio, in 1845, 80 out of 144 members were former Millerites. And cases of smaller groups and individual conversions were scattered across Ohio and elsewhere.[6]

Shakers may have been but one of several sectarian groups to which Millerites retreated after the Disappointment. For some believers, both Millerism and Shakerism proved stops along a winding path through a variety of outsider religions. Millerite leader Enoch Jacobs, for example, joined the Shakers in 1846 but later moved on into spiritualism.[7] Joshua Himes certainly remained outside the mainstream, although his attachments were not always specifically religious; his later commitments included a return in full force to radical abolitionism and to non-resistance as well as to the movement for Christian Union.[8]

Scholars agree that the majority of Millerites returned to mainstream churches after the disappointment.[9] As the case of the Baptist church in Williamson, New York, indicates, even where adventists were organized, their ranks were often decimated within a few years after the Great Disappointment. Initiation of disciplinary proceedings was, in part, an effort to facilitate just such returns to the fold. Not all former Millerites who returned to churches associated with major denominations went back to those they had belonged to before, of course. Perhaps they chose their new affiliation because of changes in principle; an individual who had taken up abolitionist views along with Millerism might have moved into the Wesleyan Methodist church, for example. Or perhaps they switched churches primarily to move on, to escape from the lingering stigma attached to their earlier commitment to a now-discredited movement. The influence of their Millerism within such churches on an individual basis is impossible to track. Stepping back to look at the broader picture, however, it is possible to speculate on the long-term influence of the Millerite movement on American religious culture as a whole.

MILLERISM AND MID-NINETEENTH-CENTURY AMERICAN RELIGION

Writing in the 1880s, Jane Marsh Parker, daughter of a Millerite, asserted that the effect of Millerism "upon the aggregate" was "the evolution of its effect upon the individual."[10] Certainly, those who had been Millerites or had associated with the Millerite movement helped to define its legacy, to mold the ways in which it entered the collective memory. Intimate acquaintance with the Millerite movement was not, however, any more necessary for the manipulation of Millerism as a symbol of deviance after the Disappointment than it had been before. Millerites continued to play prominent roles in the tale-telling, scoffing, and warnings of nineteenth-century Americans, while the surviving and later thriving Seventh-day Adventists escaped such strong and frequent ridicule. The image of Millerites remained meaningful in the popular imagination and in common discourse. It is reasonable to suggest, then, that Millerites continued to function as a negative reference group that helped to define acceptable belief and behavior.

Millerism was far from the dominant influence in the changing culture of the mid-nineteenth century. It was not, in fact, even the dissenting movement that most concerned contemporaries. Nonetheless, Millerism as a popular movement that drew a good deal of mostly negative attention did have effects on Americans and the American culture of the age. To a great extent, rejection of Millerism reinforced changes associated with revolutions in economic, social, and intellectual life. In reinforcing broad changes, still, Millerism left its own peculiar imprint—a certain twist—on those changes that defined a legacy specifically its own. An examination of some of the trends in American culture, especially in American religious life, between the 1840s and the 1880s introduces some possibilities for areas in which that influence played a role.

The main category of change in which the influence of Millerism might be related is the sweeping one of secularization. The terms secular and secularization mean so many things as to have become almost meaningless, at least without further elaboration.[11] In terms of the present discussion these words can best be made meaningful by focusing initially on the definition of secularization as "the transposition of belief and patterns of behavior from the religious to the secular sphere."[12] This definition allows for sidestepping such sticky issues as the relative quality of subjective faith in one age as opposed to another, and opens the way for concentration on changes in institutions and social relations that are more easily observed and analyzed.

In so rapid a summary, examples of the transferral of social authority and the definition of acceptable social behavior from the religious to the secular sphere will have to suffice. One example has already been examined: the decline of church discipline as a means to define and reinforce acceptable behavior and, to a lesser extent, acceptable belief. The quick reduction in the number of disciplinary cases brought before churches in the 1840s and 1850s attests to the loss of power of that mode of identification and control. This does not mean that the members of a community could no longer exercise pressure for conformity upon one another. Individuals and communities could turn to the courts, or to threats exercised in the economic realm, or to other forms of social pressure, to influence the behavior and belief of others. It would prove less effective to work through specifically religious institutions to apply such pressure after the 1840s. And as long as dissenters remained in sectarian seclusion, of course, members of more mainstream denominations had little recourse to influencing them through religious means.

A second area in which it is possible to perceive a shift in social authority from the religious to the secular sphere is in what might be called the domestication of the revival. The revival gave form and impetus to changes in belief and fed denominational rivalry, of course. But the revival in its manifestation as the camp meeting or the protracted meeting also became a symbolic demand for a choice: would one drop the everyday to pursue salvation, or would one remain on the farm or in the store while neighbors turned their backs on worldly things for a few days of devotion to the religious? The camp meetings of the Cane Ridge variety or the Finney revivals some decades later may have issued in a new order, but in their origins tended to introduce economic and social disorder. The contrast between the disruption that was at least perceived in the revivals of the early part of the nineteenth century and the orderly nature of the businessman's revival makes the point. Earlier revivals called potential or previous converts away from economic pursuits to focus on the message of salvation and the community of the saved. The revival of 1857–1858 fit the religious message into lunch hours, reversing the order of priority and dramatizing the domestication of the revival.[13] Amariah Brigham would, presumably, have been pleased. He had associated religious insanity with both Millerism and the protracted meeting; by 1857 Millerism had been reduced to a specter and the protracted meeting to a noon-hour prayer.[14]

Millerism, or the symbol of Millerism, took part in changes of belief as well as of social action during the decades after 1840. The sets of beliefs and assumptions that Millerism can be most clearly related to are those about apocalypse, millennium, and the end of time. In Millerism's heyday, the most widely held conception of the course of history toward the final days combined what scholars have separated out as postmillennial optimism and premillennial cataclysm. Millerism dealt a blow to that precarious combination—not a fatal blow, by any means, but one that nonetheless helped to issue in realignments and reassessments that would become important later in the century. There was, first of all, a resurgence of explicitly premillennial theology in the middle of the century. This makes sense in the context of the reaction against Millerism only if it is noted that Millerism drew scorn not as much for premillennialism, *per se*, as for supernaturalism symbolized by the image of the immediate, personal, dramatic, and physical return of Christ. The premillennialists who gathered strength in the 1840s, 1850s, and 1860s strove to distance themselves from Millerites, of course. Their stance was, therefore, defined in part by reaction against Millerism. Premillennialists emphasized their orthodoxy on just those points at which Millerism had been attacked. As one author explained, premillennialism was "not only reasonable but consoling to the Saint" and it would tend "to arouse the dormant energies of the Church." The writer introduced his subject by asserting, "*Millerism* and *Pre-Millennialism* are two different things."[15] In fact, that judgment hit on the mark. The premillennialism that was on the rise in those decades was a theological construct, appealing on an intellectual level to a certain group of writers, but only thinly connected to any popular religious movements. It is not by chance that, as the nation entered the late nineteenth century, premillennialism was associated with Princeton Theological Seminary. As an intellectual movement, this premillennialism did not function on the same level that Millerism, widespread and popular if amorphous, had. That the appeal of this way of thinking differed from that of Millerism is also apparent from the substance of the prophetic interpretation that issued from Princeton and elsewhere. Charles Hodge and George Duffield, among others, drew on the tradition of those millenarians whose chronology for the end posited delays—most importantly, the return of the Jews. The sense of crisis associated with the cry that Christ would come suddenly and above all soon was missing from such an interpretation. Ernest Sandeen has characterized the tone of one millenarian periodical in this tradition as "restrained and conservative."[16] In a sense, it was as if the Princeton theologians and their confreres sought to slow down time—to resist the encroachments of change that the onrush of time brought—while

Millerites had sought to speed up time to the point at which it collapsed and ended altogether.

Even with their expanding ranks, premillennialists probably held a minority position among religious spokespersons of the mid-nineteenth century. Postmillennialists held sway. Millerites have often been given partial credit for that predominance, in fact.[17] Much of the evidence presented here would tend to reinforce that conclusion, but it also points to a possible impact of Millerism on the nature of postmillennialism as well. Not the idiot optimists of caricature, spokespersons for postmillennialism reflected broadly shared assumptions as they worked to balance faith in progress with anticipation of crisis. For some among this majority, however, Millerism disrupted that balance. The sense of crisis, the anticipation of cataclysm, looked absurd when painted in the tones used in popular portraits of Millerites. Only later in the century, or even in the twentieth century, would adherents of that popular eschatological position recognize how equally foolish the other extreme, the emphasis on progress to the neglect of a sense of crisis or judgment, might seem.

Some would go further. In part in reaction against Millerism, some believers at mid-century internalized their hopes. Angelina Grimké Weld clearly stated such a position: "Once I was a believer in the Second personal advent of Christ," she wrote, "but now I see that his second coming is to be in the hearts of the people."[18] The smaller group to which Weld belonged found in the image of Millerism a glaring error against which they could define their conception of a radically immanent God and his workings in history. Their position, and not postmillennialism, was the true opposite of Millerism. Whereas premillennialists and postmillennialists had their differences, emphasized especially in decades after the Millerite excitement, they also bore similarities. In general, American Protestants in those years did maintain some belief in a transcendent power, even if that power seemed bound ever more closely to worldly processes of change. Weld and others foreshadowed a later age when transcendence would lose its significance among a large and influential portion of American Protestants. That later erasure of traces of supernaturalism among liberals and former postmillennialists cannot, of course, be attributed to the influence of Millerism. Yet early inroads were made by a radical minority in part in response to the outburst of extreme supernaturalism in the 1840s.[19]

If a radically immanent God did not always pervade popular assumptions during the period after the demise of Millerism, there was, again, a sense in which a more orthodox God was tied more firmly to worldly ideals and processes. The 1840s introduced a period during which national and political concerns took precedence over religious concerns. Or perhaps it would be more accurate to say that religious concerns were subsumed under, even defined by, secular hopes and conflicts. William McLoughlin would have it that such a shift in priorities was part of a cycle in American history, a cycle in which religious revivals are followed by the emergence of social and political questions at the forefront of popular concern. The story here can be considered complementary to that interpretation if Millerism and the response it aroused can be taken as part of the process of moving from revival phase to reforming or political phase.[20]

In any case, the burning questions of the 1850s, 1860s, and 1870s tended to center not on conceptions of God and the nature of the supernatural, but on loyalties to and relationships among sections and nation. The Civil War revitalized the jeremiad form for understanding the trials of the American nation and with it the balance of progress and crisis that still held sway in postmillennial thought. Yet as revitalization is never in actuality a return to some original purity, so the reinvigoration of millennial rhetoric carried with it different meaning in the context of the political and military crisis. In wartime the categories of the cosmic battle came to be defined in ways that tied warnings and hopes ever more closely to secular plans and visions of national destiny.[21] Appeals to a transcendent God of judgment asked him to judge not according to moral or spiritual imperatives, but according to political loyalties surrounded by the trappings of sacred imagery.

Insofar as some Americans retained the assumptions and beliefs associated with the radical supernaturalism of the Millerites, then, they could only have found themselves in a state of disarray. It was, perhaps, that state that Sandeen had in mind when he observed that "the Millerite movement appears to have virtually destroyed premillenialism in America for a generation."[22] The rhetoric of judgment and crisis had been appropriated by the culture at large and put in service of the cause of the war. It should perhaps not be surprising that it was during the war decade that Ellen White and her fellows drew together the symbols and prophecies that would give form to Seventh-day Adventism. With millennial rhetoric put in service to the dominant culture, those who would reassert the primacy of the supernatural over the political could find their best opportunities in retreating to a sectarian stance. The times were not propitious for the development of a broad-based popular movement that would express the doubts and hopes of the supernaturalists while working in the world at large.[23]

The reemergence of the stance of radical supernaturalism on a popular basis came late in the nineteenth century. Anticipation of the personal, imminent, premillennial return of

Christ took on new life, perhaps not in the hearts of individual believers—ultimately we can never know how vital such personal belief remained through the decades of war and reconstruction—but in new organizational forms and with new foci for belief. What would become the Fundamentalist movement began to take form in part through the organizational focus provided by Bible conferences in the 1870s and later. Similarly, Fundamentalism would draw force through an ideological focus clarified and popularized in confrontations over the issues of evolution and biblical criticism.[24] At the same time, the beliefs and assumptions—perhaps it would be accurate even to say yearnings—of radical supernaturalism found alternative expression in the related emergence of the Holiness and Pentecostal movements of the late nineteenth and early twentieth centuries.[25] Perhaps the ethos of radical supernaturalism has persisted throughout the nineteenth and into the twentieth centuries, and perhaps its resurgence is less a rebirth than a return to a level of social power and social visibility. Whatever the nature of the reemergence, those who seek to order their lives with reference to what they conceive to be a transcendent supernatural power continue to meet the scorn and reproach, sometimes humorous but often serious, that takes its most familiar form in the picture of an old man with vacant eyes, robed in white, proclaiming that the end is near.

Conclusion

David Brion Davis has described how some Americans have projected onto their enemies attributes that stirred up great ambivalence in themselves. He evokes the fear, and also the fearful attraction, that Masons, Mormons, and Catholics raised among their contemporaries in the 1820s, 1830s, and 1840s. Davis' description introduces an important question in this book: why have people feared, hated, and attacked certain groups? And it reminds us that the answer is never simply that the rejected presented an objective threat.[1] This work has built upon Davis' insights in fleshing out the interaction between the "mainstream" and dissenters—and sometimes between different groups of dissenters—and indicating the process of cultural change into which that interaction fed.

There are implicit contrasts in this work that should perhaps be made explicit here. The Millerites were and were perceived to be different from other groups that stood outside the bounds of orthodoxy in antebellum America. Millerites were, in their origins, good evangelical Protestant Americans. So were abolitionists, of course. Whitney Cross has made the classic statement on the movement from the spread of evangelical Christianity in the revival to the logical extension of that religious impulse beyond acceptable limits into what he called "ultraism."[2] In some ways, Millerites—and abolitionists, too—became American in the extreme in carrying such attributes as the "show-me" literalism and the moralism of America beyond their usual limits. That tremendous American-ness of dissenters in the United States has been more common than exceptional. One need look only at the Mormons, first of all, but also at Christian Scientists and even the Millerites' descendants, the Seventh-day Adventists, to see that opting out of the dominant modes of belief and organization has often led, in the fulness of time, to an adoption of virtual caricatures of American structures and faiths.[3] In spite of the similar paths, in the long run, of so many American dissenters, however, they did not begin by heading down any single byway, nor did they inspire a uniform response from their detractors.

It is true, as Davis has said, that Americans molded their images of the dissenters among them to fit their own fears and to express their own ambivalence. But two other generalizations also apply. First, those middle Americans responded not only out of fear and neurotic reaction but also out of hopes for a new and better order. It is to be hoped that it will not come across as glorifying bigotry to point out that there can be a creative process involved in discovering, analyzing, and repudiating those things that one is not or does not want to be. It was part and parcel of the development of new ideals for American thought and life to discover the limits of those new ideals, to say "no" at the point where it seemed that some had gone too far. The Millerites provided a foil against which many of their contemporaries clarified their new visions of the future. Other dissenters played a similar role, but came to embody or represent different limits. This raises the second generalization beyond Davis' exploration of antebellum responses to the different. When opponents drew up graphic images of the dissenters who seemed to threaten present stability and future opportunity in the

1830s and 1840s, they had to stick close to at least a grain of truth to make the negative images of the alternatives realistic and compelling. In the case of the Millerites, the genuinely radical supernaturalism of the dissenters, and its expression in an attachment to literalism and a denigration of existing structures, became the starting point for negative images that could easily have been outgrowths of that fundamental heresy. A classic example of that development of a detailed, though exaggerated picture of the rejected group by picking up and fleshing out a piece of the truth is the appearance, spread, and popularity of the ascension robe stories.

The dissenters helped to define the precise role that they would play in the long and complex process of testing, analyzing, and often rejecting alternatives for belief, organization, and behavior. This fact becomes clear through a comparison of attacks on Millerites with those made on another unorthodox group. One of the dissenting groups that drew the most attention in the antebellum years was the Latter-day Saints, popularly known as the Mormons.

Early accounts of Mormonism scoffed at the "new Bible" and attacked the "money-digging" Joseph Smith. The Book of Mormon, such commentaries noted, seemed to tell a story drawn from contemporary rather than ancient experience and perhaps bore too striking a similarity to certain recently written works. When Smith claimed to have discovered the book by digging in a hillside, it seemed too obvious that he had taken to an extreme the common practice of going digging for treasure and that his original inspiration was greed rather than angelic visitation. As Mormonism grew in structure and strength, as it became clear that a good number of people actually believed in the new Book and were actually prepared to follow the money-digger, hostile accounts of the new religion became increasingly vehement and followed a few specific lines. Criticism of the Mormons sometimes paralleled that directed against Millerites and sometimes ran on different themes. In either case, the criticism picked up and elaborated on points that reflected both Mormon belief and behavior and the hopes and fears of their detractors.[4]

Mormons shared with Millerites a number of condemnations by their peers. If Millerites were suspected of claiming a new revelation and direct guidance from God, Mormons announced with pride that they had exactly those inspirations and authorities. In tandem with special knowledge went an expectation of exclusive salvation—at least so opponents read Millerite and Mormon doctrine. The repetition of such accusations, of course, points directly to a dilemma of early American Protestantism. Christian teachings had drawn a line between saved and damned; the promise to the saints was, by its nature, an exclusive promise. In an America founded on the Declaration of Independence and inspired by the likes of the mythic Andrew Jackson, however, democracy and equality were supposed to take their places among the highest of ideals. How could a God who seemed to look with special favor upon the democratic republic set up his own ultimate order on such aristocratic terms? Traditional teachings ran up against new hopes and produced anxieties and tensions expressed in condemnations of outsiders. In addition, many Americans shared the conviction that, under the new order of liberty and equality, only religion could provide the glue to hold the nation together. Not only did Mormons and Millerites seem to say that only a few would possess true religion, leaving all others to sink in chaos, but both groups seemed destined to cast negative light on the supposedly true religion upon which the nation was assumed to depend so heavily. Again, a central problem facing the populace at large—the problem of cohesion in the face of liberty and diversity—was expressed in part through attacks on those who appeared peculiar and threatening.[5]

Mormons and Millerites faced similar charges, too, in less specifically religious terms. Perhaps Millerties did not seem to go as far as the Mormons supposedly did in "violating . . . every command of the decalogue, save the first and second," but Millerites came in for their share of accusations of immorality. Both groups were pictured, on the one hand, as the product of silly delusions, but also, on the other hand, as the perpetrators of fanatical delusions that would rip through the fabric of entire communities. No one of firm Christian principles or good character, said the critics, would follow either of those ridiculous systems. At the same time, evidence abounded that the influence of self-serving or crazy blackguards could effectively play on the excitability of too large a proportion of the population. Both Mormonism and Millerism took high rank among the "greatest humbugs of the age."[6]

If Mormons and Millerites shared public images that derived as much from the fears of their contemporaries as from the realities of the movements themselves, Mormons also came under attack for characteristics that were not—or were rarely—attributed to Millerites. Joseph Smith was accused of establishing a new papacy. The hierarchy and centralized power that others found reminiscent of Rome was buttressed by a flair for ritual and display. Even the Catholic menace did not seem an adequate analogy for such oriental-style splendor and mystery, and attacks on Mormonism often replaced or supplemented the image of papal power with the even more exotically threatening parallel of Mohammedanism. The simple virtue and egalitarianism that were supposed to characterize the new republic were, in fact, being left behind by many besides the Mormons. The dissenters once again became the obvious target for the unleashing of tensions that ran deeply through the whole society. Similarly, observers discovered that Mormons indulged in political and military pageantry to match the religious. There was Joseph Smith, "with his sword, and pistols, with his military hat and three ostrich feathers, like a Mohammedan pacha with three tails." His power, like that of the Pope, held sway in a "Politico-Religion-Military Government." It took little imagination to find military conspiracy among the supporters of the Nauvoo legion or to discover political plotting in a group that already governed a section of Illinois and would, in 1844, run its leader for the presidency.[7]

Attacks against Mormonism, like those against Millerism, took form from what the dissenters actually said and did as well as from the amorphous fears of their contemporaries. In the case of the Mormons, the threat was, in many ways, more obvious. A private army and, in effect, a private government posed a direct threat to safety and stability on a larger scale than Millerite defections from churches, for example. Yet the functions of the two groups were very similar in terms of the process of cultural change and the establishment of a revised cultural orthodoxy. Cultural change in the northern United States during the middle period of this country's history was both accelerated and defined, in part, through confrontations between the "mainstream" and the "marginal." Both dissenting groups gave others a chance to define what they were not and what they did not intend to be; both challenged others to clarify, and in the process modify, what they were and what they hoped for.

In the 1830s, the supernaturalism represented most dramatically by the Millerites was still a live option in the northern United States. It was not clear, when the Millerites first burst upon the scene, that belief in the imminent, personal advent of Christ was to be associated with—and repudiated with—the rejection of such beliefs and values as growth in holiness, the prominence and efficacy of humankind in God's providence, wide possibilities for human salvation, new approaches to the authority of both the Bible and the Holy Spirit within, and right action in the world—in the family, in the workplace, in efforts to change society, and in promoting the destiny of the nation as a whole. Some—sometimes many, and perhaps all—Millerites combined their anticipation of the physical and fast-approaching return of Christ with beliefs and behaviors that their detractors thought of as being inconsistent with their first principles. Some adventists, for example, emphasized the need for growth in grace. Others hoped that many conversions would precede the advent and open the way for salvation for most of humanity. Many believed that dutiful action in the family and in work had to continue until the Lord's arrival. A number never gave up their association with movements for reform, and some believed, even, that a commitment to abolitionism was necessary for salvation.

A variety of attitudes and standards for behavior coexisted, then, with anticipation of the imminent, personal advent. The stereotype of the "premillennialist," nonetheless, grew largely out of attacks on believers in the advent near. Critics of Millerism forged that stereotype from materials provided not only by the actual expectations, interpretations, and actions of the majority of adventists but also by generalizations drawn from a few to the many, by their own assumptions about where supernaturalism would lead, and by the voices of their own hopes and fears. They created the crabby and crazy Millerite, pessimistic, passive, and out of touch with the forces of history.

The more those people spoke and acted against the Millerites, the more the dissenting group shifted its center—

through the psychology of sectarianism and through force of numbers—toward a reality that resembled more closely that pictured by the critics. The evidence that gave new force to the arguments against Millerism in 1843 and 1844 bolstered the authority of the opponents, but such evidence had hardly been necessary to the development of the stereotype in the first place. Nor was it the evidence provided by the Millerites who acted as the opponents had predicted all along that gave the final stamp of legitimacy to the anti-Millerite position. For all of the complexity of the Millerite subculture, Millerism began and ended with a date. Miller had drawn the attention of early converts with his announcement that Christ would return in 1843. Opponents of Millerism achieved a clear victory when Jesus did not descend through the clouds on October 22, 1844. Date-setting may not have been the only, or even the most important, foundation for Millerism. But date-setting did give the greatest force to Millerism's ironic and unintentional legacy to American culture.

There is little force to arguments founded on what might have been. Had there been no date announced for the return of Christ, Miller would have lacked the dramatic point that brought his movement briefly to center stage. Without a date as the symbol for his belief, he might not have attracted so many converts. Without a date, the Millerites might not have gained the attention of so many opponents. It is hard to resist further speculation, nonetheless. If Henry Jones, for example, had defined adventism and put date-setting aside, might the movement have charted a different course? Might it have made a place for supernaturalism within the mainstream of American culture? Without a date, critics of supernaturalism would not have attained so final and resounding a victory. One factor in the acceleration of a set of changes within the culture would have been defused.

The point of the counterfactual is less to raise a vision of what might have been than to reemphasize the force of what was. The dates were set, and the final date passed. The nonevent of October 22, 1984, gave legitimacy to opponents of Millerism not only on the matter of time, but also, by association, on all of those pieces of the system that they had lined up as part of the repudiation of the time. Those pieces included belief in a benevolent God working within and through men and social processes, hope for gradual growth in time and on earth toward a better day, an assumption that the good was achievable through energetic action within existing structures, and turning to the world outside and the sense within for cues to understanding. None of these pieces was totally new in the 1830s and 1840s. Existing pieces were, rather, brought together and articulated as a new orthodoxy during those and later years. The social base for the new cultural orthodoxy centered on a liberalized evangelicalism lay, in part, in the churches and denominations. The challenges of the antebellum years, however, had circumscribed the power of the churches. American culture in the Victorian era grew out of nurture and discipline within the family and restrictive control in such institutions as the asylum as much as it took social definition from the churches.

The Millerite excitement gave rise to one of a number of conflicts through which the new orthodoxy was hammered out. The furor over abolitionism was, perhaps, the key point of cultural conflict in the 1840s. Abolitionism and anti-abolitionism followed a pattern and fed into a process very similar to those described here. The dissenters spoke from a position derived in large part from evangelical Protestantism. They presented a challenge that struck close to home among their contemporaries and so demanded a response. Opponents of abolitionism formulated an image of that which they refused to be, and they called that image the true nature of abolitionism. In the process, they articulated their own position, clarified the changing beliefs that gave a new foundation to their approach, and shifted their stance to widen the distance between themselves and the threatening minority. Abolitionism, too, shifted its ground as the polarization of the two sides pressed them apart. In the end, a new center arose out of the process of debate, polarization, and retrenchment. In addition, the challenge of the abolitionists, along with and even more than the challenge of the Millerites, revealed the limits of congregational and denominational authority. Millerites threw individual churches into turmoil that sometimes resulted in schism. Even in those cases, abolitionism often took a role. On the larger scene, abolitionism not only tore through one congregation at a time but also drove wedges through the middle of entire denominations.

The abolitionists played a more significant role in the transformation of nineteenth-century culture than did the Millerites. The abolitionists—and their opponents—have rightly attracted the interest of a number of historians. Focus on the problem of abolitionism can, however, narrow the understanding of cultural change. The turmoil of the 1830s and 1840s did not boil up only out of abolitionism. Americans at the time responded excitedly—often fearfully—to Mormons, Universalists, Catholics, and others, including Millerites. Study of the furor surrounding Millerism, then, broadens and deepens the portrait of cultural transformation in those years. The process of defining the evolving center of nineteenth-century American culture involved confrontations on a number of fronts.

Each battle drew many Americans into articulating their beliefs, fleshing out their hopes for the future, and defining the limits beyond which they would not happily allow their contemporaries to go. Each battle was important for the larger process. The hypothetical common man who attended to spokesmen for orthodoxy in the 1840s might have denied that Christ would return visibly and personally, but he turned only partially toward an immanence as radical as that posited by the Transcendentalists. He retreated from the exclusivity of salvation only for believers in the advent near, but he stopped short of embracing Universalism. He rejected the peculiar biblical literalism of Miller's prophetic numbers, but he was not ready to jump on the bandwagon of new revelation as the Mormons rode by. He balked at attacks on existing institutions, but he struck out against the stolid church of Roman Catholicism. Of course, a number of Americans followed one or another of these courses out to its conclusion. More sought a firm center ground. Thrown into a chaos of alternatives, this archetypal resident of antebellum America drew limits to acceptable belief. At the same time, the constant eruption of new schemes, opportunities, and visions pressed him toward formulating his own position. He might well have said that he believed in 1840, or 1845, or 1850, what he had believed all along. But the questions had changed, the terms of debate had changed, the social context of his belief had changed, and the reformulation of his belief was bound to take many if not all such changes into account. He emerged from the tumultuous 1830s and 1840s with new aspirations, new assumptions, and new visions of the future. He emerged, also, with new fears, new hatreds, and new stereotypes defining those with whom he disagreed.

The Millerite movement gave a particular form to a unique outpouring of supernaturalism in the midst of the chaotic Jacksonian era. The interest that the movement holds consists not only of the peculiar forces that converged to create adventism, nor only of the specific arguments, objections, and accusations that arose in response to that movement. Millerism broke forth into a particular process that was but one of many shaking loose and unfolding in the tumult of the antebellum years. In this sense, Millerism serves as example more than eccentricity. All of those processes of debate and interaction fed into the larger transformation of American culture in the nineteenth century. In this sense, Millerism becomes part rather than peculiarity. By putting Millerites and other marginal groups into the context of these broader cultural processes, we can begin to take seriously the notion that dissent revitalizes the culture. We take that notion seriously only when we examine the role of dissenters who did not "win," when we study dissenters with whom we disagree as well as those with whom—with the benefit of the great wisdom born of hindsight—we agree, and when we are prepared to recognize that the added vitality may have issued in results that bore little relation to the intentions either of the dissenters or of those who grappled with the challenges that those dissenters presented.

The story of the Miller heresy is a story of millennialism. For the Millerites themselves, millennialism—broadly defined as an anticipation of a great culmination to come at the end of time—became central to their understanding of themselves, of their society, and of the place of both in a larger scheme of meaning. Their apocalyptic brand of millennialism expressed an orientation that I have called "radical supernaturalism." That orientation took as its ultimate point of reference a reaffirmation of faith in an objective, powerful, transcendent order that gave meaning to and imposed demands upon individual lives and, indeed, all of human history. In a sense, Millerites sought to turn back the clock, to return to a perhaps mythical state in which awed submission before God was the foundation for social and religious order and the source of norms and values. In a sense, too, Millerites were people very much of their time, for they drew on the culture around them to interpret and express their supernaturalism, and they also organized their lives in ways remarkably similar to those of their more orthodox neighbors. Finally, however, Millerites hoped that the clock would be broken rather than turned back and that the culture of their time would be torn asunder rather than nurtured. While their central assumptions offered an alternative basis—a God-centered and supernaturalist one—for emerging ideals of identity, behavior, and order, those assumptions also carried an inherent judgment against any activities and structures in the world.

The story of the Miller heresy is also a story of American culture, and of some of the dramatic changes that that culture underwent in the nineteenth century. Millerism grew out of the influential evangelical culture of the early decades of that century. The movement became a heresy because it emphasized one side of evangelicalism at the moment when the dominant center of American religious culture was shifting to another set of emphases. In part in response to the outburst of Millerism, Americans outside the movement articulated and refined new boundaries for cultural orthodoxy. In a fairly strictly religious sense, the changes made apparent and accelerated in reaction to Millerism were to become the foundations of religious liberalism—movements toward acceptance of an immanent divinity, belief in human ability, and emphasis on the importance of social action as a form of religious behavior and expression. In a broader sense, those changes were part of the development of a vague but powerful "culture Protestantism" that diffused the authority of specifically religious beliefs and institutions but imposed a general orthodoxy on the life of the nation as a whole. Millerites, like other dissenters of their day, grew out of the booming possibilities opened up by independence, religious liberty, Jacksonian democracy, and the Second Great Awakening. But Millerites, again like their fellow dissenters, became participants, if unwilling ones, in the process of tightening up the acceptable implications of those possibilities as American culture moved from the experimentation of the new nation into the restriction of the Victorian age.

Notes

ABBREVIATIONS

CP   Whitney Cross Papers, Department of Manuscripts and University Archives, Cornell University, Ithaca, N.Y.

ERL   "Early Religious Life" (microfilm), Department of Manuscripts and University Archives, Cornell University, Ithaca, N.Y.

MCS   Methodist Collection, Syracuse University Archives, Syracuse, N.Y.

WKP   Woodruff-Kaercher Papers, Department of Manuscripts and University Archives, Cornell University, Ithaca, N.Y.

WMC   William Miller, Correspondence, "Millerites and Early Adventists Microfilm Collection," University Microfilms International, Ann Arbor, Mich., 1979, sec. 5, reels 11–12

JVH   Joshua V. Himes Collection, Massachusetts Historical Society, Boston, Mass.

AHE   Alice L. Hoag, "Essays on Spiritualism and Millerism," Department of Manuscripts and University Archives, Cornell University, Ithaca, N.Y.

INTRODUCTION

1. For decades, the study of Millerism was almost frozen at the poles of Clara Endicott Sears' attack, *Days of Delusion: A Strange Bit of History* (Boston: Houghton Mifflin, 1924), and Francis D. Nichol's defense, *The Midnight Cry: A Defense of the Character and Conduct of*

William Miller and the Millerites, Who Mistakenly Believed That the Second Coming of Christ Would Take Place in the Year 1844 (Takoma Park, Washington, D.C.: Review and Herald Publishing Assoc., 1944). The context for the emergence of Millerism, as well as the movement itself, was considered in Alice Felt Tyler's *Freedom's Ferment: Phases of American Social History from the Colonial Period to the Outbreak of the Civil War* (New York: Harper and Row, 1944) and Whitney R. Cross' *The Burned-Over District: The Social and Intellectual History of Enthusiastic Religion in Western New York, 1800–1850* (Ithaca, N.Y.: Cornell University Press, 1950; New York: Harper Torchbooks, 1965). A collection of essays first presented as conference papers, *The Rise of Adventism: Religion and Society in Mid-Nineteenth-Century America* (New York: Harper and Row, 1974), edited by Edwin Scott Gaustad, presaged a renewed interest in Millerism. J. F. C. Harrison discussed the movement, along with others in both England and America, in *The Second Coming: Popular Millenarianism, 1780–1850* (New Brunswick, N.J.: Rutgers University Press, 1979). David L. Rowe has finally offered a full scholarly study of Millerism, much of which applies beyond the geographical boundaries that he has set, in his *Thunder and Trumpets: Millerites and Dissenting Religion in Upstate New York, 1800–1850* (Chico, Calif.: Scholars Press, 1985). While the present work was in process, additional studies appeared that are advancing our understanding of Millerites and related subjects; I have tried to incorporate the insights of these authors insofar as has been possible: R. Laurence Moore, *Religious Outsiders and the Making of Americans* (New York: Oxford University Press, 1986); Jonathan Butler, "From Millerism to Seventh-day Adventism: 'Boundlessness to Consolidation,'" *Church History* 55 (March 1986): 50–64; Michael Barkun, *Crucible of the Millennium* (Syracuse, N.Y.: Syracuse University Press, 1986); and a collection of articles that have contributed to this work in their original form as conference papers, *The Disappointed: Millerism and Millenarianism in the Nineteenth Century* (Bloomington: Indiana University Press, 1987), edited by Ronald L. Numbers and Jonathan Butler.

2. See Rowe, *Thunder and Trumpets*, p. 47, on estimates of numbers of Millerites.

The geographical distribution of correspondents to the *Signs of the Times* and the *Advent Herald* provides a general picture of where Millerites attracted the most adherents. Not surprisingly, New Yorkers provided the largest number: 131 correspondents' names appeared with letters indicating that they lived in that state. Vermonters were not far behind in total numbers of Millerites, however, with 107 correspondents counted, the Green Mountain state showed Millerite strength out of proportion to its size. Outside Vermont, New England accounted for another 279 of the 615 total correspondents recorded—giving New England as a whole a healthy 386 (Connecticut, 52; Maine, 54; Massachusetts, 88; New Hampshire, 73; Rhode Island, 12). Beyond New York and New England, representation of Millerites grew sparse: 23 in New Jersey, Pennsylvania, Delaware, and Maryland together; 65 in the West (20 of those in Ohio); and only 10 in the South (from *Signs of the Times* and *Advent Herald*, 1840–1847). On the geography of the "Burned-Over District," see Cross, *Burned-Over District*, and Donal Ward, "Religious Enthusiasm in Vermont, 1761–1847," Ph.D. diss., Notre Dame University, 1980.

There were some adventists across the Atlantic. See Louis Billington, "The Millerite Adventists in Great Britain, 1840–1850," *Journal of American Studies* 1 (Oct. 1967): 191–212.

3. Quotations here are from the King James Version.

4. Norman Cohn, *The Pursuit of the Millennium: Revolutionary Millenarians and Mystical Anarchists of the Middle Ages* (New York: Oxford University Press, 1957; rev. ed., 1970). Cohn describes the common factors in millenarian expectation in the Introduction, rev. ed., p. 15.

5. Samuel Danforth's sermon "A Brief Recognition of New England's Errand Into the Wilderness" (1670) provided the starting point for Perry Miller's "Errand into the Wilderness," in Miller, *Errand Into the Wilderness* (Cambridge, Mass.: Harvard University Press, 1956), see esp. pp. 10–13. See also Miller, *The New England Mind: The Seventeenth Century* (Cambridge, Mass.: Harvard Univer-

sity Press, 1939), and Sacvan Bercovitch, *The American Jeremiad* (Madison: University of Wisconsin Press, 1978).

6. Sacvan Bercovitch, *The Puritan Origins of the American Self* (New Haven, Conn.: Yale University Press, 1975).

7. James W. Davidson analyzes the "afflictive model of progress" in *The Logic of Millennial Thought: Eighteenth-Century New England* (New Haven, Conn.: Yale University Press, 1977); C. C. Goen discusses Edwards' millennial expectations in "Jonathan Edwards: A New Departure in Eschatology," *Church History* 28 (1959): 25–40.

8. Nathan O. Hatch, *The Sacred Cause of Liberty: Republican Thought and the Millennium in Revolutionary New England* (New Haven, Conn.: Yale University Press, 1977); also Ruth H. Bloch, *Visionary Republic: Millennial Themes in American Thought, 1756–1800* (Cambridge, Eng.: Cambridge University Press, 1985).

9. Major works on nineteenth-century evangelicalism and the evangelical empire include John Boles, *The Great Revival, 1787–1805: The Origins of the Southern Evangelical Mind* (Lexington: University Press of Kentucky, 1972), Clifford S. Griffin, *Their Brothers' Keepers: Moral Stewardship in the United States* (Westport, Conn.: Greenwood Press, 1960), Timothy L. Smith, *Revivalism and Social Reform in Mid-Nineteenth-Century America* (Nashville: Abingdon Press, 1957), Donald G. Mathews, *Religion in the Old South* (Chicago: University of Chicago Press, 1977), and William G. McLoughlin, *Revivals, Awakenings, and Reform: An Essay on Religion and Social Change in America* (Chicago: University of Chicago Press, 1978).

10. On Finney and the "new measures," see, for example, William McLoughlin, "Revivalism," in Gaustad, ed., *Rise of Adventism*, and Charles Grandison Finney, *Memoirs of Rev. Charles Grandison Finney Written by Himself* (New York: A. S. Barnes and Co., 1876).

11. Emphasis on the distinction between postmillennialism and premillennialism may be found in Ernest Lee Tuveson, *Millennium and Utopia: A Study in the Background of the Idea of Progress* (New York: Harper Torchbooks, 1964), in Smith, *Revivalism and Social Reform*, and in Goen, "Jonathan Edwards," and has appeared in more recent works such as Harrison, *The Second Coming*, pp. 6–7, and Peter W.

Williams, *Popular Religion in America: Symbolic Change and the Modernization Process in Historical Perspective* (Englewood Cliffs, N.J.: Prentice-Hall, 1980), pp. 125–126. Very recent works seem, however, to be moving away from the earlier concentration on the premillennial/postmillennial dichotomy. See, for example, Rowe, *Thunder and Trumpets*, p. 123 (but see also p. 13), and Bloch, *Visionary Republic*, pp. 32 and 41.

12. James Moorhead, "Between Progress and Apocalypse: A Reassessment of Millennialism in American Religious Thought, 1800–1880," *Journal of American History* 71 (Dec. 1984): 524–542.

13. Cross, *Burned-Over District*. See also Tyler, *Freedom's Ferment*.

14. David Brion Davis, "Some Ideological Functions of Prejudice in Ante-Bellum America," *Mississippi Valley Historical Review* 39 (Dec. 1952): 441–445; Davis, "Some Themes of Counter-Subversion: An Analysis of Anti-Masonic, Anti-Catholic, and Anti-Mormon Literature," *Mississippi Valley Historical Reveiw* 47 (1960): 205–224; John Higham, *From Boundlessness to Consolidation: The Transformation of American Culture, 1848–1860* (Ann Arbor, Mich.: Bobbs-Merrill, 1969).

15. Biographical information on Miller is available in William Miller, *Apology and Defence* (Boston: J. V. Himes, 1845); Sylvester Bliss, *Memoirs of William Miller, Generally Known as a Lecturer of the Prophecies, and the Second Coming of Christ* (Boston: J. V. Himes, 1853); and Nichol, *Midnight Cry*. See also Rowe, *Thunder and Trumpets*.

16. Bliss, *Memoirs*, p. 22.

17. For a new perspective on the problem of the "mainstream" versus the "marginal," see Moore, *Religious Outsiders*.

18. See Daniel Walker Howe, *The Unitarian Conscience: Harvard Moral Philosophy, 1805–1861* (Cambridge, Mass.: Harvard University Press, 1970); also William G. McLoughlin, *New England Dissent, 1630–1833: The Baptists and the Separation of Church and State* (Cambridge, Mass.: Harvard University Press, 1971).

19. Perry Miller's "From Edwards to Emerson" (in *Errand*, pp. 184–203) searches out the continuities spanning the generations between those two prominent figures; Donald Scott, "The Popular

Lecture and the Creation of a Public in Mid-Nineteenth-Century America," *Journal of American History* 66 (March 1980): 791–809 (he notes Emerson's popularity on p. 794).

20. Martin Marty, *Pilgrims in Their Own Land: 500 Years of Religion in America* (Boston: Little, Brown, 1984), p. 210.

21. William G. McLoughlin, *Modern Revivalism: Charles Grandison Finney to Billy Graham* (New York: Ronald Press, 1959); McLoughlin, *Revivals, Awakenings, and Reform*. Writing in the mid-nineteenth century himself, Robert Baird imposed a categorization on American religious groups that set orthodox evangelicals against others, (Henry Warner Bowden, ed., *Religion in America* [New York: Harper and Row, 1970; orig. pub. 1856]).

22. Richard Carwardine, "The Know-Nothing Party, the Protestant Evangelical Community, and American National Identity," in Stewart Mews, ed., *Religion and National Identity*, Studies in Church History, vol. 18 (Oxford: Basil Blackwell, 1982), p. 450. Moorhead lists, among cultural ideals prevalent by the 1820s, "egalitarianism, individual freedom, repudiation of arbitrary authority, diffusion of power, and translocal unity based on ideology" ("Between Progress and Apocalypse," p. 531). Sidney Mead summarizes the "fundamental beliefs" of the democratic experience in "Abraham Lincoln's 'Last, Best Hope of the Earth': The American Dream of Destiny and Democracy," in Mead, *The Lively Experiment: The Shaping of Christianity in America* (New York: Harper and Row, 1963), pp. 80–83.

23. Kai T. Erikson, *Wayward Puritans: A Study in the Sociology of Deviance* (New York: John Wiley and Sons, 1966), pp. 3–4, citing Emile Durkheim, esp. *The Division of Labor in Society*, trans. George Simpson (New York: Free Press, 1933).

24. Erikson, *Wayward Puritans*, pp. 9–12.

25. *Ibid.*, pp. 69–70.

26. Rowe sees Millerism as having been shaped by revivalism, millennialism, and pietism (*Thunder and Trumpets*, esp. p. 69).

27. Higham, *Boundlessness to Consolidation*. The point here differs from that made by Butler, "From Millerism to Seventh-day Adventism." Butler examines the transition from Millerism to Seventh-day

Adventism between the 1830s and the 1860s. I refer to a more general transition over a shorter period of time.

28. Moorhead, "Between Progress and Apocalypse."

29. On the problem of secularization, a respected view comes from Owen Chadwick, *The Secularization of the European Mind in the Nineteenth Century* (Cambridge, Eng.: Cambridge University Press, 1975). A critic of the concept is David Martin, for example in his *A General Theory of Secularization* (New York: Harper and Row, 1978). On a related topic, see James Turner's *Without God, Without Creed: The Origins of Unbelief in America* (Baltimore: John Hopkins University Press, 1985).

CHAPTER I
THE TIME

1. The summary of Miller's calculation of the time in Chapter 1 derives from William Miller, *Evidence from Scripture and History of the Second Coming of Christ, About the Year 1843: Exhibited in a Course of Lectures* (Troy, N.Y.: Kemble and Hooper, 1836; Boston: J. V. Himes, 1842); Miller, *Apology and Defence* (Boston: J. V. Himes, 1845); Sylvester Bliss, *Memoirs of William Miller, Generally Known as a Lecturer of the Prophecies, and the Second Coming of Christ* (Boston: J. V. Himes, 1853).

2. See *Signs of the Times*, March 20, 1840, p. 6; Miller to Bro. Marsh, Aug. 30, 18??, and Miller to Truman Hendryx, July 21, 1836, UMC.

3. Bliss, *Memoirs*, p. 8; Miller, in his *Apology*, p. 24, claims that he was never positive about the day or time. See also Miller to J. Atwood and family, May 31, 1831, WMC.

4. Miller, *Evidence* (1836), p. 222. See also Miller to Truman Hendryx, Oct. 1, 1832, WMC.

5. Miller, *Evidence* (1836), p. 138.

6. Miller to Truman Hendryx, March 26, 1822, WMC.

7. Miller to Truman Hendryx, Oct. 23, 1834, WMC.

8. Miller to Atwood and family, May 31, 1831.

9. Miller to Truman Hendryx, Feb. 8, 1833, WMC.

10. Seth Ransom to Miller, March 19, 1838, WMC; Lewis Perry, *Childhood, Marriage and Reform: Henry Clarke Wright, 1797–1870* (Chicago: University of Chicago Press, 1980), p. 179; Lewis C. Gunn, *The Age to Come!: The Present Organization of Matter Called Earth, to Be Destroyed by Fire at the End of This Age or Dispensation,* rev. ed. (Boston: J.V. Himes, 1844).

11. Charles Cole to William Miller, Jr., Jan. 25, 1838, WMC; *Signs of the Times,* Feb. 1, 1843, p. 155; 3rd General Conference of Christians, *Report of the Proceedings of the Third Session of the General Conference Expecting the Advent of the Lord, Held in Portland, Me., Oct. 12–14, 1841* (Boston: J. V. Himes, 1841), pp. 6–7; John Pearson to Miller, June 11, 1841, WMC. See also, again on Portland, Joshua V. Himes to Miller, July 27, 1840, WMC.

12. Joshua V. Himes to Miller, Jan. 17, 1840, WMC.

13. F. S. Parke to Miller, March 1839, WMC; *Signs of the Times,* June 1, 1840, p. 37 (letter from R. B. Medbury, May 21, 1840); *Disciple,* Jan. 1, 1842, p. 15.

14. *Signs of the Times,* June 1, 1840, p. 37 (letter from Medbury, May 21, 1840). See also Hiram Weed to George J. Kaercher, April 25, 1843, WKP; *Signs of the Times,* Jan. 1, 1842, p. 149, and Feb. 15, 1842, p. 172.

15. *Disciple,* Jan. 1, 1842, p. 15.

16. Donal Ward, "Religious Enthusiasm in Vermont, 1761–1847," Ph.D. diss., Notre Dame University, 1980, pp. 223–227. See also Francis D. Nichol, *The Midnight Cry: A Defense of the Character and Conduct of William Miller and the Millerites, Who Mistakenly Believed That The Second Coming of Christ Would Take Place in the Year 1844* (Takoma Park, Washington, D.C.: Review and Herald Publishing Assoc., 1944).

17. Henry Jones to Miller, Sept. 1, 1833, and May 19, 1834, WMC.

18. Henry Jones, *American Views of Christ's Second Advent, Consisting Mostly of Lectures Delivered Before Late General Conventions in the Cities of Boston, Lowell, and New York; Vindicating the Lord's Personal and Glorious*

NOTES TO CHAPTER I 237

Appearing on Earth, to Judge the World, "At Hand," Without Fixing the Time; Without a Previous Millennium; or Return of the Jews to Palestine (New York: Saxton and Miles, 1842), pp. 6–7 and 22; *Zion's Watchman,* July 25, 1840, p. 117.

19. *Signs of the Times,* Feb. 1, 1841, p. 164; Joshua V. Himes to Miller, Jan. 1, 1841, WMC.

20. 1st General Conference of Christians, *Report of the General Conference of Christians Expecting the Advent of the Lord Jesus Christ, Held in Boston, Oct. 14, 15, 1840* (Boston: J. V. Himes, 1841).

21. Andreas Bernardus Smolnikar to Miller, Nov. 17, 1839, WMC; *Signs of the Times,* Sept. 15, 1840, pp. 95–96, and July 1, 1840, p. 56; John T. Matthews, *A Key to the Old and New Testaments, Exhibited by the Initials of the White Stone, on the Coming of the Millenium; Also, an Exhortation to the Word,* 3rd ed. (New York: n. pub., 1842), pp. 6, 13, and *passim; Liberator,* Jan. 5, 1844, p. 4.

22. *Advent Herald,* Feb. 21, 1844, p. 21, and Feb. 28, 1844, p. 30.

23. William G. McLoughlin, *New England Dissent, 1630–1833: The Baptists and the Separation of Church and State,* vol. 2 (Cambridge, Mass.: Harvard University Press, 1971), p. 110n.

24. The *Signs of the Times* reported such predictions in Scotland and Ireland, from a Baptist layman in Belgrade, Maine, and from a minister in Falmouth, Maine (*Signs of the Times,* Aug. 2, 1843, p. 171, Nov. 15, 1843, p. 108, March 1, 1842, p. 182, and Sept. 1, 1840, p. 85). The Shakers in North Union, Ohio, found Christ already among them—"spiritually"—in the same year, 1843 (Robert S. Ellwood, Jr., *Alternative Altars: Unconventional and Eastern Spirituality in America* [Chicago: University of Chicago Press, 1979], p. 77, quoting from Marguerite Fellows Melcher, *The Shaker Adventure,* p. 185). One newspaper even gave credit for the 1843 date to the Mormons (Dover *Gazette,* April 28, 1840).

25. New York *Evangelist,* Feb. 16, 1843, pp. 41–44, March 2, 1843, pp. 65–66, March 16, 1843, pp. 81–82, March 30, 1843, p. 49, and April 13, 1843, pp. 57–58; *Christian Reflector,* March 1, 1843, p. 35.

26. Samuel Farmer Jarvis, *Two Discourses on Prophecy: With an Appendix in Which Mr. Miller's Scheme, Concerning Our Lord's Second Ad-*

vent, Is Considered and Refuted (New York: James A. Sparks, 1843), pp. 41–47 and 50–51.

27. John Dowling, *Reply to Miller: A Review of Mr. Miller's Theory of the End of the World in 1843*, 3rd ed. (New York: J. R. Bigelow, 1843), pp. 9–12, 19–20, 28–30, and 42.

28. The *Advent Herald* summarized the arguments of several of these critics in the December 4, 1844, issue, pp. 129–130.

29. *Christian Reflector,* Nov. 16, 1842, [pp. 1–2].

30. New York *Evangelist,* Feb. 22, 1844, p. 30; *Evangelical Magazine and Gospel Advocate,* May 5, 1843, p. 144.

31. *Signs of the Times* April 15, 1840, pp. 12–13.

32. James A. Hazen, *The False Alarm: A Discourse Delivered in the Congregational Church, South Wilbraham, Sabbath Evening, June 12th, 1842* (Springfield, [Mass.]: Wood and Rupp, 1842), pp. 21–22 and 22n.

33. Luther Fraseur Dimmick, *The End of the World Not Yet: A Discourse Delivered in the North Church, Newburyport, on the Last Evening of the Year 1841*, 3rd ed. (Newburyport, [Mass.]: C. Whipple, 1842), pp. 42–43.

34. *Christian Reflector,* Aug. 17, 1842, [p. 3].

35. Miller to Truman Hendryx, Nov. 28, 1834, and Dec. 23, 1836, WMC.

36. Miller, *Evidence* (1836), p. 97.

37. Timothy Cole to Miller, July 25, 1839 (from Lowell); George Phillips to William Miller, Jr., Aug. 27, 1839 (from Newfane, Vt.); William Storrs to Miller, Sept. 2, 1839 (from Harpersville, Broome County, N.Y.), all from WMC.

38. Otis A. Skinner, *Theory of William Miller, Concerning the End of the World in 1843, Utterly Exploded: Being Five Discourses with Some Other Essays on the Same Subject* (Boston: Thomas Whittemore, 1840), pp. 49–50, 146–148, and 186–187; John M. Austin, "Brief Review of William Miller's Destruction of the World," in Skinner, *Theory Exploded,* p. 204; *Signs of the Times,* Oct. 15, 1840, p. 112.

39. *Signs of the Times,* Sept. 15, 1840, p. 92.

40. 1st General Conference of Christians, p. 3.

NOTES TO CHAPTER I

41. 3rd General Conference of Christians, pp. 41–42.
42. *Signs of the Times*, June 1, 1842, p. 69.
43. David Tallmadge Arthur, "'Come Out of Babylon': A Study of Millerite Separatism and Denominationalism, 1840–1865," Ph.D. diss., University of Rochester, 1970.
44. *Ibid.*, p. 33.
45. Miller later claimed that he was pushed into public affirmation of this dating (Miller, *Apology*, p. 24).
46. For example, Oxford *Times*, March 1, 1843.
47. *Ibid.*
48. Samuel Luckey, *Strictures on Millerism, or the Second Advent Doctrines, as Taught by Its Advocates, and Particularly the System of Measures by Which They Are Disseminated* (Rochester, N.Y.: R.M. Colton, 1843), pp. 6–8.
49. *Niles National Register*, Dec. 9, 1843, p. 240, and March 23, 1844, p. 64.
50. *Niles National Register*, Sept. 17, 1842, p. 48, Dec. 9, 1843, p. 240, April 29, 1843, p. 144, and May 6, 1843, p. 160; *Liberator*, Sept. 9, 1842, p. 143; Silas Hawley, *The Second Advent Doctrine Vindicated: A Sermon Preached at the Dedication of the Tabernacle, with the Address of the Tabernacle Committee* (Boston: J. V. Himes, 1843), p. 99.
51. *Niles National Register*, Oct. 29, 1842, p. 144, and Nov. 12, 1842, p. 176; *Liberator*, April 14, 1843, p. 60; *Niles National Register*, July 29, 1843, p. 352; *Christian Reflector*, July 12, 1843, p. 111.
52. *Christian Reflector*, May 16, 1844, p. 77. The signature is printed "J. B. Coles" but may have been written by Millerite physician Larkin B. Coles. I would like to thank Ronald L. Numbers for raising this possibility.
53. *Advent Herald*, April 24, 1844, pp. 92–93, and May 1, 1844, p. 100.
54. George Storrs, *Six Sermons on the Inquiry Is There Immortality in Sin and Suffering?: Also, a Sermon on Christ the Life-Giver, or the Faith of the Gospel* (New York: Bible Examiner, 1855), pp. 9–10; *Christian Reflector*, May 16, 1844, p. 77. See also David L. Rowe, *Thunder and*

Trumpets: Millerites and Dissenting Religion in Upstate New York, 1800–1850 (Chico, Calif.: Scholars Press, 1985), chap. 7, "A Babel in Zion."
55. *Advent Herald,* April 10, 1844, p. 69.
56. *Advent Herald,* Oct. 23, 1844, pp. 87–88.
57. *Advent Herald,* Sept. 11, 1844, p. 47, and Sept. 18, 1844, pp. 52–53.
58. Himes to Miller, Sept. 31, 1844, MHS.
59. *Niles National Register,* Sept. 14, 1844, p. 32, Oct. 19, 1844, p. 112, and Oct. 26, 1844, [p. 128]; *Advent Herald,* Oct. 23, 1844, pp. 87–88, and Nov. 6, 1844, pp. 98–99.
60. *Advent Herald,* Oct. 9, 1844, pp. 73–74, 76, and 80, Oct. 16, 1844, p. 81, and Oct. 23, 1844, p. 88.
61. *Advent Herald,* Oct. 23, 1844, pp. 87–88, and Nov. 6, 1844, pp. 98–99. See also Nichol, *Midnight Cry.*

CHAPTER II
THE MEANING OF SUPERNATURALISM

1. *Christian Reflector,* Feb. 8, 1843, [p. 2].
2. Ronald Knox proposed "ultrasupernaturalism" as a synonym for "enthusiasm" in his famous study *Enthusiasm: A Chapter in the History of Religion with Special Reference to the XVII and XVIII Centuries* (New York: Oxford University Press, 1950), p. 2. Hans W. Frei labels one school of biblical criticism "Supernaturalism," with connotations similar to those implied here, in *The Eclipse of Biblical Narrative: A Study in Eighteenth and Nineteenth Century Hermeneutics* (New Haven, Conn.: Yale University Press, 1974), pp. 86–95.
3. Peter W. Williams notes, "The supernatural, which modernization would discredit and discard, by no means disappeared, and divine agency or the intrusion of divine power into the mundane world has been a frequent characteristic of American Protestant belief, especially at the popular level. Miraculous healings, expectations of the imminent return of Christ, seizures of individuals with the power of the Spirit, all have been manifestations of direct appearances of the divine—*hierophanies*—into the realm of the ordinary" (*Popular Religion in America: Symbolic Change and the*

NOTES TO CHAPTER II

Modernization Process in Historical Perspective [Englewood Cliffs, N.J.: Prentice-Hall 1980], p. 13).

4. David L. Rowe recounts the story of a group of Millerites awaiting the resurrection of a dead woman (*Thunder and Trumpets: Millerites and Dissenting Religion in Upstate New York, 1800–1850* [Chico, Calif.: Scholars Press, 1985], pp. 64–65).

5. Henry Jones, *American Views of Christ's Second Advent, Consisting Mostly of Lectures Delivered Before Late General Conventions in the Cities of Boston, Lowell, and New York; Vindicating the Lord's Personal and Glorious Appearing on Earth, to Judge the World, "At Hand," Without Fixing the Time; Without a Previous Millennium; or Return of the Jews to Palestine* (New York: Saxton and Miles, 1842), pp. 8 and 17. See also Anthony Lane to Miller, April 4, 1838, WMC.

6. Jones, *American Views*, p. 17; *Advent Shield and Review* 1 (Jan. 1845): 287–288.

7. William Miller, *Evidence from Scripture and History of the Second Coming of Christ, About the Year 1843: Exhibited in a Course of Lectures* (Troy, N.Y.: Kemble and Hooper, 1836; Boston, J. V. Himes, 1842), p. 138.

8. *Ibid.*, p. 177.

9. Miller to Truman Hendryx, March 26, 1832, WMC.

10. *Signs of the Times*, June 15, 1842, p. 88 (from *Investigator*).

11. *Liberator*, Sept. 22, 1843, p. 152 (from New York *Tribune*), and April 14, 1843, p. 60.

12. *National Anti-Slavery Standard*, May 12, 1842, p. 195 ("Letters from New York.—No. 24").

13. *Liberator*, Oct. 25, 1844, p. 172.

14. Samuel Luckey, *Strictures on Millerism, or the Second Advent Doctrines, as Taught by Its Advocates, and Particularly the System of Measures by Which They Are Disseminated* (Rochester, N.Y.: R. M. Colton, 1843), p. 4; *Christian Reflector*, March 31, 1841, p. 49 (italics in original); S. W. Lynd, *The Second Advent of Christ* (Cincinnati: J. B. Wilson, 1843), p. 13. See also Ethan Smith in New York *Evangelist*, June 23, 1838, p. 97, June 30, 1838, p. 101, July 7, 1838, p. 105, and Aug. 25, 1838, p. 133.

15. Miller, *Evidence* (1836), p. 135; Jones, *American Views*, pp. 1 and 5; *Signs of the Times*, May 25, 1842, p. 60; Miller, *Apology and Defence* (Boston: J. V. Himes, 1845), p. 7; *Jubilee Standard*, April 17, 1845, p. 45, and June 5, 1845, p. 101.

16. Silas Hawley, *The Second Advent Doctrine Vindicated: A Sermon Preached at the Dedication of the Tabernacle, with the Address of the Tabernacle Committee* (Boston: J. V. Himes, 1843), pp. 18, 19, and 91; Jones, *American Views*, p. 17; *Jubilee Standard*, June 26, 1845, p. 127, and June 5, 1845, p. 101.

17. *Signs of the Times*, April 12, 1843, p. 46 (from New York *Observer*) and Francis D. Nichol, *The Midnight Cry: A Defense of the Character and Conduct of William Miller and the Millerites, Who Mistakenly Believed That the Second Coming of Christ Would Take Place in the Year 1844* (Takoma Park, Washington, D.C.: Review and Herald Publishing Assoc., 1944), pp. 377–378; *Niles National Register*, May 6, 1843, p. 160 (from Providence *Journal*); Alice L. Hoag, "Millerism," AHE. Although Nichol skewed his evidence in order to deny accusations against Millerism, he may yet have been right about the lack of evidence behind ascension robe stories. Jane Marsh Parker remembered no robes ("A Little Millerite," *Century Magazine* 11 [Nov. 1886–April 1887]: 316). More on ascension robes can be found in: *Signs of the Times*, Feb. 22, 1843, p. 179 (from *New Hampshire Telegraph*), March 8, 1843, p. 4 (from *Investigator*), May 17, 1843, p. 88 (from the Pawtucket *Gazette*), and Nov. 20, 1844, p. 113; Oxford *Times*, March 1, 1843; New York *Evangelist*, March 23, 1843, pp. 94–95; *Niles National Register*, Jan. 18, 1845, p. 320.

18. C. Sprague to Miller, Nov. 18, 1839, WMC. Again, Kai T. Erikson notes that during boundary crises certain issues come into focus; beliefs defined as deviant need not be new (*Wayward Puritans: A Study in the Sociology of Deviance* [New York: John Wiley and Sons, 1966], p. 69).

19. Angelina Grimké Weld to Sarah Grimké, Jan. 1845, CP, copy of original in Library of Congress.

20. Miller to J. Atwood and family, May 31, 1831, WMC.

21. Miller to Hendryx, March 26, 1832, WMC. See also Miller, *Evidence* (1836), p. 198.

22. For example, N. N. Whiting to Miller, Jan. 27, 18??, WMC; *Signs of the Times,* Nov. 15, 1843, p. 107; Jones, *American Views,* p. 14; *Advent Tracts,* vol. 2 (Boston: J. V. Himes, 1845?), "World to Come," pp. 71–82.

23. Kittredge Haven, *The World Reprieved, Being a Critical Examination of William Miller's Theory That the Second Coming of Christ and the Destruction of the World Will Take Place About A.D. 1843* (Woodstock, Vt.: Haskell and Palmer, 1839), PP. 16–17; John M. Austin, "Brief Review of William Miller's Destruction of the World," in Otis A. Skinner, *Theory of William Miller, Concerning the End of the World in 1843, Utterly Exploded: Being Five Discourses with Some Other Essays on the Same Subject* (Boston: Thomas Whittemore, 1840), p. 196; *Albany Weekly Journal,* Oct. 5, 1844.

24. *Signs of the Times,* July 5, 1843, p. 140 (from "The Balm of Gilead").

25. *Christian Reflector,* Nov. 7, 1844, p. 177; Lynd, *Second Advent,* p. 32; *Signs of the Times,* June 28, 1843, p. 134 (from *Herald of Freedom*).

26. Austin, "Brief Review," p. 191; Skinner, *Theory Exploded,* p. 6, also pp. 3–4; Thomas Whittemore, "Sermon," in Skinner, *Theory Exploded,* p. 154; James A. Hazen, *The False Alarm: A Discourse Delivered in the Congregational Church, South Wilbraham, Sabbath Evening, June 12th, 1842* (Springfield, Mass.: Wood and Rupp, 1842), p. 21.

27. "Cosmopolite," *Miller Overthrown; or, The False Prophet Confounded* (Boston: Abel Tompkins, 1840), pp. 5–6; Skinner, *Theory Exploded,* pp. 6 and 81–82; Whittemore, "Sermon," pp. 155–157.

28. *Signs of the Times,* July 19, 1843, p. 156 (from *Puritan*).

29. Theodore Parker, "A Sermon of the Dangerous Classes in Society—Preached at the Melodeon, on Sunday, January 31, 1847," in Parker, *Discourses on Social Science* (London: Trubner and Co., 1864), p. 66; George Junkin, *The Little Stone and the Great Image; or, The Lectures on the Prophecies Symbolized in Nebuchadnezzar's Vision of the*

Golden Headed Monster (Philadelphia: J. M. Campbell, 1844), pp. vii–viii.

30. *Christian Reflector,* Nov. 7, 1844, p. 177; Lynd, *Second Advent,* pp. 21–22 and 32. See also Lewis Perry, *Childhood, Marriage and Reform: Henry Clarke Wright, 1797–1870* (Chicago: University of Chicago Press, 1980), esp. pp. 34, 35, 137, 170, 179, 234, and 237.

31. *Methodist Review* 8, no. 4 (Oct. 1837): 445 and 456; *Liberator,* Feb. 10, 1843, p. 23; A. Gregory Schneider, "Perfecting the Family of God: Religious Community and Family Values in Early American Methodism," Ph.D. diss., University of Chicago, 1981, esp. pp. 158 and 207. See also William McLoughlin, "Revivalism," in Edwin Scott Gaustad, ed., *The Rise of Adventism: Religion and Society in Mid-Nineteenth-Century America* (New York: Harper and Row, 1974), p. 141; Timothy L. Smith, "Righteousness and Hope: Christian Holiness and the Millennial Vision in America, 1800–1900," *American Quarterly* 31 (Spring 1979): 21–45.

32. *Signs of the Times,* July 13, 1842, p. 118, and May 31, 1843, p. 104. See also *Advent Herald,* July 17, 1844, p. 188.

33. *Liberator,* June 2, 1843, p. 88. The common conception of holiness discussed here should be distinguished from the more specific "holiness movement" that focused on an experience of sanctification and the possibility of Christian perfection. On the second blessing and perfectionism, see Chapter 3.

34. Apollos Hale, *Herald of the Bridegroom in Which the Plagues That Await the Enemies of the King Eternal Are Considered; and the Appearing of Our Lord to Gather His Saints Is Shown to Be the Next Event Before Us, by a Scriptural Exhibition of the Order of Events from the Fall of the Papacy Down to the Establishment of the Everlasting Kingdom* (Boston: J. V. Himes, 1843), p. 11; Miller, *Apology,* p. 9; Miller, *Evidence* (1836), pp. 175 and 197.

35. Miller to Truman Hendryx, April 2, 1836, and Oct. 23, 1834, WMC.

36. Jones, *American Views,* pp. 7 and 17. See also *Advent Tracts,* vol. 1 (Boston: J. V. Himes, [1845?]), "That Blessed Hope," p. 110, "Pres-

ent Dispensation—Its Course," p. 15, and "Present Dispensation—Its End," p. 35.

37. New York *Evangelist*, Dec. 21, 1839, p. 202; *Advent Herald*, Dec. 16, 1846, p. 148 (from *Olive Branch* and [Christian] *Intelligencer*); John Dowling, *Reply to Miller: A Review of Mr. Miller's Theory of the End of the World in 1843*, 3rd ed. (New York: J. R. Bigelow, 1843), pp. 35 and 39; *Christian Reflector*, Nov. 7, 1844, p. 177.

38. Dowling, *Reply to Miller*, p. 41; Lynd, *Second Advent*, pp. 21 and 23; Luther Fraseur Dimmick, *The End of the World Not Yet: A Discourse Delivered in the North Church Newburyport, on the Last Evening of the Year 1841*, 3rd ed. (Newburyport, Mass.: C. Whipple, 1842), pp. 10, 12–15, and 45.

39. *Liberator*, Sept. 22, 1843, p. 152; Charles Grandison Finney, *Memoirs of Rev. Charles Grandison Finney Written by Himself* (New York: A. S. Barnes and Co., 1876), p. 371.

40. Abraham Hoagland to Miller, Nov. 30, 1839, WMC; Fred Somkin, *Unquiet Eagle: Memory and Desire in the Idea of American Freedom, 1815–1860* (Ithaca, N.Y.: Cornell University Press, 1967), p. 48. See also James Moorhead, "Between Progress and Apocalypse: A Reassessment of Millennialism in American Religious Thought, 1800–1880," *Journal of American History* 71 (Dec. 1984).

41. *Christian Reflector*, March 6, 1845, p. 38. On the tradition of the jeremiad, see Sacvan Bercovitch, *The American Jeremiad* (Madison: University of Wisconsin Press, 1978).

42. Angelina Grimké, Weld to Sarah Grimké, Jan. 1845, CP.

43. For example, see Ethan Smith in New York *Evangelist*, June 23, 1838, p. 97, June 30, 1838, p. 101, July 7, 1838, p. 105, and Aug. 25, 1838, p. 133.

44. Miller, *Evidence* (1836), pp. 19–21; Miller to Silas Bush, n.d., WMC; Hawley, *Second Advent*, p. 53; Jones, *American Views*, pp. 16–17; *Advent Shield and Review* 1 (Jan. 1845): 287–288.

45. Oberlin *Evangelist*, Jan. 19, 1842, p. 14, and April 13, 1842, p. 57; New York *Evangelist*, Nov. 6, 1841, p. 177.

46. *Signs of the Times*, June 28, 1843, p. 134 (from *Herald of Freedom*). See also *Liberator*, Feb. 10, 1843, p. 23.

47. See R. Laurence Moore, "Spiritualism," in Gaustad, *Rise of Adventism*, on fusing the natural and the supernatural.

48. New York *Evangelist*, March 26, 1846, p. 49; *Christian Reflector*, Jan. 5, 1842, [p. 2]; Dimmick, *End Not Yet*, p. 21.

49. New York *Evangelist*, Aug. 25, 1838, p. 133, and Feb. 6, 1841, p. 22; Luckey, *Strictures on Millerism*, p. 4; *Christian Reflector*, March 31, 1841, p. 49; Lynd, *Second Advent*, pp. 9, 13, and 14.

50. *Advent Herald*, Dec. 16, 1846, p. 148 (from *Olive Branch*); *Christian Reflector*, March 31, 1841, p. 49; Lynd, *Second Advent*, p. 9; New York *Evangelist*, June 30, 1838, p. 101 (italics in original).

51. New York *Evangelist*, Nov. 20, 1841, p. 185.

52. *Signs of the Times*, July 12, 1843, p. 150.

53. Skinner, *Theory Exploded*, pp. 51–52; Whittemore, "Sermon," pp. 153–154; Haven, *World Reprieved*, p. 9; *Perfectionist*, July 1, 1843, p. 39.

54. *Liberator*, Feb. 10, 1843, p. 23, and May 5, 1843, p. 71.

55. Dowling, *Reply to Miller*, pp. 35 and 41; Lynd, *Second Advent*, pp. 3 and 18; Dimmick, *End Not Yet*, pp. 10 and 14–15; *Oberlin Evangelist*, Jan. 19, 1842, p. 14, and June 22, 1842 (from Haverhill *Gazette*); New York *Evangelist*, Nov. 20, 1841, p. 185 (Ethan Smith).

56. New York *Evangelist*, Oct. 7, 1837, p. 161; Dowling, *Reply to Miller*, p. 35.

57. *Liberator*, Sept. 22, 1842, p. 152.

58. *Methodist Review* 8, no. 4 (Oct. 1837): 445; Lynd, *Second Advent*, p. 14; *Oberlin Evangelist*, March 3, 1841, p. 37.

59. Weld to Grimké, Jan. 1845. See also Finney, *Memoirs*, p. 371.

60. *Hierophant* 3 (Aug. 1842): 7; *Liberator*, June 2, 1843, p. 88.

61. Lewis C. Gunn, *The Age to Come: The Present Organization of Matter Called Earth, to Be Destroyed by Fire at the End of This Age or Dispensation*, rev. ed. (Boston: J. V. Himes, 1844), p. 9; *Advent Tracts*, vol. 2, "World to Come," pp. 74–75.

62. Jones, *American Views*, pp. 18–19.

63. *Advent Tracts*, vol. 1, "Present Dispensation–Its Course," p. 2; *Advent Herald*, March 27, 1844, p. 64.

64. Miller to Truman Hendryx, July 21, 1836, and Dec. 23, 1836, WMC; Miller, *Evidence* (1842), p. 271.

65. Miller, *Evidence* (1836), pp. 175–176; Joshua V. Himes to William S. Miller, Nov. 12, 1840, JVH; Henry Jones to Miller, Sept. 1, 1833, WMC; Miller to Hendryx, March 26, 1832.

66. Miller, *Evidence* (1842), pp. 268, 290, and 291.

67. Joseph Eldridge, *Reform and Reformers: A Sermon Delivered at Norfolk, Conn., November 30, 1843* (New Haven, Conn.: B. L. Hamlen, 1844), p. 5; *Methodist Review* 9, no. 3 (July 1838): 342 (italics in original).

68. *Christian Reflector*, Nov. 7, 1844, p. 177.

69. *Christian Reflector*, Jan. 19, 1842 [p. 1]; Dimmick, *End Not Yet*, p. 45; New York *Evangelist*, Oct. 7, 1837, p. 161; Sept. 30, 1937, p. 157, and Oct. 7, 1837, p. 161; *Methodist Review* 9, no. 3 (July 1838); 344 345; *Christian Reflector*, Nov. 7, 1844, p. 177.

70. *Oberlin Evangelist*, Dec. 22, 1841, p. 204; Finney quoted in McLoughlin, "Revivalism," p. 145.

71. Dimmick, *End Not Yet*, p. 45; *Christian Reflector*, Jan. 4, 1844, p. 2; *Methodist Review* 9, no. 1 (Jan. 1838): 72–73, and 9, no. 3 (July 1838): 344–345.

72. Oberlin *Evangelist*, July 7, 1841, pp. 110–111.

73. Dimmick, *End Not Yet*, pp. 45–46; *Advent Herald*, May 27, 1846, p. 124 (from *Vermont Observer*); Lynd, *Second Advent*, pp. 23–24; Oberlin *Evangelist*, April 13, 1842, p. 57.

74. New York *Evangelist*, June 22, 1842, p. 172.

75. Miller, *Evidence* (1842), p. 281. Also [Joshua V. Himes?], *Protestantism: Its Hope of the World's Conversion Fallacious* (Boston: J. V. Himes, 1847), pp. 66–67.

76. Miller to Hendryx, March 26, 1832.

77. Miller to Truman Hendryx, April 28, 1835, WMC; [Himes?] *Protestantism*, p. 61.

78. *Signs of the Times*, Aug. 2, 1843, p. 171 (from *Herald of Freedom*).

79. Dimmick, *End Not Yet*, pp. 12–13; New York *Evangelist*, Nov. 20, 1841, p. 185; Auburn *Banner*, Jan. 5, 1837.

80. Miller to Truman Hendryx, Oct. 1, 1832, WMC; Miller to Truman Hendryx, Sept. 8, 1838, WMC; *Signs of the Times*, March 20, 1840, p. 6.

81. Jones, *American Views*, pp. 21–22. The differences between Miller and Jones on this point again raise the problem of characterizing the tone of the Millerite movement. Just as the burning of the world could, on the one hand, take on the implication of angry punishment and, on the other, of the sweeping away of impediments to glory, so similarly, Millerites differed in their estimates of the prospects for the majority of people.

82. *Advent Tracts*, vol. 1, "Present Dispensation—Its Course," p. 22.

83. For example, letter from "J.W." in the *Christian Reflector*, Feb. 8, 1843 [p. 42]. See Chapter 3.

84. William Miller, *Review of a Discourse, Delivered in the North Church, Newburyport, on the Last Evening of the Year 1841, by L. F. Dimmick, Pastor of the Church* (Boston: J. V. Himes, 1842), p. 3; Hale, *Herald*, pp. 23–25; Miller, *Evidence* (1836), pp. 27–29 and 84–85.

85. Skinner, *Theory Exploded*, p. 109, also p. 57.

86. *Liberator*, Oct. 26, 1844, p. 172.

87. Lynd, *Second Advent*, p. 18; Oberlin *Evangelist*, Jan. 19, 1842, p. 14.

88. Oberlin *Evangelist*, Jan. 19, 1842, p. 14, and April 13, 1842, p. 57.

89. Oberlin *Evangelist*, April 13, 1842, p. 57.

90. Jones, *American Views*, p. 3; *Advent Herald*, Jan. 13, 1846, p. 178; *Signs of the Times*, June 1, 1840, p. 37.

91. *Christian Reflector*, Nov. 23, 1842, [p. 4] (from New York *Evangelist*).

92. Hoag, "Millerism," p. 7.

93. *Signs of the Times*, Aug. 24, 1842, p. 166 (from *Connecticut Observer*). See also *Advent Herald*, Dec. 30, 1846, p. 163 (from *Prot[estant] Church[man]*); New York *Evangelist*, Feb. 6, 1841, p. 22.

94. *Christian Reflector*, March 11, 1840, p. 41; *Signs of the Times*, Jan. 1, 1842, p. 148 (from *Christian Herald*).

95. *National Anti-Slavery Standard,* May 12, 1842, p. 195.
96. For example, Miller to Hendryx, July 21, 1836.

CHAPTER III

REVELATION AND AUTHORITY

1. Miller to Truman Hendryx, March 26, 1832, WMC (italics in original).
2. Miller to Truman Hendryx, Oct. 1, 1832, WMC.
3. *Signs of the Times,* May 20, 1846, p. 117.
4. Miller to Truman Hendryx, Nov. 28, 1834, WMC (italics in original).
5. *Signs of the Times,* June 15, 1840, p. 45.
6. James A. Hazen, *The False Alarm, A Discourse Delivered in the Congregational Church, South Wilbraham, Sabbath Evening, June 12th, 1842 (Springfield, [Mass.]: Wood and Rupp, 1842), p. 21; Signs of the Times,* March 29, 1842, pp. 31–32; *Advent Herald,* Jan. 1, 1845, p. 161.
7. This summary comes from Hans W. Frei, *The Eclipse of Biblical Narrative: A Study in Eighteenth and Nineteenth Century Hermeneutics* (New Haven, Conn.: Yale University Press, 1974), pp. 1–16 and *passim.*
8. See Timothy P. Weber, "The Two-Edged Sword: The Fundamentalist Use of the Bible," in Nathan O. Hatch and Mark A. Noll, eds., *The Bible in America: Essays in Cultural History* (New York: Oxford University Press, 1982), esp. pp. 104–105.
9. *Signs of the Times,* May 15, 1840, p. 31.
10. Miller to J. Atwood and family, May 31, 1843, WMC.
11. William Miller, *Apology and Defence* (Boston: J. V. Himes, 1845), p. 6.
12. Miller to J. Atwood and family, May 31, 1831, WMC.
13. See L. E. Lincoln, *Disquisitions on the Prophecies of Daniel, with an Appendix, Exhibiting the Fulfilment of the Prophecy, "In the Third Year of Cyrus, King of Persia," to the Present Time* (Lowell, Mass.: Stearns and Taylor, 1843), p. 92.
14. Oberlin *Evangelist,* June 8, 1842, pp. 91–92 (letter from Charles Fitch).

15. Henry Jones, *American Views of Christ's Second Advent, Consisting Mostly of Lectures Delivered Before General Conventions in the Cities of Boston, Lowell, and New York; Vindicating the Lord's Personal and Glorious Appearing on Earth, to Judge the World, "At Hand," Without Fixing the Time; Without a Previous Millennium; or Return of the Jews to Palestine* (New York: Saxton and Miles, 1842), p. 2; William Miller, *Miller's Reply to Stuart's "Hints on the Interpretation of Prophecy"; in Three Letters, Addressed to Joshua V. Himes* (Boston: J. V. Himes, 1842), pp. 5–6; Apollos Hale, *The Second Advent Manual, in Which the Objections to Calculating the Prophetic Times Are Considered; the Difficulties Connected with the Calculation Explained; and the Facts and Arguments on Which Mr. Miller's Calculations Rest, Are Briefly Stated and Sustained* (Boston: J. V. Himes, 1843), pp. 5–6; *Liberator,* Dec. 11, 1840, p. 197.

16. Otis A. Skinner, *Theory of William Miller, Concerning the End of the World in 1843, Utterly Exploded: Being Five Discourses with Some Other Essays on the Same Subject* (Boston: Thomas Whittemore, 1840), p. 125.

17. For example, Dexter Dickson, *A Key to the Prophecies, and Second Advent of Christ, with the Time of His First and Second Manifestations* (Boston: n. pub., 1843), pp. 8–19.

18. Henry Clarke Wright, for example: Lewis Perry, *Childhood, Marriage and Reform: Henry Clarke Wright, 1797–1870* (Chicago: University of Chicago Press, 1980), pp. 143–146.

19. *Christian Reflector,* April 1, 1840, p. 56 (quoting from *Zion's Herald*).

20. Mark A. Noll notes the continued use of Old Testament "types" in American popular culture in "The Image of the United States as a Biblical Nation, 1776–1865," in Hatch and Noll, eds., *Bible,* pp. 39–58.

21. Nathan O. Hatch, "The Christian Movement and the Demand for a Theology of the People," *Journal of American History* 67 (Dec. 1980): 545–567, and Hatch, "*Sola Scriptura* and *Novus Ordo Seclorum,*" in Hatch and Noll, eds., *Bible,* pp. 59–78.

22. George M. Marsden, "Everyone One's Own Interpreter?: The Bible, Science, and Authority in Mid-Nineteenth-Century America,"

in Hatch and Noll, eds., *Bible*, pp. 79–100; Marsden, *Fundamentalism and American Culture: The Shaping of Twentieth-Century Evangelicalism, 1870–1925* (New York: Oxford University Press, 1982); Theodore Dwight Bozeman, *Protestants in an Age of Science: The Baconian Ideal and Antebellum Religious Thought* (Chapel Hill, N.C.: University of North Carolina Press, 1977).

23. Hatch, "*Sola Scriptura*," p. 71.
24. *Signs of the Times*, Dec. 20, 1843, p. 150.
25. Miller to Joshua V. Himes, n.d., WMC. See also Miller to [Nathaniel] Southard, n.d., WMC; Silas Hawley, *The Second Advent Doctrine Vindicated: A Sermon Preached at the Dedication of the Tabernacle, with the Address of the Tabernacle Committee* (Boston: J. V. Himes, 1843), "Address," p. 101.
26. Joshua V. Himes to Miller, Jan. 27, 1840, MHS.
27. *Signs of the Times*, Dec. 27, 1843, p. 156 (from Hartford *Universalist*).
28. *Signs of the Times*, Aug. 10, 1842, p. 148 (from Hazen's *False Alarm*).
29. The classic statement on individualism and the "tyranny of the majority" is, of course, Alexis de Tocqueville, *Democracy in America*, ed. Phillips Bradley, trans. Henry Reeve (New York: Vintage Books, 1945; orig. pub. in English in 1835).
30. *Signs of the Times*, Aug. 10, 1842, p. 152 (from Portland *Tribune*); Hale, *Second Advent Manual*, pp. 30–31. Also Thomas Whittemore, "Sermon," in Skinner, *Theory Exploded*, p. 154; *Advent Message to the Daughters of Zion* 1, no. 2 (Sept. 1844): 31–34.
31. New York *Evangelist*, June 15, 1843, p. 96.
32. Samuel Farmer Jarvis, *Two Discourses on Prophecy: With an Appendix in Which Mr. Miller's Scheme, Concerning Our Lord's Second Advent, Is Considered and Refuted* (New York: J. R. Bigelow, 1843), pp. 16–29. Also Luther Fraseur Dimmick, *The End of the World Not Yet: A Discourse Delivered in the North Church, Newburyport, on the Last Evening of the Year 1841*, 3rd ed. (Newburyport, [Mass.]: C. Whipple, 1842), p. 45.
33. John Dowling, *Reply to Miller: A Review of Mr. Miller's Theory of*

252 NOTES TO CHAPTER III

the End of the World in 1843, 3rd ed. (New York: J. R. Bigelow, 1843), pp. 2–3; John Henry Hopkins, *Two Discourses on the Second Advent of the Redeemer, with Special Reference to the Year 1843*, 3rd ed. (Burlington, [Vt.]: Chauncey Goodrich, 1843), p. 9; *Signs of the Times*, March 15, 1841, p. 191 (from *Christian Watchman*).

34. Dowling, *Reply to Miller*, p. 3; *Christian Reflector*, Jan. 18, 1843, [p. 2], and Feb. 22, 1843, p. 31; *American Millenarian and Prophetic Review*, Dec. 1, 1843, p. 106; Hopkins, *Two Discourses*, p. 14.

35. William Miller, *Evidence from Scripture and History of the Second Coming of Christ, About the Year 1843: Exhibited in a Course of Lectures* (Troy, N.Y.: Kemble and Hooper, 1836; Boston: J. V. Himes, 1842), pp. 256–257 (1836), See also *Advent Tracts*, vol. 1 (Boston: J. V. Himes, [1845?]), "Looking Forward," p. 9.

36. Miller to J. Atwood and Family, May 31, 1831, WMC; L. Hersey, *Review of Professor Chases's "Remarks on the Book of Daniel"* (Boston: J. V. Himes, 1844), p. 14; Gunn, *Age to Come*, pp. 23 and 31.

37. See Bozeman, *Protestants in an Age of Science*: Marsden, *Fundamentalism*. As in Marsden's work, the findings here indicate that "Baconianism" was widespread in popular culture, not just among elites and not just among Presbyterians.

38. Patricia Cline Cohen, *A Calculating People: The Spread of Numeracy in Early America* (Chicago: University of Chicago Press, 1982), esp. pp. 127–138.

39. Jane Marsh Parker described drawing and calculating on her slate in "A Little Millerite," *Century Magazine* 11 (Nov. 1886–April 1887): 315. David L. Rowe and J. F. C. Harrison both note the innovations of Millerites in the use of "visual aids," and Harrison also emphasizes the "do-it-yourself" character of biblical interpretation in that group (Rowe, *Thunder and Trumpets: Millerites and Dissenting Religion in Upstate New York, 1800–1850* [Chico, Calif.: Scholars Press, 1985], p. 45, and Harrison, *The Second Coming: Popular Millenarianism, 1780–1850* [New Brunswick, N.J.: Rutgers University Press, 1979], pp. 200–201).

40. *Signs of the Times*, Feb. 22, 1843, p. 179 (from New York

Mercury); also in Penn-Yan *Democrat*, Feb. 21, 1843 (quoting from Cleveland *Plain Dealer*).

41. *Niles National Register*, May 23, 1844, p. 208; "Cosmopolite," *Miller Overthrown; or, the False Prophet Confounded* (Boston: Abel Tompkins, 1840), pp 37–38.

42. *Christian Reflector*, Oct. 18, 1843, p. 167.

43. "An Enquirer after truth" to Miller, Feb. 19, 1840, WMC (italics in original).

44. *Signs of the Times*, Feb. 1, 1843, pp. 159–160 (from Boston *National Champion*); *Vermont Chronicle*, June 3, 1831, quoted in Donal Ward, "Religious Enthusiasm in Vermont, 1761–1847," Ph.D. diss., Notre Dame University, 1980, p. 136.

45. *Signs of the Times*, April 6, 1842, p. 5 (from Hartford *Christian Secretary*).

46. *Christian Reflector*, March 1, 1843, p. 35.

47. John M. Austin, "Brief Review of William Miller's Destruction of the World," in Skinner, *Theory Exploded*, p. 191.

48. Miller, *Evidence* (1836), *passim;* Hawley, *Second Advent*, pp. 71–82.

49. Miller, *Evidence* (1836), pp. 124–127 and 208–233; *Signs of the Times*, March 20, 1840, pp. 3–6.

50. Sylvester Bliss, "The Advent, the Next Prophetic Event," in Hersey, *Review of Chase*, pp. 23–24; Miller, *Evidence* (1836), p. 217.

51. Harrison; *The Second Coming*, esp. pp. 39–43.

52. R. Laurence Moore's *caveat* is to the point here: "Historians of religion are always going to have trouble holding firm the distinction drawn by Frazier, Malinowski, Durkheim, and others, between a religious confession of human impotence before superior powers and magical, occult attempts to control nature by tapping hidden sources of power" (Moore, "The Occult Connection?: Mormonism, Christian Science, and Spiritualism," in Howard Kerr and Charles L. Crow, eds., *The Occult in America: New Historical Perspectives* [Urbana: University of Illinois Press, 1983], p. 136).

53. *Signs of the Times*, Oct. 11, 1843, pp. 62–63.

54. Note the balance expressed in a late adventist publication:

"While the Word of God is the arbitrator on all points of faith, our faith cannot be complete, so as to obtain the testimony, without recognizing the fulfilment of that Word in all those occurrences which, according to the prophecy, transpire around us" (*Jubilee Standard*, June 5, 1845, p. 99). Miller himself was not immune to the awesome potential of nature as well as history as a source of knowledge of divine purpose, and although he presented some vivid images of the end before his public audiences, he reserved the most magical of his visions for his private correspondence, especially with his confidant Hendryx: "Hark, hear those dreadful bellowings of the angry nations. It is the presage of horrid and terrific war, Look! Look again! See crowns, and kings, and kingdoms, tumbling to the dust—see Lords, and Nobles, captains, and mighty men all arming for the bloody [?] fight. See the carnivorous fowls screaming through the air. See, see these signs, behold the heavens grow black with clouds, the sun has vailed himself, the moon pale and forsaken hangs in the middle air, the hails descend, the seven thunders utter loud their voices" (Miller to Hendryx, March 26, 1832).

55. Jarvis, *Two Discourses on Prophecy*, pp. 55–56.

56. New York *Evangelist*, June 23, 1838, p. 97 (Ethan Smith).

57. New York *Evangelist*, Feb. 16, 1843, pp. 41–42, March 2, 1843, pp. 65–66, March 16, 1843, pp. 81–82, March 30, 1843, p. 49, and April 13, 1843, pp. 57–58.

58. Kittredge Haven, *The World Reprieved, Being a Critical Examination of William Miller's Theory That the Second Coming of Christ and the Destruction of the World Will Take Place About A.D. 1843* (Woodstock, Vt.: Haskell and Palmer, 1839), pp. 31–39; Dowling, *Reply to Miller*, pp. 23–24 and p. 10.

59. For example, Austin, "Brief Review," p. 193.

60. Dowling, *Reply to Miller*, p. 35. See also, for example, New York *Evangelist*, Nov. 9, 1939, p. 178; *Christian Reflector*, Jan. 5, 1842, [p. 2].

61. *Signs of the Times*, Aug. 3, 1842, p. 143 (from *Utican*).

62. See, for example, *Liberator*, Feb. 17, 1843, p. 27.

63. S. W. Lynd, *The Second Advent of Christ* (Cincinnati: J. B. Wilson, 1843), p. 28.

NOTES TO CHAPTER IV 255

64. *Signs of the Times,* April 12, 1843, p. 44 (from Portland *Bulletin*).
65. *Christian Reflector,* March 15, 1843, p. 43.
66. Albany *Weekly Journal,* Feb. 4, 1843 (and quoting from Boston *Transcript*), and Dec. 2, 1843, "Progress of Superstition!"
67. *Niles National Register,* March 18, 1843 (from Newark *Daily Advertiser*); *Christian Reflector,* March 29, 1843, p. 51.
68. *Christian Reflector,* March 15, 1843, p. 43.
69. *Signs of the Times,* May 17, 1843, p. 86.
70. Sylvester Bliss, *Memoirs of William Miller, Generally Known as a Lecturer of the Prophecies, and the Second Coming of Christ* (Boston: J. V. Himes, 1853), p. 71.
71. E. J. Marden, *A Letter from Mrs. E. J. Marden, of Bangor, Me., Containing Her Experience in the Blessing of Entire Sanctification; Also an Account of Her Receiving, by Faith, the Doctrine of the Second Advent of Our Lord Jesus Christ in 1843* (Haverhill, [Mass.]: Essex Banner, 1842), esp. pp. 19–21.
72. *Ibid.,* p. 32.
73. *Signs of the Times,* May 17, 1843, p. 86; *Advent Herald,* April 10, 1844, p. 78. See also John Starkweather, *A Scriptural Test of Saving Faith, Exhibited in an Exposition of Daniel 12:10* (Boston: A. J. Wright, 1844), esp. pp. 8 and 10.
74. Samuel Luckey, *Strictures on Millerism, or the Second Advent Doctrines, as Taught by Its Advocates, and Particularly the System of Measures by Which They Are Disseminated* (Rochester, N.Y.: R. M. Colton, 1843), pp. 20–24 (italics in original).
75. *Signs of the Times,* May 10, 1843. See also a reprint from *Zion's Herald* in *Signs of the Times,* May 15, 1840, and the circular letter of the Fairfield (Conn.) County Baptist Association in *Signs of the Times,* Dec. 20, 1843, p. 149.

CHAPTER IV
OUT OF BABYLON

1. Nathan O. Hatch, "*Sola Scriptura* and *Novus Ordo Seclorum,*" in

Hatch and Mark A. Noll, eds., *The Bible in America: Essays in Cultural History* (New York: Oxford University Press, 1982); Hatch, "The Christian Movement and the Demand for a Theology of the People," *Journal of American History* 67 (Dec. 1980).

2. Sydney E. Ahlstrom, "The Scottish Philosophy and American Theology," *Church History* 24 (1955): 257—272; Theodore Dwight Bozeman, *Protestants in an Age of Science: The Baconian Ideal and Antebellum Religious Thought* (Chapel Hill, N. C.: University of North Carolina Press, 1977); George M. Marsden, "Everyone One's Own Interpreter?: The Bible, Science, and Authority in Mid-Nineteenth-Century America," in Hatch and Noll, eds., *Bible*.

3. The best example is that of the Disciples of Christ/Churches of Christ. See Hatch, "Christian Movement."

4. See, for example, Ronald P. Formisano, "Political Character, Antipartyism and the Second Party System," *American Quarterly* 21 (Winter 1969): 683—709; David Brion Davis, "Some Themes of Counter-Subversion: An Analysis of Anti-Masonic, Anti-Catholic, and Anti-Mormon Literature," *Mississippi Valley Historical Review* 47 (1960), esp. pp. 211–212.

5. On antipartyism, see Formisano, "Political Character," and Michael Holt, "The Politics of Impatience: The Origins of Know Nothingism," *Journal of American History* 60 (Sept. 1973): 309—331. David L. Rowe uses the term "antiformalism" when interpreting this thrust among Millerites (*Thunder and Trumpets: Millerites and Dissenting Religion in Upstate New York, 1800–1850* [Chico, Calif.: Scholars Press, 1985), pp. 71–79).

6. Davis, "Some Themes of Counter-Subversion"; Richard Hofstadter, "The Paranoid Style in American Politics," in Hofstadter, *The Paranoid Style in American Politics and Other Essays* (New York: Vintage Books, 1967; first pub. 1952).

7. Miller to Truman Hendryx, July 21, 1836, and Dec. 23, 1836, WMC. By Miller's reckoning, the church emerged from her 1,260 days (years) in the wilderness in 1798, when the papal power in France fell before the forces of Napoleon. See William Miller, *Evidence from Scripture and History of the Second Coming of Christ, About the*

NOTES TO CHAPTER IV 257

Year 1843: Exhibited in a Course of Lectures (Troy, N. Y.: Kemble and Hooper, 1836, and Boston: J. V. Himes, 1842), pp. 178–179. (1836).

8. Miller, *Evidence* (1842), pp. 278–281.

9. Miller, *Evidence* (1836), pp. 99 and 120–128. See also Josiah Litch, *Eight Fundamental Errors in Miller's Theory Pointed Out by Charles K. True and William C. Brown, in Zion's Herald, March, 1840* (n. pub., [1840?]), p. 31, and Sylvester Bliss, "The Advent, the Next Prophetic Event," in L. Hersey, *Review of Professor Chase's "Remarks on the Book of Daniel"* (Boston: J. V. Himes, 1844), p. 22.

10. *Signs of the Times*, June 14, 1843, p. 114.

11. Miller, *Evidence* (1836), pp. 177, 187, 87, and *passim*.

12. See David Tallmadge Arthur, "'Come Out of Babylon': A Study of Millerite Separatism and Denominationalism, 1840–1865," Ph.D. diss., University of Rochester, 1970, pp. 12–41.

13. Charles Fitch, *Come Out of Her My People* (Rochester, N.Y.: J. V. Himes, 1843).

14. *Advent Herald*, June 5, 1844, p. 137; *Gospel Standard*, July 25, 1844, p. 16. The withdrawal took place in July of 1843.

15. *Advent Herald*, April 10, 1844, p. 78.

16. First Baptist Church of Eden, N.Y., *Minutes*, Jan. 1844, Oct. 12, 1844, and March 22, 1845, ERL.

17. *Advent Herald*, April 10, 1844, p. 78 (italics in original).

18. Rowe cites examples of Millerites who withdrew from their churches in *Thunder and Trumpets*, p. 116.

19. Examples of confessions of faith are in First Baptist Church of Romulus, N.Y., *Records*, and First Presbyterian Church of Palmyra, N.Y., *Records*, both in ERL.

20. On Universalism: First Presbyterian Church in Bath, N.Y., *Records*, Feb. 24, 1833; First Baptist Church of Romulus, *Records*, 1840; First Baptist Church of Marion, N.Y., *Records*, Jan. 1, 1842, all in ERL. On Mormonism: quotation from Baptist Church of Prattsburg Village, N.Y., *Records*, March 12, 1843; also Baptist Church of Prattsburg, N.Y., *Records*, Aug. 5, 1843, and Jan. 6, 1844; First Baptist Church of Marion, *Records*, Nov. 21, 1835; Congregational

Church of Prattsburg, N.Y., *Records*, July 10, 1844, all in ERL (italics in original).

21. Presbyterian Church of Pulteney, N.Y., *Records*, ERL (fear of adultery); Immorality Trials, MCS (adultery); First Baptist Society, N.Y., *Minutes*, Jan. 13, 1838, Syracuse University Archives (conversation leading to jealousies); First Presbyterian Church in Bath, *Records*, Feb.–Dec. 1836 (Sunday work); Presbyterian Church of Newark, N.Y., *Records*, Oct. 14, 1844 ERL; First Baptist Church of Marion, *Records*, June 12, 1830 (debts); Immorality Trials (debts); First Baptist Church of Newark, N.Y., *Records*, June 24, 1843, and March 6, 1847, ERL (disorderly walk).

22. Immorality Trials, MCS.

23. *Ibid.*, First Baptist Society, Pompey, *Minutes*, Oct. 8, 1838.

24. The argument here borrows from Glenn C. Altschuler, "Varieties of Religious Activity: Conflict and Community in the Churches of the Burned-Over District," in Altschuler and Jan M. Saltzgaber, *Revivalism, Social Conscience, and Community in the Burned-Over District: The Trial of Rhoda Bement* (Ithaca, N.Y.: Cornell University Press, 1983), pp. 143–169.

25. On the problem of "scrupulosity," see Robert G. Pope, "New England vs. the New England Mind: The Myth of Declension," *Journal of Social History* 3 (1969–1970): 95–108; First Baptist Church of Palmyra, New York, *Records*, Dec. 10 and Dec. 24, 1842, ERL, (italics in original).

26. Donal Ward, "Religious Enthusiasm in Vermont, 1761–1847," Ph.D. diss., Notre Dame University, 1980, p. 245; *Signs of the Times*, Aug. 1, 1840, p. 70, and July 20, 1842, p. 128.

27. *Advent Herald*, June 26, 1844, p. 166. A tangential effect of the use of this charge is that it frustrates the historian in search of the exclusion of Millerites. Most of such cases are presumably hidden in the records among a large number of individuals charged with neglect who had nothing to do with Millerism.

28. First Presbyterian Church of Palmyra, *Records*, "Names of the members of this Church." The total membership of the church probably did not exceed one hundred in any of these years.

29. First Presbyterian Church of Seneca Falls, N.Y., *Records*, 1832–1840, ERL.

30. The transcript of the Bement trial is printed in Altschuler and Saltzgaber, *Revivalism, Social Conscience, and Community,* pp. 89–140, and is taken from the First Presbyterian Church of Seneca Falls, *Records*.

31. Altschuler and Saltzgaber, *Revivalism, Social Conscience, and Community,* p. 109.

32. *Ibid.*, p. 134.

33. On Millerites and abolitionists, see Chapter 6.

34. Altschuler and Saltzgaber, *Revivalism, Social Conscience, and Community,* p. 109. Bogue was a colonizationist.

35. First Baptist Church of Seneca Falls, *Records,* July 29, 1843, and Jan. 14, 1844. See also Rowe, *Thunder and Trumpets,* pp. 42 and 44, and E. R. Pinney to Miller, Aug. 15, 1845, JVH. Mob action as well as church division broke out in Seneca Falls; see Rowe, *Thunder and Trumpets,* p. 139; also Chapter 6.

36. Second Baptist Church of Walworth, N.Y., *Records,* 1840–1841, ERL.

37. First Baptist Church of Williamson, N.Y., *Records,* 1837–1841, ERL.

38. A number of committees were appointed in June and July of 1842 to question members about "neglect of the church" and, in some cases, about unspecified "unfavorable reports." These labors continued through the fall, with additional cases arising for "neglect" and "unchristian conduct" (*Ibid.*, July–Nov. 1842).

39. There was some confusion as to where Elijah Greenfield was a member at the time of his trial, causing some procedural complications.

40. Presumably Greenfield's Millerism caused Brother Gilbert to say that he "cannot hear him [Greenfield] preach," and Gilbert's difficulties with the pastor went back at least to the first days of 1843 (First Baptist Church of Williamson, *Records,* Jan. 25, 1845, and Jan. 4, 1843).

41. *Ibid.*, Feb. 26, 1845.

42. *Ibid.*, April 16, 1845.

43. *Ibid.*, 1845–1846.

44. For cases of excommunication and schism not covered here, see, for example, Abigail Mussey, *Life Sketches and Experience* (Cambridge, [Mass.]: Dakin and Metcalf, 1865), pp. 61–66, and Ellen G. White, *Life Sketches . . . , Being a Narrative of Her Experience to 1881 as Written by Herself; with a Sketch of Her Subsequent Labors and of Her Last Sickness, Composed of Original Sources* (Mountain View, Calif.: Pacific Press Publishing, 1915). Rowe mentions the divisions in Miller's church and in Elon Galusha's church in Lockport, New York *(Thunder and Trumpets,* pp. 100–101).

CHAPTER V
THE INDIVIDUAL: IDEALS AND CONTROL

1. The humbug of P. T. Barnum is discussed in Neil Harris' work, *Humbug: The Art of P. T. Barnum* (Chicago: University of Chicago Press, 1981). A recent study of the problems of character and confidence men in mid-nineteenth-century America is Karen Halttunen, *Confidence Men and Painted Women: A Study of Middle-Class Culture in America, 1830–1870* (New Haven, Conn.: Yale University Press, 1982). See also Gilbert Seldes, *The Stammering Century,* sometimes subtitled "Minor movements, cults, manias, fads, sects and religious excitements in 19th Century America" (New York: Harper and Row, 1928; Harper Colophon ed., 1965).

2. David Riesman *et al., The Lonely Crowd: A Study of the Changing American Character* (New Haven, Conn.: Yale University Press, 1950; pbk. ed., 1969); Daniel Walker Howe, "Victorian Culture in America," in Howe, ed., *Victorian America* (Philadelphia: University of Pennsylvania Press, 1976), pp. 3–28; Warren I. Susman, "'Personality' and the Making of Twentieth-Century Culture," in John Higham and Paul K. Conkin, eds., *New Directions in American Intellectual History* (Baltimore: Johns Hopkins University Press, 1979), pp. 212–226.

3. Rufus W. Clark, *Lectures on the Formation of Character, Temptations and Mission of Young Men* (Boston: John P. Jewett and Co., 1853), p. 29, quoted in Halttunen, *Confidence Men,* p. 43.

NOTES TO CHAPTER V   261

4. Quoted in Susman, "Personality," p. 214.
5. *Christian Reflector*, Nov. 28, 1844, p. 192; *Advent Herald*, Feb. 25, 1846, p. 21 (quoting from Rochester *Democrat*).
6. New York *Evangelist*, May 4, 1843, p. 69; *Christian Reflector*, Jan. 16, 1845, p. 9.
7. *Advent Herald*, July 24, 1844, p. 196.
8. *Signs of the Times*, Dec. 20, 1843, p. 149 (quoting from *Biblical Recorder*), and Feb. 22, 1843, p. 180 (quoting from New York *Observer*).
9. *Signs of the Times*, July 13, 1842, p. 114 (quoting from *Daily Mail*); *Advent Herald*, July 24, 1844, p. 196 (quoting from and responding to *Christian Freeman*).
10. Silas Hawley, "Address," in Hawley, *The Second Advent Vindicated: A Sermon Preached at the Dedication of the Tabernacle, with the Address of the Tabernacle Committee* (Boston: J. V. Himes, 1843), p. 103.
11. *Advent Tracts*, vol. 1 (Boston: J. V. Himes, [1845?], "Practical Doctrine," pp. 108–113.
12. John Dowling, *Reply to Miller: A Review of Mr. Miller's Theory of the End of the World in 1843*, 3rd ed. (New York: J. R. Bigelow, 1843), p. 1; Albany *Weekly Journal*, Nov. 9, 1844 (quoting from Boston *Daily Mail*); New York *Evangelist*, Oct. 31, 1844, p. 174; Dover *Gazette*, April 28, 1840; Otis A. Skinner, *Theory of William Miller, Concerning the End of the World in 1843, Utterly Exploded: Being Five Discourses with Some Other Essays on the Same Subject* (Boston: Thomas Whittemore, 1840), p. 81; "Asmodeus in America, or the Devil on Two Sticks," *The Millerite Humbug; or, The Raising of the Wind!!: A Comedy in Five Acts, as Performed with Unbounded Applause in Boston and Other Parts of the Union* (Boston: For the author, 1845); John M. Austin, "Brief Review of William Miller's Destruction of the World," in Skinner, *Theory Exploded*, p. 194; *Christian Reflector*, Nov. 7, 1844, p. 178; *Signs of the Times*, May 1, 1840, p. 23 (from Universalist *Trumpet*), and April 6, 1842, p. 8; *Advent Herald*, Oct. 8, 1845, p. 72 (from Philadelphia *Ledger*), and April 15, 1846, p. 80 (from Cleveland *Herald*).
13. *Signs of the Times*, May 17, 1843, p. 88 (quoting from *Olive Branch*).
14. *Evangelical Magazine and Gospel Advocate*, March 13, 1840,

p. 87; *Signs of the Times,* March 15, 1843, pp. 11–12 (quoting from Oberlin *Evangelist*).

15. *Signs of the Times,* May 10, 1843, p. 78 (quoting from letter to Universalist *Trumpet*); *Signs of the Times,* March 15, 1843, pp. 11–12 (quoting from Oberlin *Evangelist*); *Signs of the Times,* Oct. 19, 1842, p. 36 (quoting from *New Hampshire Sentinel*); also *Advent Herald,* Feb. 28, 1844, p. 28 (quoting from Hartford *Christian Secretary*); *Signs of the Times,* April 15, 1841, p. 16. See also *Signs of the Times,* April 15, 1840, p. 13 (quoting from *Christian Mirror*).

16. *Signs of the Times,* May 17, 1843, p. 88 (quoting from *Olive Branch*); *Advent Herald,* Oct. 8, 1845, p. 72 (quoting from Philadelphia *Ledger*); New York *Evangelist,* Nov. 7, 1844, p. 178; *Advent Herald,* July 24, 1844, p. 197 (quoting from *Christian Freeman*).

17. One report even accused Himes of buying up and selling off anti-Millerite literature in order to turn higher profits (*Signs of the Times,* Oct. 5, 1842, p. 16 [quoting from Hartford *Times*]). See also *Signs of the Times,* March 22, 1843, p. 24 (quoting from Universalist *Trumpet*).

18. *Signs of the Times,* Nov. 20, 1844, p. 113 (quoting from *Christian Watchman*).

19. *Advent Herald,* Nov. 6, 1844, p. 99 (quoting from a letter from the Baptist "Rev. Dr." John Dowling); more stories of duping for gain, and responses to those accusations follow on pp. 100–102. See also *Christian Reflector,* Oct. 31, 1844, p. 175; "Asmodeus," *Millerite Humbug,* pp. 2–5; and *Advent Herald,* Oct. 30, 1844, p. 96 (quoting from New York *Herald*).

20. *Advent Herald,* Nov. 13, 1844, p. 105 (quoting from *Daily Mail*). See also *Advent Herald,* Oct. 30, 1844, p. 96 (quoting from New York *Herald*).

21. *Signs of the Times,* July 5, 1843, p. 144 (quoting from Rochester *Evening Post*).

22. *Signs of the Times,* May 15, 1841, p. 29 (quoting from *Christian Publisher*). See also *Signs of the Times,* March 15, 1841, p. 188 (quoting from Lynn *Record*).

23. Eliza C. A. Sprague to Lucy Miller, Nov. 4, 1839, WMC; *Signs*

NOTES TO CHAPTER V 263

of the Times, Oct. 19, 1842, p. 36 (quoting from *New Hampshire Sentinel*), Feb. 1, 1843, p. 159, and March 15, 1843, pp. 11–12 (quoting from Oberlin *Evangelist*); *Christian Reflector,* Jan. 18, 1843, [p. 2].

24. *Christian Reflector,* July 31, 1845, p. 123; *Advent Herald,* Sept. 3, 1845, p. 29 (from *Congregational Journal*); *Signs of the Times,* Feb. 22, 1843, p. 179 (from Fitchburg *Sentinel*), March 20, 1840, p. 8, and July 15, 1840, p. 64 (from Rev. Parsons Cooke, editor of the *Puritan*), Nov. 8, 1843, p. 96 (from *Olive Branch*), Dec. 12, 1843, pp. 140–141 (from *Christian Reflector* and *Christian Watchman*); *Advent Herald,* Jan. 1, 1845, p. 165 (from *Olive Branch*).

25. Daniel T. Rodgers, *The Work Ethic in Industrial America, 1850–1920* (Chicago: University of Chicago Press, 1974; pbk. ed., 1978), pp. xi–xii.

26. *Circular,* Jan. 8, 1853, p. 62 (italics in original).

27. *Advent Tracts,* vol. 1, "Practical Doctrine" (italics in original).

28. Skinner, *Theory Exploded,* p. 6. See also *Evangelical Magazine and Gospel Advocate,* March 13, 1840, p. 87.

29. *Courtland County Whig,* Jan. 24, 1843 (and quoting from Boston *Journal*); *Signs of the Times,* Feb. 22, 1843, p. 179 (from Bellows Falls *Gazette* and p. 180 (from New York *Sun*); *Signs of the Times,* July 20, 1842 (p. 128); *Christian Reflector,* Jan. 18, 1843, [p. 2].

30. *Advent Herald,* Nov. 6, 1844, pp. 98–100.

31. Albany *Weekly Journal,* Oct. 26, 1844 (from Philadelphia *Gazette*), and Nov. 9, 1844; *Christian Reflector,* Nov. 28, 1844, p. 191; *Liberator,* Oct. 18, 1844, p. 168 (from Philadelphia *Ledger*).

32. Timothy Weber, *Living in the Shadow of the Second Coming: American Premillennialism, 1875–1925* (New York: Oxford University Press, 1979).

33. *Liberator,* Oct. 25, 1844, p. 172; *Niles National Register,* March 4, 1843, p. 16 (from *Berks and Schuylkill Journal*); Alice L. Hoag, "Millerism," AHE pp. 7–8; *Christian Reflector,* Oct. 5, 1842, [p. 3] (from New Brunswick *Mercury*).

34. *Advent Herald,* Feb. 11, 1846, p. 5 (from Palmer, Mass., *Sentinel*).

35. Dowling, *Reply to Miller; Advent Herald,* Nov. 6, 1844, p. 99.

36. *Signs of the Times,* Aug. 10, 1842, p. 152 (from Portland *Tribune*).
37. Howe, "Victorian Culture," p. 24.
38. Rodgers, *Work Ethic;* E. P. Thompson, "Time, Work-Discipline, and Industrial Capitalism," *Past and Present* 38 (1967): 56–97.
39. *Signs of the Times,* Feb. 22, 1843, p. 180 (quoting from New York *Observer*); *Christian Reflector,* Nov. 28, 1844, p. 191, and Nov. 7, 1844, p. 179; *Liberator,* May 26, 1843, p. 84 (quoting from Cleveland *Plain Dealer*).
40. *Signs of the Times,* July 26, 1843, p. 167, (quoting from *Daily Democrat*); *Christian Reflector,* Nov. 7, 1844, p. 179 (quoting from *Republican*); *Advent Herald,* May 1, 1844, p. 100 (quoting from *Zion's Herald*); *Christian Reflector,* March 8, 1843, p. 39; *Liberator,* Nov. 25, 1842, p. 187; *Niles National Register,* March 18, 1843, p. 48.
41. William Lloyd Garrison to Elizabeth Pease, April 4, 1843, in Garrison, *Letters,* vol. 3: *No Union with Slaveholders, 1841–1849,* ed. Walter M. Merrill, (Cambridge, Mass.: Harvard University Press, 1974), p. 150; *Liberator,* April 26, 1844, p. 68; *Christian Reflector,* March 27, 1845, p. 52.
42. This account draws from the following: Michel Foucault, *Madness and Civilization: A History of Insanity in the Age of Reason,* trans. Richard Howard (New York: Random House, 1965); Gerald N. Grob, *Mental Institutions in America: Social Policy to 1875* (New York: Free Press, 1973); Grob, *The State and the Mentally Ill: A History of the Worcester State Hospital in Massachusetts, 1830–1920* (Chapel Hill: University of North Carolina Press, 1966); David J. Rothman, *The Discovery of the Asylum: Social Order and Disorder in the New Republic* (Boston: Little, Borwn, 1971); and Norman Dain, *Concepts of Insanity in the United States, 1789–1865* (New Brunswick, N.J.: Rutgers University Press, 1964). Material on the founding of mental institutions is in Grob, *Mental Institutions,* app. 1, pp. 343–370. On the problem of Millerite insanity, see Ronald L. Numbers and Janet S. Numbers, "Millerism and Madness: A Study of 'Religious Insanity' in Nineteenth-Century America," *Bulletin of the Menninger Clinic* 49 (1985): 289–320, and Numbers and Numbers, in Ronald L. Numbers and

Jonathan Butler, eds., *The Disappointed: Millerism and Millenarianism in the Nineteenth Century* (Bloomington: Indiana University Press, 1987).

43. *Signs of the Times,* May 3, 1843, p. 69.

44. *American Journal of Insanity* 1, no. 2 (Oct. 1844): 97.

45. Ronald Knox, *Enthusiasm: A Chapter in the History of Religion with Special Reference to the XVII and XVIII Centuries* (New York: Oxford University Press, 1950), p. 524; Gerald N. Grob, "Introduction," in Edward Jarvis, *Insanity and Idiocy in Massachusetts: Report of the Commission on Lunacy, 1855,* ed. Grob (Cambridge, Mass.: Harvard University Press, 1971), p. 52. See Thomas S. Szasz, *Manufacture of Madness: A Comparative Study of the Inquisition and the Mental Health Movement* (New York: Harper and Row, 1970), p. 13: in the seventeenth century, says Szasz, "the inquisitor-witch complex disappeared and in its place there arose the alienist-madman complex."

46. See the statistics from the Worcester Asylum reprinted in *Signs of the Times,* June 28, 1843, p. 132, and the causes cited by Gerald Grob from the Worcester Asylum *Annual Report* for 1845 in *The State and the Mentally Ill,* p. 55. See also cases in the *American Journal of Insanity* 1, no. 3 (Jan. 1845): 246–248.

47. *American Journal of Insanity* 1, no. 3 (Jan. 1845): 249–253 (italics in original).

48. *Liberator,* March 17, 1843, p. 44 (quoting from Lowell *Advertiser*), March 31, 1843, p. 52, and May 26, 1843, p. 84 (quoting from Cleveland *Plain Dealer*); New York *Evangelist,* March 16, 1843, p. 86.

49. *Christian Reflector,* Feb. 15, 1843, p. 27 [p. 3]; also printed in Albany *Argus,* Feb. 14, 1843, with credit given to New York *Evening Post.*

50. *Advent Herald,* Nov. 27, 1844, p. 124 (quoting from *New Hampshire Patriot*); *Christian Reflector,* March 27, 1845, p. 52 (quoting from *Asylum Journal of the Vermont Asylum for the Insane*); also *Advent Herald,* Dec. 18, 1844, p. 152 (quoting from *Olive Branch*).

51. *Advent Herald,* Dec. 31, 1845, pp. 164–165 (quoting from *Investigator*); *Advent Herald,* Dec. 18, 1844, p. 152 (quoting from *Olive Branch*).

52. *Liberator,* March 31, 1843, p. 52 (quoting from Philadelphia *North American*); *Niles National Register,* April 1, 1843, p. 80, and *Liberator,* March 17, 1843, p. 44 (both quoting from Essex *Banner*); *Advent Herald,* Nov. 27, 1844, p. 123, and *Christian Reflector,* Nov. 7, 1844, p. 179 (quoting from *New Hampshire Patriot* and "Buffalo papers"); *Signs of the Times,* June 1, 1841, p. 40 (quoting from Providence *Republican Herald*); *Liberator,* March 17, 1843, p. 44, and May 26, 1843, p. 84 (quoting from Cleveland *Plain Dealer*), and *Christian Reflector,* March 8, 1843, p. 39.

53. *Liberty Press,* Nov. 29, 1842, p. 10 (quoting from Boston *Traveller*); also in *Liberator,* Nov. 25, 1842, p. 187.

54. *Signs of the Times,* Feb. 22, 1843, p. 180 (quoting from New York *Observer*); *Niles National Register,* March 18, 1843, p. 48; *Christian Reflector,* Nov. 28, 1844, p. 191 (quoting from Essex County *Washingtonian*); *Liberator,* April 26, 1844, p. 68; *Advent Herald,* May 1, 1844, p. 100 (quoting from *Zion's Herald* and from Portland *Transcript*). The numbers cited here are those reported by the press and are not necessarily an accurate reflection of asylum records.

55. *Christian Examiner and General Review* 16 (March 1834): 136, quoted in Grob, *The State and the Mentally Ill,* pp. 50–51; *Niles National Register,* Dec. 30, 1843, p. 279; *Christian Reflector,* Sept. 9, 1840, p. 148.

56. *Liberator,* Oct. 25, 1844, p. 172 (quoting from Boston *Times*); *Advent Herald,* Feb. 11, 1846, p. 5 (quoting from Palmer, Mass., *Sentinel*).

The careful studies by Ronald L. and Janet S. Numbers have produced evidence that Millerites committed to asylums in the 1840s were not committed for heterodox belief but rather for "pathological" behavior and belief. Their research is not altogether incompatible with the argument here, which emphasizes popular assumptions about Millerism, insanity, and asylums rather than the actual diagnosis in individual cases. Numbers and Numbers do note that "by the late 1840s, Millerism had come to occupy a prominent place in the literature of American psychiatry as the stereotype of epidemic 'religious insanity.'" The two approaches do, nonetheless, differ in their perspectives on the problem (Numbers and Numbers, "Millerism and Madness," pp. 301 and 299).

57. Paul Boyer and Stephen Nissenbaum argue that there were significant parallels between the witch hysteria in Salem in the 1690s and the revivals of the eighteenth century; in fact, they imply that the two may have been the same phenomenon and that the differences lay in the interpretation (*Salem Possessed: The Social Origins of Witchcraft* [Cambridge, Mass.: Harvard University Press, 1974], esp. pp. 26–27).

58. John O. King discusses the experience of temptation to "self-murder" among Puritans and notes that, in the nineteenth century, such an experience would be taken as evidence of "moral insanity" and lead to commitment to an asylum (*The Iron of Melancholy: Structures of Spiritual Conversion from the Puritan Conscience to Victorian Neurosis* [Middletown, Conn.: Wesleyan University Press, 1983], pp. 49–54). Boyer and Nissenbaum also cite a case of temptation to suicide as part of a Puritan's religious experience (*Salem Possessed*, p. 28).

CHAPTER VI

THE SOCIETY: IDEALS AND CONTROL

1. Barbara Welter, "The Cult of True Womanhood, 1820–1860," reprinted in Michael Gordon, ed., *The American Family in Social-Historical Perspective* (New York: St. Martin's Press, 1978), pp. 313–333; Mary P. Ryan, *Cradle of the Middle Class: The Family in Oneida County, New York, 1790–1865* (Cambridge, Eng.: Cambridge University Press, 1981), esp. pp. 98–104, and 145–155; Ann Douglas, *The Feminization of American Culture* (New York: Avon Books, 1977).

2. *Advent Herald*, Dec. 25, 1844, p. 153; *Niles National Register*, March 11, 1843, p. 32 (from *U.S. Gazette*); Samuel Farmer Jarvis, *Two Discourses on Prophecy: With an Appendix in Which Mr. Miller's Scheme, Concerning Our Lord's Second Advent, Is Considered and Refuted* (New York: James A. Sparks, 1843), p. 59.

3. *Liberator*, June 16, 1843, p. 95 (from Detroit *Daily Advertiser*).

4. *Signs of the Times,* June 1, 1841, p. 40 (from Providence *Republican Herald*). See also Dover *Gazette,* June 4, 1839, for an account of a father, "victim of [an undefined] religious phrenzy," who killed his child with an axe.

5. *Christian Reflector,* Sept. 27, 1843, p. 155 (from New York *Journal of Commerce*).

6. George Addison Throop to D. D. W. C. Throop, April 23, 1843 WKP (italics in original). Olive Maria Rice recognized the opposition, but declared that she "dare not stop, for the only reason that I am a sister. And though men may censure and condemn," she went on, "I feel justified before God" (*Signs of the Times,* May 17, 1843, p. 87). See also *Signs of the Times,* June 28, 1843, p. 133: "it was very *immodest* for *ladies* to be studying and explaining the prophecies."

7. *Advent Herald,* April 1, 1846, p. 61 (from *Signal of Liberty*).

8. *Christian Reflector,* Oct. 31, 1844, p. 175, and March 8, 1843, p. 39; *Liberator,* May 26, 1843, p. 84 (from Cleveland *Plain Dealer*).

9. Some of the titles on a single page of the New York *Evangelist* of 1837 reflected the new importance given to woman and the domestic sphere: "Home"; "The Wife"; "The Family State"; "The Mechanic's Wife"; "The Call Again System" (on a lady and a wet nurse); "The Importance of a Holy Life" (New York *Evangelist,* Nov. 11, 1837, p. 184).

10. *Signs of the Times,* Sept. 15, 1840, p. 96 (italics in original). Note the—perhaps intentional—confusion of Miller with Mormon prophet "Joe" Smith.

11. There is little specific evidence on Millerite attitudes or behavior with regard to family life and the role of women in the family. The lack of evidence may indicate an unremarkable adherence to community norms. On the other hand, Millerites did include female lecturers among their number. The *Advent Message to the Daughters of Zion,* a periodical addressed specifically to women in the movement, did not explicitly call for conformity to the cult of domesticity and sometimes printed articles that could have been construed as subversive. (For example, "To the Advent Sisters" and "Individual Judgment of the Truth" in vol. 1, no. 2, pp. 26 and 33–35.) David L. Rowe

discusses female itinerants in *Thunder and Trumpets: Millerites and Dissenting Religion in Upstate New York, 1800–1850* (Chico, Calif.: Scholars Press, 1985), pp. 128–129.

12. Henry Jones to Miller, Feb. 21, 1833, WMC (italics in original). On Himes (and some others), see *Liberator,* 1839–1846. Also, in general on leaders, Nichol, *The Midnight Cry: A Defense of the Character and Conduct of William Miller and the Millerites, Who Mistakenly Believed That the Second Coming of Christ Would Take Place in the Year 1844* (Takoma Park, Washington, D.C.: Review and Herald Publishing Assoc., 1944), chaps. 12–13 (pp. 174–205), and Donal Ward, "Religious Enthusiasm in Vermont, 1761–1847," Ph.D. diss., Notre Dame University, 1980, pp. 145–155 (on Jones, Galusha, and others); Joseph Bates, *The Autobiography of Elder Joseph Bates; Embracing a Long Life on Shipboard . . . and a Brief Account of the Great Advent Movement of 1840–44* (Battle Creek, Mich.: Steam Press of the Seventh-day Adventist Publishing Assoc., 1868), pp. 228–241. See also Ronald Graybill, "The Abolitionist-Millerite Connection," in Ronald L. Numbers and Jonathan Butler, eds., *The Disappointed: Millerism and Millenarianism in the Nineteenth Century* (Bloomington: Indiana University Press, 1987).

13. Miller to Truman Hendryx, Feb. 25, 1834, WMC; Philander Barbour to Miller, Nov. 8, 1844, WMC; *Liberator,* Feb. 14, 1840, p. 27.

14. First Baptist Church of Williamson, N.Y., *Records,* ERL; note also the case of Eleanor Lum in Seneca Falls (Glenn C. Altschuler and Jan M. Saltzgaber, *Revivalism, Social Conscience, and Community in the Burned-Over District: The Trial of Rhoda Bement* [Ithaca, N.Y.: Cornell University Press, 1983]); First Presbyterian Church of Seneca Falls, N.Y., *Records,* ERL.

15. Whitney R. Cross, *The Burned-Over District; The Social and Intellectual History of Enthusiastic Religion in Western New York, 1800–1850* (Ithaca, N.Y.: Cornell University Press, 1950); Lewis Perry, *Radical Abolitionism: Anarchy and the Government of God in American Antislavery Thought* (Ithaca, N.Y.: Cornell University Press, 1973); David Brion Davis, "The Emergence of Immediatism in British and American

Antislavery Thought," *Mississippi Valley Historical Review* 49 (Sept. 1962): 209–230; Anne C. Loveland, "Evangelicalism and 'Immediate Emancipation' in American Antislavery Thought," *Journal of Social History* 32 (May 1966): 172–188; Angelina Grimké Weld to Sarah Grimké, Jan. 1845, CP.

16. *Liberator,* May 5, 1843, p. 70, and June 16, 1843, p. 94; *Advent Herald,* June 3, 1846, p. 133; *Gospel Standard,* July 18, 1844, p. 10.

17. *Liberator,* Feb. 14, 1840, p. 27.

18. *Signs of the Times,* March 15, 1841, p. 188 (from Lynn *Record*).

19. *Liberator,* Feb. 10, 1843, p. 23, April 15, 1844, p. 53, and Nov. 26, 1845, p. 125.

20. William Lloyd Garrison to Amos Farnsworth, Sept. 6, 1840, in Garrison, *Letters,* vol. 2: *A House Dividing Against Itself, 1836–1840,* ed. Louis Ruchames (Cambridge, Mass.: Harvard University Press, 1972), pp. 695 and 695–696n.

21. *Liberator,* Nov. 25, 1842, p. 187, Nov. 1, 1844, p. 176, Nov. 29, 1844, p. 192, and May 26, 1843, p. 84.

22. William Lloyd Garrison to Henry Clarke Wright, March 1, 1843, in Garrison, *Letters,* vol. 3: *No Union with Slaveholders, 1841–1849,* ed. Walter M. Merrill (Cambridge, Mass.: Harvard University Press, 1974), p. 135.

23. *Liberator,* Feb. 10, 1843, p. 23.

24. *Liberator,* April 5, 1844, p. 53.

25. Weld, quoted in Perry, *Radical Abolitonism,* p. 51 (italics in original).

26. Miller to Truman Hendryx, Oct. 23, 1834, WMC.

27. This account derives from a letter from T. M. Preble to the *Signs of the Times* written on December 22, 1841 (*Signs of the Times,* Jan. 15, 1842, pp. 159–160).

28. *Ibid.;* Edwin Scott Gaustad, *Dissent in American Religion* (Chicago: University of Chicago Press, 1973); see also Lydia Maria Child in the *Liberator,* Oct. 25, 1844, p. 172.

29. *Signs of the Times,* Aug. 24, 1842, p. 164, Oct. 4, 1843, p. 54, July 12, 1843, p. 152, and July 19, 1843, p. 157.

30. Pauline Maier, "Popular Uprisings and Civil Authority in

Eighteenth-Century America," *William and Mary Quarterly* 27 (Jan. 1970): 3–35; Leonard L. Richards, *"Gentlemen of Property and Standing": Anti-Abolition Mobs in Jacksonian America* (New York: Oxford University Press, 1970), *passim* and pp. 11–12; David Grimsted argues that the mob in the 1830s returned to its eighteenth-century status "as a frequent and tacitly accepted if not approved mode of behavior" ("Rioting in the Jacksonian Setting," *American Historical Review* 77 [April 1972]: 364).

31. *Christian Reflector*, April 18, 1844, p. 63 (quoting from Portsmouth *Journal*); *Advent Herald*, Nov. 6, 1844, p. 104; *Advent Herald*, Oct. 1, 1845, p. 61, Nov. 19, 1845, p. 117, Jan. 13, 1846, p. 183, and Feb. 11, 1846, p. 7.

32. In contrast, Richards found that the appearance of anti-abolitionist mobs was directly related to an increase in abolitionist organization in a given area (*"Gentlemen of Property and Standing,"* pp. 73–81).

33. Miller to I. O. Orr, Dec. 13, 1844; *Signs of the Times*, Jan. 15, 1842, pp. 159–160; *Advent Herald*, Feb. 11, 1846, p. 7; *Advent Herald*, Oct. 1, 1845, p. 61.

34. *Signs of the Times*, March 1, 1843, p. 189 (quoted in Nichol, *Midnight Cry*, p. 130), and *Christian Reflector*, Feb. 22, 1843, p. 31; Philadelphia *Public Ledger*, Oct. 14, 1844, Oct. 19, 1844, p. 132 (quoted in Nichol, *Midnight Cry*, p. 223); New York *Herald*, Oct. 23, 1844 (quoted in Nichol, *Midnight Cry*, pp. 243–244), and N. N. Whiting to Miller, Oct. 24, 1844, WMC; Nichol, *Midnight Cry*, pp. 220–221 and p. 93 (quoting from New York *Herald*, Oct. 30, 1844), Baltimore *Sun*, Oct. 17, 1844, and *Daily Eastern Argus* (Portland, Me.), Oct. 15, 1844.

35. *Liberator*, Feb. 10, 1843, p. 23.

36. Sylvan S. Tompkins, "The Psychology of Commitment," in Martin Duberman, ed., *The Antislavery Vanguard: New Essays on the Abolitionists* (Princeton, N.J.: Princeton University Press, 1965), pp. 270–298.

37. *Liberator*, April 14, 1843, p. 59. The comparison could cut both ways, however. When Miller lectured successfully in Baltimore,

the *Liberator* asked if he could have "delivere[d] eleven lectures against slavery in that city, without being driven beyond its precincts, or lynched?" The "inference" drawn by that abolitionist writer was "that Satan and his minions are incomparably less excited in view of the burning of the world by material fire, than they would be if the proposition to abolish the slave system were enforced upon them with equal boldness and fidelity." The fiercer the opposition, some abolitionists believed, the surer and greater the truth (*Liberator*, April 5, 1844, p. 53).

38. Joshua V. Himes to Miller, May 17, 1844, JVH.

39. *Liberator*, Oct. 25, 1844, p. 172.

40. Joshua V. Himes to Miller, Jan. 29, 1840, April 2, 1840 (italics in original), and Oct. 21, 1840, JVH.

41. Miller to William Miller, Jr., Feb. 2, 1843, quoted in Nichol, *Midnight Cry*, p. 129.

42. *Advent Tracts*, vol. 1 (Boston: J. V. Himes, [1845?]), "The Saviour Nigh," pp. 118–119; William Miller, *Evidence from Scripture and History of the Second Coming of Christ, About the Year 1843: Exhibited in a Course of Lectures* (Troy, N.Y.: Kemble and Hooper, 1836; Boston: J. V. Himes, 1842), p. 215 (1836).

43. *Christian Reflector*, April 19, 1843, p. 62 (italics in original).

44. *Christian Reflector*, Jan. 18, 1844, p. 10; New York *Evangelist*, Oct. 16, 1841, p. 165, and June 2, 1842, p. 172 (quoting William Ellery Channing).

45. New York *Evangelist*, March 26, 1846, p. 49; *Christian Reflector*, April 20, 1842, [p. 1].

46. Ernest Lee Tuveson, *Redeemer Nation: The Idea of America's Millennial Role* (Chicago: University of Chicago Press, 1968); James W. Davidson, *The Logic of Millennial Thought: Eighteenth Century New England* (New Haven, Conn.: Yale University Press, 1977); Norman O. Hatch, *The Sacred Cause of Liberty: Republican Thought and the Millennium in Revolutionary New England* (New Haven, Conn.: Yale University Press, 1977).

47. *Christian Reflector*, April 19, 1843, p. 62; Luther Fraseur Dimmick, *The End of the World Not Yet: A Discourse Delivered in the North*

Church, Newburyport, on the Last Evening of the Year *1841*, 3rd ed. (Newburyport, [Mass.]: C. Whipple, 1842), pp. 13–14; *Signs of the Times*, May 11, 1842, p. 44 (from *Journal of Commerce*).

48. *Signs of the Times*, July 19, 1843, p. 156 (from *Puritan*); *Signs of the Times*, Sept. 1, 1840, p. 86 (from *Buffalo Tattler*).

49. Fred Somkin, *Unquiet Eagle: Memory and Desire in the Idea of American Freedom, 1815–1860* (Ithaca, N.Y.: Cornell University Press, 1967).

50. Davidson, *Logic of Millennial Thought*.

51. For example, *Christian Reflector*, Dec. 14, 1838, [p. 3].

52. George Peck, "National Evils and Their Remedy," George Peck Papers, Syracuse University Archives, Syracuse, N.Y.

53. *Christian Reflector*, Feb. 9, 1842, [p. 2], and May 23, 1844, p. 82; *Methodist Review*, n.s., 9, no. 1 (Jan. 1838): 65–80. Also D. H. Meyer, "American Intellectuals and the Victorian Crisis of Faith," in Daniel Walker Howe, ed., *Victorian America* (Philadelphia: University of Pennsylvania Press, 1976), p. 67.

54. *Herald*, May 1, 1844, p. 102; Jonathan Butler, "Adventism and the American Experience," in Edwin Scott Gaustad, ed., *The Rise of Adventism: Religion and Society in Mid-Nineteenth-Century America* (New York: Harper and Row, 1974).

CHAPTER VII
EPILOGUE

1. Leon Festinger, Henry W. Riecken, and Stanley Schachter, *When Prophecy Fails: A Social and Psychological Study of a Modern Group That Predicted the Destruction of the World* (New York: Harper and Row, 1956; Harper Torchbooks, 1964) is the classic study of disconfirmation and cognitive dissonance. The case of the Millerites is summarized on pp. 12–23. David L. Rowe takes issue with the application of this theory to the Millerites in *Thunder and Trumpets: Millerites and Dissenting Religion in Upstate New York, 1800–1850 (Chico, Calif.: Scholars Press, 1985), p. 133.*

2. See David Tallmadge Arthur, "'Come Out of Babylon': A Study

of Millerite Separatism and Denominationalism, 1840–1865," Ph.D. diss., University of Rochester, 1970.

3. In addition to Miller's *Apology and Defence* (Boston: J. V. Himes, 1845), see *Time of the Advent; or, What Do the Adventists Teach Now on the Time?*, Tracts on Prophecy, no. 14 (Boston: J. V. Himes, 1853), for statements opposing the setting of a specific time but favoring the expectation that "the coming of the Son of Man is nigh, even at the door."

4. On White, see Ellen G. White, *Life Sketches . . . , Being a Narrative of Her Experience to 1881 as Written by Herself; with a Sketch of Her Subsequent Labors and Her Last Sickness, Composed of Original Sources* (Mountain View, Calif.: Pacific Press Publishing Assoc., 1915); also Ronald L. Numbers, *Prophetess of Health: A Study of Ellen G. White* (New York: Harper and Row, 1976); on the formation of the Seventh-day Adventist denomination, see Arthur, "Come Out of Babylon," and Jonathan Butler, "From Millerism to Seventh-day Adventism: 'Boundlessness to Consolidation,'" *Church History* 55 (March 1986).

5. Lawrence Foster, "Had Prophecy Failed?: Contrasting Perspectives of the Millerites and Shakers," in Ronald L. Numbers and Jonathan Butler, *The Disappointed: Millerism and Millenarianism in the Nineteenth Century* (Bloomington: Indiana University Press, 1987).

6. Foster, "Had Prophecy Failed?"; Henry B. Bear, "Henry B. Bear's Advent Experience," Harrison, Ohio, n.d. I am indebted to Lawrence Foster for providing me a copy of Bear.

7. Foster, "Had Prophecy Failed?"; N. Gordon Thomas, "The Millerite Movement in Ohio," *Ohio History* 81 (Spring 1972): 101.

8. David Tallmadge Arthur, "Joshua V. Himes and the Cause of Adventism, 1839–1845," M. A. thesis, University of Chicago, 1961, is one of the few good sources on Himes' life.

9. Rowe, *Thunder and Trumpets*, pp. 142–143; Thomas, "Millerite Movement in Ohio," p. 106.

10. Jane Marsh Parker, "A Little Millerite," *Century Magazine* 11 (Nov. 1886–April 1887): 317.

11. Martin Marty summarizes the five definitions of "secular" laid

out by Larry Shiner in "Religion in America Since Mid-Century," in Mary Douglas and Stephen Tipton, eds., *Religion and America: Scriptural Life in a Secular Age* (Boston: Beacon Press, 1983), p.277. David Martin has made much of a career out of critiquing scholars' use of the concept of secularization. See, for example, his *A General Theory of Secularization* (New York: Harper and Row, 1978). Influential approaches to the problem of secularization include that of Owen Chadwick, *The Secularization of the European Mind in the Nineteenth Century* (Cambridge, Eng.: Cambridge University Press, 1975), and Thomas Luckmann, *The Invisible Religion: The Problem of Religion in Modern Society* (New York: Macmillan, 1967).

12. Marty, "Religion in America since Mid-Century," p. 277.

13. Timothy L. Smith, *Revivalism and Social Reform in Mid-Nineteenth-Century America* (Nashville: Abingdon Press, 1957), esp. pp. 60–62 and chap. 4, "*Annus Mirabilis*—1858."

14. See Chapter 5 on insanity.

15. Joseph M. Weaver, *Pre-Millennialism; the Two-Fold Resurrection as Taught in the Scriptures: The "Reviewer" Reviewed* (Louisville: Waller, Sherrill, 1865), p. 3 (italics in original). Ernest Sandeen emphasized the efforts of premillennalists or millenarians to distance themselves from Millerism in *The Roots of Fundamentalism* (Chicago: University of Chicago Press, 1970), pp. xvi, 95–96, and 150. On millenarians see also Robert Kieran Whalen, "Millenarianism and Millennialism in America, 1790–1880," Ph.D. diss., SUNY–Stony Brook, 1971.

16. Sandeen, *Roots of Fundamentalism*, p. 97.

17. For example, Smith, *Revivalism and Social Reform*, p. 228; J. F. C. Harrison, *The Second Coming: Popular Millennarianism, 1780–1850* (New Brunswick, N.J.: Rutgers University Press, 1979), p. 197.

18. Angelina Grimké Weld to Sarah Grimké, Jan. 1845, CP.

19. James Moorhead has noted that "the erosion of postmillennialism was part of the waning of supernaturalism" (Moorhead, "The Erosion of Postmillennialism in American Religious Thought, 1865–1925," *Church History* 53 [March 1984]: 76; see also p. 67).

20. William G. McLoughlin, *Revivals, Awakenings, and Reform: An*

Essay on Religion and Social Change in America (Chicago: University of Chicago Press, 1978).

21. See James H. Moorhead, *American Apocalypse: Yankee Protestants and the Civil War* (New Haven, Conn.: Yale University Press, 1978).

22. Sandeen, *Roots of Fundamentalism*, p. 54.

23. John Nelson Darby tapped the surviving impulse toward such radical supernaturalism during his visits to the United States in the 1860s and 1870s, but he did not succeed in stirring up a high level of public recognition or viable enthusiam (Sandeen, *Roots of Fundamentalism*, pp. 76–77).

24. On the rise of Fundamentalism see Sandeen, *Roots of Fundamentalism;* Timothy Weber, *Living in the Shadow of the Second Coming: American Premillennialism, 1875–1925* (New York: Oxford University Press, 1979); George M. Marsden, *Fundamentalism and American Culture: The Shaping of Twentieth-Century Evangelicalism, 1870–1925* (New York: Oxford University Press, 1982); and Grant Wacker, "The Holy Spirit and the Spirit of the Age in American Protestantism, 1880–1920," *Journal of American History* 72 (June 1985): 45–62.

25. Robert Mapes Anderson, *Vision of the Disinherited: The Making of American Pentecostalism* (New York: Oxford University Press, 1979).

CONCLUSION

1. David Brion Davis, "Some Themes of Counter-Subversion: An Analysis of Anti-Masonic, Anti-Catholic, and Anti-Mormon Literature," *Mississippi Valley Historical Review* 47 (1960); also Davis, "Some Ideological Functions of Prejudice in Antebellum America," *American Quarterly* 15 (Summer 1963): 115–125; and again Kai T. Erikson, *Wayward Puritans: A Study in the Sociology of Deviance* (New York: John Wiley and Sons, 1966).

2. Whitney R. Cross, *The Burned-Over District: The Social and Intellectual History of Enthusiastic Religion in Western New York, 1800–1850* (Ithaca, N.Y.: Cornell University Press, 1950; New York: Harper Torchbooks, 1965).

3. See Klaus J. Hansen, *Mormonism and the American Experience*

(Chicago: University of Chicago Press, 1981), and Catherine Albanese, *America: Religion and Religions* (Belmont, Calif.: Wadsworth Publishing, 1981), esp. pp. 137–154.

4. Fawn Brody, *No Man Knows My History: The Life of Joseph Smith the Mormon Prophet* (New York: Alfred A. Knopf, 1946).

5. Lucius Smith to Mary G. Brockway, June 20, 1843, Brockway Papers, Syracuse University Archives, Syracuse, N.Y.; New York *Evangelist*, Jan. 27, 1838, p. 13; *Christian Reflector*, March 14, 1844, p. 43; *Liberator*, April 15, 1842. See also unpublished paper by Whitney Cross, "Revivalism and Eccentric Religion," p. 40, CP.

6. *Christian Reflector*, Oct. 16, 1845, p. 167; Albany *Argus*, Sept. 30, 1842. See also *Liberator*, June 10, 1842, and March 20, 1840; *Christian Reflector*, Nov. 9, 1838, [p. 3], and July 5, 1843, p. 107; *Advent Herald*, Nov. 12, 1845, p. 111; *Saturday Courier*, July 17, 1841, and July 24, 1841; *Evangelical Magazine and Gospel Advocate*, Nov. 15, 1839, pp. 364–365; *Liberty Press*, Aug. 22, 1843, p. 163; *Signs of the Times*, June 8, 1842, p. 80 (from *Olive Branch*).

7. *Liberty Press*, Aug. 1, 1843, p. 153; *Signs of the Times*, July 27, 1842, p. 135. See also *Methodist Review* 13, no. 3 (July 1842): 483, and 14, no. 1 (Jan. 1843): 111–127; *Evangelical Magazine and Gospel Advocate*, Sept. 13, 1839, pp. 294–295; *Niles National Register*, April 1, 1843, p. 80, July 15, 1843, p. 320, Nov. 18, 1843, pp. 180–181, Dec. 9, 1843, p. 229.

Index

Abolitionism: against Millerism, 184–187; and anti-abolitionism, 16, 223–224; and come-outerism, 125, 134–135; conversion to, 115, 186, 215; and Millerites, 37, 134–135, 181–183, 187, 193–194, 197, 205, 206, 221. *See also* Reform
Advent Christian Church, 203
Adventists. *See* Millerites
Albany Conference (1845), 203
American Evangelical Adventist Conference, 203
Annihilationism, 49, 203
Anti-creedalism, 121–122
Anti-Millerism. *See* Opposition to Millerism
Antipartyism, 122
Ascension robes, 60–61, 185, 214, 217, 242 n. 17
Asylums, 158–174, 223; Brattleboro, Vt., 158, 159, 169; Bloomingdale (N.Y.), 161; Concord, N.H., 158, 169; founding of, 160, 165; Friends' (Pa.), 160; McLean (Mass.), 160; superintendents of, 159, 160, 162–167, 169, 170, 173; Utica, N.Y., 169; Worcester, Mass., 159, 160, 169. *See also* Insanity

Bacon, Francis, 98, 100
Baconianism, 98–102, 121
Baptists: and church discipline, 126–127, 128; and come-outerism, 125; and date-setting, 40; Eden, N.Y., 125; and Miller family, 17; and Millerites, 3–4; and orthodoxy, 25; Palmyra, N.Y., 129; Parma, N.Y., 139; Pompey, N.Y., 128; and revivals, 24; Seneca Falls, N.Y., 136; and slavery, 137–138; Walworth, N.Y., 136–137; Williamson, N.Y., 136–140, 206
Barnum, P. T., 141
Bates, Joseph, 181
Bement, Rhoda, 134–135
Beverly, Thomas, 43
Bible, 83–93; authority of, 83–85, 112–113, 221; and Baconian induction, 99; interpretation of, 87–92, 93–102, 214,

225; "literal-realistic" approach to, 87–88; Miller and, 31–33, 66; and "populist hermeneutic," 94; societies, 180; and "year-day" principle, 105. *See also* Prophecy
Bliss, Sylvester, 51
Bogue, Horace, 134–135
Boutelle, Luther, 183, 184
Brigham, Amariah, 160, 209
Burned-over district, 136, 137
Bush, George, 72

Calvinism, 24, 25, 80, 178
Cataclysm, 14, 62–64, 65–66, 67, 72, 200–201, 209, 211
Catholic. *See* Roman Catholic Church
Character, 142–151, 156, 158, 173, 175–176, 178, 180, 186
Child, Lydia Maria, 59, 77, 79, 194
Christian Connection, 3, 24
Christian Science, 216
Church discipline, 126–140, 172; and Millerites, 130–133, 134–135, 138–140, 187, 197, 206, 208
Church of God (Seventh Day), 203
Civil War, 212
Cognitive dissonance, 273 n. 1
Cohn, Norman, 9
Cole, Charles, 35
Come-outerism, 121–125, 132–133, 134–135, 138–140

Common Sense philosophy, 94, 100, 121
Congregationalists, 22; Millerite, 36; as orthodox, 21, 25; Seneca Falls, N.Y., 133
Conversion, 84, 113–114, 117, 118, 178, 186; death and, 79–80; of Miller, 17–18; in Second Great Awakening, 11–12, 114, 171. *See also* Second blessing
Cowles, Henry, 75, 77–78
Cross, Whitney, 16, 182, 215

Darby, John Nelson, 276 n. 23
Davis, David Brion, 215, 216
Death and individual salvation, 78–80
Deism, 22
Dimmick, Luther, 44, 199
Disciples of Christ, 24, 121
Dissent, 21–25, 26–27, 49, 56, 81–82, 106, 127, 133, 194, 195, 197, 202, 207, 208, 215, 216, 217, 219–228. *See also* Church discipline
Dix, Dorothea, 165, 169, 170
Dowling, John, 42, 109, 155
Duffield, George, 210
Durkheim, Emile, 26

Earle, Pliny, 160
Edson, Hiram, 203–204
Edwards, Jonathan, 10, 199
Emerson, Ralph Waldo, 23, 144
Emperor of the Last Days, 8–9

Episcopalians, 25
Erikson, Kai, 25–26
Evangelicalism, 11–16, 23–24, 27, 84, 117, 223; and church discipline, 126, 128–129; definition, 11; and evangelical empire, 12, 180; and insanity, 165; of Miller, 17–18; and Millerism, 28, 195, 196, 215, 227; and reform, 15, 180, 182, 215
Evolution, 214
Excommunication of Millerites, 126, 133, 135. *See also* Church discipline

Family, 175–180, 221, 223
Finney, Charles Grandison, 25, 171, 208; and the millennium, 75; and Miller, 67; and new measures, 13, 24. *See also* Great Awakening
Fitch, Charles, 48, 124, 144, 147, 181
Forman, Daniel W., 134
Foster, Lawrence, 205
Fourierism, 119, 141
Free Spirit, cult of the, 9
Frei, Hans, 87–88
French, Calvin, 188
Fuller, Isaac, 34
Fundamentalism, 214

Galusha, Elon, 144
Garrison, William Lloyd, 119, 158, 184, 185

General Conference of Believers in the Advent Near: First, 38–39, 46; of May 1842, 46
Giles the Prophet of God and Branch of Christ, 40
Great Awakening, First, 10–11
Great Awakening, Second, 228; and biblical interpretation, 94; and conversion, 13, 114, 171; and millennium, 11; and reform, 15
Great Disappointment, 52, 157, 182, 190, 191, 202, 204, 205, 206, 222, 223. *See also* Millerites
Greenfield, Elijah G., 136–140
Gunn, Lewis C. and Elizabeth, 35

Hale, Apollos, 192
Hale, Ezekiel, Jr., 181
Hall, Benjamin, 184
Harrison, J. F. C., 107
Haven, Kittredge, 108
Hawley, Silas, 48, 60, 70, 145, 184
Hazen, James A., 44
Hendryx, Truman, 85, 122
Higham, John, 16, 27
Himes, Joshua V.: attacks on, 146–148, 185, 196, 199–200; and date-setting, 38, 51; against "D.D.s," 94–95; and holiness, 65; and insanity, 170; joins Millerite movement, 19, 35, 195; on mobs, 194; and

282 INDEX

politics, 73; praise for, 149, 185; and reform, 181–182, 205; threats against, 189
Hodge, Charles, 210
Holiness, 65, 66, 71, 115, 178, 182, 221; movement, 115, 214, 244 n. 33
Hospitals for the insane. *See* Asylums
Howe, John, 44
Howe, Samuel Gridley, 165

Immanence, 28, 56, 70–71, 72, 82, 108, 153, 157, 211, 212, 223, 225, 227
Influence, 64–65, 69, 142, 145–146, 148, 176, 179
Inner-directedness, 143, 144, 150, 156
Insanity, 158–174; causes of, 160–161, 164–165; diagnosis of, 162–163; popular views on, 165–167, 173; as possession, 164–165, 172–173; religious, 161, 163–165, 166, 171–172, 266–267 n. 56, 267 n. 58; treatment of, 161–162. *See also* Asylums

Jacobs, Enoch, 205
Jarvis, Edward, 160
Jarvis, Samuel Farmer, 41–42
Jeremiad, 67, 200, 212
Joachim of Fiore, 9
Jones, Henry, 36–37, 57, 60, 66, 73, 77; and Millerism, 36–37, 46, 47, 222; and reform movements, 37, 181, 195
Junkin, George, 64

Kelley, Abby, 134–135

Lee, Mother Ann, 205
Litch, Josiah, 50, 51
Luckey, Samuel, 48, 117
Lum, Eleanor, 133–135
Lutherans, 25

McLoughlin, William, 212
Magic, 107, 110
Marden, Mrs. E. J., 115–116
Marty, Martin, 23
Masons, 16, 215
Matthews, John T., 40
Matthias (Robert Matthews), 141
Methodists, 121; and church discipline, 127; and come-outerism, 125; and date-setting, 40; and human ability, 56; and insanity, 163; and Millerites, 3; and orthodoxy, 25; and revivals, 24; and second blessing, 114–115, 117; Wesleyan, 134, 206
Millennialism, 5–11, 20–21, 28, 69, 71, 119, 209, 226–227; biblical, 5–8; in colonial period, 9–11, 199; and come-outerism, 122; definition, 9; and human effort, 74–75; medieval, 8–9; of Miller, 18–19, 31–33; political, 10–11, 12, 30, 56,

71–72, 198–201, 213, 218, 221; in Reformation, 9. *See* Postmillennialism; Premillennialism; Second coming

Miller, William, 3; antislavery stand of, 182; and arithmetic, 99–102; and Bible, 18, 31–33, 85–86, 88–91, 94, 99–102, 109; and Calvinist heritage, 80–81; and the churches, 122–123; conversion of, 17–18; and date-setting, 32–34, 51, 99–102; death of, 203; deism of, 17, 195; early life of, 17; evangelistic activity of, 19, 34–36, 120, 136; after Great Disappointment, 203; and Great Disappointment, 52; and human ability, 73–74, 75; and millennialism, 18–19; on mobs, 192; and personal return, 58, 203; and politics, 73; praise for, 149; in Seneca Falls, 136; and signs in nature, 106–107. *See also* Millerites; Opposition to Millerism

Millerites: and American destiny, 201; and ascension robes, 60–61; and the Bible, 84, 85–91, 93, 94, 96–98, 99–100, 101–102; and burning of the earth, 62–63, 68; and character, 144–145, 219; and the churches, 3–4, 124–125, 132–135, 136–140; and collective salvation, 78–81; and comeouterism, 124–125, 132–133, 134–135, 138–140; and conversion to Millerism, 34–37, 115–116, 194, 196; and date-setting, 35–39, 44–53, 54, 115, 203, 222; defense of, 148–150; definition of, 4–5; and deviant behavior, 51–52, 144–145, 146–148, 151, 219; and dissent, 27, 202, 217, 221–222, 225–226; and family, 221, 268 n. 11; and the future, 30, 72–73, 156–157, 173–174, 201, 227; after Great Disappointment, 202–206; and history, 88–90, 102–106; and human effort, 75–76, 187; and insanity, 158–159, 163, 164, 166, 167–169, 170–174, 266–267 n. 56; membership in, 4; organization of, 46–47, 120, 123–124, 139–140, 188, 203, 206; and particular providence, 103–104; and politics, 73; and reform, 37, 180–187, 221; and second blessing, 115–116, 117; and signs in nature, 106–108; and special knowledge, 112–113, 117; and typology, 91; and Victorian values, 176; and work, 152–154, 180, 221. *See also* Opposition to Millerism *and names of individual Millerites*

Miracles, 55, 107, 240 n. 3, 241 n. 4

Mobs, 187–197
Moorhead, James H., 14
Mormonism, 21, 127, 131, 141, 197, 215, 216, 217–220, 224, 225
Munzer, Thomas, 9, 44

New Birth. *See* Conversion
Noyes, John Humphrey, 152

Opposition to Millerism, 20, 27–30, 39–44, 82, 120; and alternate prophecies, 40–44; and arithmetic, 100–102; and ascension robes, 60–61, 185, 214, 217; and Bible, 91–93, 95–96, 96–97, 100–102, 108–109; and burning of the earth, 63–65, 68–69; and character, 144, 146–148, 219; and church discipline, 130–140, 172, 197; and date-setting, 40–44, 52; and death, 79–80; and family, 176–180; after Great Disappointment, 207, 222; and history, 91–93, 108–110; and human ability, 74–75, 157; and immorality, 151, 177, 219; and insanity, 158–159, 163, 166, 167–169, 170–172, 185, 209; and limited salvation, 77–78; and mob violence, 187–197; and murder, 168, 177, 178, 185; and passivity, 151, 152–153, 154–158, 185–187; and personal return, 58–59, 60–62, 209; and postmillennialism vs. premillennialism, 20, 71–72; from radicals, 72, 184–187; and secular progress, 199–201; as sign of last days, 106; and signs in nature, 110–112; and special religious experience, 116–117; and sudden return of Christ, 66–72; and suicide, 168, 173, 185; timing of, 197; and women's roles, 177–180
Orthodoxy, 21–25, 26–27, 56, 81–82, 140, 173, 175, 196, 212, 215, 220–221, 223, 224–225, 227. *See also* Church discipline; Dissent

Parker, Jane Marsh, 206
Parker, Theodore, 64
Peabody, William, 192
Pearson, John, 35
Pentecostalism, 214
Perfectionism, 115, 117, 133, 182, 244 n. 33
Philadelphia Second Advent Association, 123
Phrenology, 141
Pinney, E. R., 136
Postmillennialism, 14, 18, 209, 211, 213; definition, 13–14. *See also* Millennialism
Preble, T. M., 189, 192
Premillennialism, 14, 29, 38, 209–211, 213, 221; definition,

INDEX

13; and Miller, 18. *See also* Millennialism
Presbyterians: and church discipline, 127; and Millerites, 3–4, 22; as orthodox, 25; Palmyra, N.Y., 131–133; and revivals, 24; Seneca Falls, N.Y., 133–135; and slavery, 134
Progress, 57, 66–72, 82, 92, 110, 151, 153, 198–201, 211, 212, 223
Prophecy: accessibility of, 96–99; and American heroes, 92–93; and arithmetic, 32–34, 99–102; of burning of the earth, 62, 82; "double sense" of, 92; of fall of Turkey, 45; medieval, 8–9; New Testament, 6–8, 32–33, 62, 66, 68, 86, 91, 105–106, 122–123; Old Testament, 5–6, 32–33, 91, 92–93, 104–105, 108–109, 113; of return of the Jews, 38–39, 210; of two resurrections, 77; and typology, 10, 91, 92. *See also* Bible; Millennialism
Puritans, 81, 143, 174; and City on a Hill, 199; and religious knowledge, 83; and salvation, 80; and temptation to suicide, 267 n. 58; and typology, 10

Quakers, 173

Ransom, Seth, 34
Rationalism, 83, 165, 173. *See also* Baconianism
Ray, Isaac, 160
Reform, 28, 72, 119, 175, 180–187, 195, 221. *See also* Abolitionism
Revivals, 23–24, 25, 34, 50, 129–130, 137, 171, 212, 267 n. 57; changes in, 208–209; and conversion to Millerism, 35–36, 64, 130, 131, 215; of 1857–1858, 209; and human ability, 77; and insanity, 164, 165, 166, 209; and reform, 182, 215. *See also* Great Awakening
Revolution, American, 11, 15, 93
Rice, Olive Maria, 177, 268 n. 6
Roman Catholic Church: attacks on, 16, 64, 197, 215, 219, 224, 225; and insanity, 163
Rowe, David L., 4
Rush, Benjamin, 160

Salvation, 73–81, 218, 221, 225; collective, 78–81; and election, 76–78; and human ability, 74; universal, 76–78
Sandeen, Ernest, 210, 213
Schism, 121, 135–140, 224
Second blessing, 49, 85, 114–117, 182
Second coming: parallel to first coming of Christ, 55, 60; as past, 20, 70–71; personal, 18, 19, 31, 33, 37–38, 46, 55, 57–62, 82, 204, 209, 213, 220,

221, 225; and Seventh-day Adventists, 204; soon, 18, 19, 31–32, 35–36, 37–39, 46, 66, 82, 174, 197, 209, 210, 213, 220, 221; spiritual, 69–70; sudden, 66, 204, 210. *See also* Millennialism; Millerites
Secularization, 29, 207–209, 212
Seventh-day Adventists, 204, 207, 213, 216
Seventh-day Baptists, 204
Shakers, 205
Sherwin, Marshall B., 131–133
Shortridge, Mr., 60
Sibylline Oracles, 8
Signs, 85, 254 n. 54; in history, 102–106, 108–109; in nature, 106–108, 110–111
Smith, Joseph, 131, 141, 217, 219, 220. *See also* Mormonism
Smolnikar, Andreas Bernardus, 40
Snow, Samuel S., 50
Somkin, Fred, 67
Southard, Nathaniel, 51, 181
Spaulding, Brother, 124
Spiritualism, 141, 205
Storrs, George, 49, 51, 181, 190
Supernaturalism, 54–82, 86, 88, 111–112, 116, 140, 142, 153, 154, 157, 172–173, 174, 179, 181, 187, 196, 197, 201, 209, 212, 213, 214, 217, 220, 222, 225, 226–227, 240 nn. 2, 3; definition, 54–56

Transcendentalism, 23, 25, 28, 56, 84, 225

Ultraism, 16, 120, 131, 182, 215
Unitarianism, 22–23, 24, 56
Universalism, 56, 77, 127, 224, 225
Ussher, Bishop, 41–42

Victorianism, 29, 142, 143, 145, 149, 150–151, 156, 175, 175–176, 178, 198, 223, 228

Ward, Henry Dana, 47
Weeks, William R., 41–42, 101, 108
Weld, Angelina Grimke, 61–62, 67, 72, 211
Weld, Theodore, 186
Wesley, John, 40, 163
Whiston, William, 43
White, Ellen Gould Harmon, 204, 213
White, James, 204
Whitefield, George, 23, 163
Williamson (N.Y.) Conference, 139–140
Witchcraft, 170, 172, 267 n. 57
Women: as Millerite leaders, 177, 268 n. 6; and reform, 184; and Victorian ideals, 176, 178–179, 268 n. 11
Woodward, Samuel, 159, 160
Work ethic, 151–158, 180, 198, 221
Wright, Henry Clarke, 185